THE GEBUSI

*Lives Transformed
in a Rainforest World*

THE GEBUSI

Lives Transformed
in a Rainforest World

SECOND EDITION

Bruce Knauft
Emory University

Mc Graw Hill **Higher Education**

Boston   Burr Ridge, IL   Dubuque, IA   New York   San Francisco   St. Louis
Bangkok   Bogotá   Caracas   Kuala Lumpur   Lisbon   London   Madrid   Mexico City
Milan   Montreal   New Delhi   Santiago   Seoul   Singapore   Sydney   Taipei   Toronto

 **Higher Education**

Published by McGraw-Hill, an imprint of The McGraw-Hill Companies, Inc., 1221 Avenue of the Americas, New York, NY 10020.

4 5 6 7 8 9 0 DOC/DOC 1 5 4 3 2 1 0

ISBN: 978-0-07-340537-7
MHID: 0-07-340537-X

Editor-in-Chief: *Michael Ryan*
Publisher: *Frank Mortimer*
Sponsoring Editor: *Gina Boedeker*
Senior Managing Editor: *Susan Gouijnstook*
Development Editors: *Phillip Butcher* and
Meghan Campbell
Editorial Assistant: *Jordan Killam*
Marketing Manager: *Leslie Oberhuber*

Production Editor: *Anne Fuzellier*
Designer: *Allister Fein*
Production Supervisor: *Tandra Jorgensen*
Production Service: *Aptara®, Inc.*
Composition: *10/12 Janson* by *Aptara®, Inc.*
Printing: *45# New Era Matte* by *R. R. Donnelley, Crawfordsville*

Cover images: Courtesy of Bruce Knauft

Library of Congress Cataloging-in-Publication Data
Knauft, Bruce M.
    The Gebusi : lives transformed in a rainforest world / Bruce Knauft. —2nd ed.
        p. cm.
    Includes index.
    ISBN-13: 978-0-07-340537-7 (alk. paper)
    ISBN-10: 0-07-340537-X (alk. paper)
    1. Gebusi (Papua New Guinean people)—Social conditions.   2. Gebusi (Papua New Guinean people)—Cultural assimilation.   3. Gebusi (Papua New Guinean people)—Social life and customs.   4. Social change—Papua New Guinea.   5. Acculturation—Papua New Guinea.   6. Papua New Guinea—Social life and customs.   I. Title.
DU740.42.K524 2010
305.89'912—dc22   2008052750

www.mhhe.com

For my Gebusi friends
May they live long and well

About the Author

Bruce Knauft is Samuel C. Dobbs Professor of Anthropology and Director of the States at Regional Risk Project at Emory University in Atlanta. He has taught a broad range of students, including many who have gone on to conduct anthropological fieldwork in diverse world areas. Author of seven books and numerous journal articles and chapters, Professor Knauft has written extensively on topics and issues in cultural anthropology. He has been interested in the Gebusi people of Papua New Guinea since his first fieldwork among them in 1980–82.

Contents

List of Map, Figures, and Photographs

Preface

BACKGROUND

Anthropology is little without powerful portrayals of peoples and cultures in diverse parts of the world. For beginning students, the wonder of learning about different ways of life can be thrilling and provocative. The range of human diversity both stretches our envelope of understanding and prods us to reconsider our own beliefs and practices. Over the years, a number of short books have filled this role in anthropology by exposing students to potent examples of cultural variety. Often, these works take the form of an ethnographic case study—a book-length description of a group of people who live in a foreign country or in underappreciated circumstances closer to home. For teaching purposes, these condensed ethnographies form useful complements and counterpoints to the textbooks commonly used in anthropology courses, which tend to be large in scope but less nuanced in portraying individuals and cultural contexts. By contrast, this is just what a short ethnography is designed to do. But even short ethnographies can be densely detailed. This occurs in part because authors want to impart as much information as possible—and because an anthropologist's scholarly reputation can suffer if his or her work does not provide as many details as possible.

In the present book, I consider myself fortunate to be able to present a more personally shaped narrative. First, I have already had the opportunity to provide a scholarly foundation by writing a number of academic books and articles about the Gebusi and their broader culture area of Melanesia, which lies north and northeast of Australia in the Pacific Ocean. Second, I have accumulated many experiences and documented many Gebusi stories that have not been otherwise published. Finally, I am fortunate that the Gebusi are—as I hope you will agree—an amazing, intriguing, fascinating, difficult, and wonderful people. So I feel privileged to write a book designed to portray important and sometimes dramatic aspects of Gebusi lives as well as of my own experiences while living among them.

Over time, I have come to believe that Gebusi experiences and my own observations provide insight into issues addressed in undergraduate anthropology courses. Beyond general topics such as subsistence, kinship, economics, politics, religion, and art, these include the aims and methods of anthropological fieldwork, the personal challenges and moral dilemmas of conducting ethnography, and the ways in which local people become enmeshed with wider influences and larger regions. Finally, because my experiences with the Gebusi have spanned a sizable arc of social and cultural transformation—from their remote isolation in the early 1980s to their active engagement with national and global lifestyles in the late 1990s to the resurgence of many traditional cultural practices in 2008—their development illustrates key issues in the study of social and cultural change.

This book has grown up with me, both personally and professionally. It was a pleasure for me to write it, and now it is a pleasure for me to revise and update it based on surprising new experiences with the Gebusi in the winter of 2008. I hope you will find the account enjoyable as well as informative, and in the best of worlds, both of these at once.

For this second edition, every chapter and the conclusion have been edited and updated. This includes the pruning of selected details, supplying broader context and comparative perspective, and linking the account as a whole through three rather than two periods of field experience: 1980–82, 1998, and 2008. Chapters 11 and 12 of the first edition are now condensed into Chapter 11. Chapter 12 in the present edition supplies information concerning the Gebusi in 2008. The "Farewell" at the end retains its original character but has been amended with artistic license to include features of my departure in 2008 as well as in 1998. The notes and references of the work are now available on Web pages as described below rather than being printed in the book itself. Study questions for each of the book's chapters and its introduction and conclusion are now included at the end of the book.

Personal names used in the book are sometimes actual names and sometimes pseudonyms. Actual names are used for persons who have given their permission and for persons whose depiction in the text is nonproblematic and/or if they have been deceased for a number of years. This reflects the fact that the Gebusi generally are pleased to have their real identities represented to the larger world. Pseudonyms have been used in cases in which persons are still alive and the information could be perceived or interpreted as embarrassing, immoral, criminal, or otherwise unflattering.

Quotations in the main text that have been taken from field notes and from Gebusi have been edited to make them more direct and succinct. I have attempted to retain the spirit and meaning of original remarks. My occasional use of quoted paraphrase is designed to make the material more understandable to a broad audience.

KEY FEATURES

This book and its associated Web sites includes a name list, study questions, reference materials, a wide range of photographs, and music sound clips for use by students and instructors.

List of Persons

An alphabetical list of persons is supplied in the endmatter for those who wish to check or remind themselves of the identity of an individual named in the book.

Study Questions

Study questions for each of the book's sections are included at the back of the book. Students and instructors can consult these questions for thematic issues of interest and for purposes of studying or configuring course assignments.

Notes and References

The book's notes and references are now posted in updated format on the Web; to access them, google the author's name and look at my Web site under "Gebusi research." A second, official copy of these materials should also be available on the McGraw-Hill "Gebusi Information Center" Web site; click on "student edition" and choose "notes" or "references" under "Choose one . . ." Taken together, the endnotes and their references can guide students and teachers who wish to use this book for developing paper topics, completing course assignments, conducting independent investigations, or to satisfy the reader's curiosity regarding practices or beliefs described in the main text. Works cited in the endnotes are listed with citations in the references, which are Web-posted as described above.

Web Site Image Library

Approximately 350 photographs of the Gebusi are Web-posted in thumbnail and in enlarged format, along with captions and supplemental information. To access these, google the Gebusi Information Center, click on "student edition" and then choose one of the book's chapters. Photos of Gebusi and the author in 2008 are posted on the author's individual Web site and on the McGraw-Hill Web site for Chapter 12. Photos and descriptive information allow readers to take a visual journey through the lives and practices of Gebusi at different time periods. The corpus of Gebusi photos and descriptions is indexed by topic on the McGraw-Hill Web site.

Sound Clips

Selected sound clips of Gebusi music, including string band singing in 2008, can be found under "Gebusi Research" on the author's home page (google "Bruce Knauft").

ACKNOWLEDGMENTS

It is hard to express the personal and professional debt that I feel toward my many Gebusi friends and acquaintances. Deepest thanks go to Sayu, Didiga, Yuway, Keda, Yamdaw, Abi, and Father Aloi. I gratefully acknowledge help in 1980–82, 1998, and 2008 from officials and staff at Nomad, Kiunga, and the Catholic Church in both of these locations.

As anthropologists are aware, field research, especially in remote locations, is difficult if not impossible to complete without financial assistance from funding and granting agencies. I gratefully acknowledge funding for my field research among the Gebusi from the U.S. National Science Foundation, the U.S. National Institutes of Mental Health, the Rackham Graduate School at the University of Michigan, the U.S. Department of Education, the Wenner-Gren Foundation, the Harry Frank Guggenheim Foundation, and Emory University.

Thanks go to numerous persons who have read and commented on various drafts of this book. For this second edition, special thanks go to McGraw-Hill editorial consultant Phil Butcher and to five anonymous reviewers, who supplied valuable feedback on the chapters of the first edition. A special thanks goes to ICIS Program Associate Kathryn Bennett, who helped edit and proof the final manuscript. Small portions of this book overlap in substance with another of my books, *Exchanging the Past*, published by the University of Chicago Press in 2002.

I deeply thank Eileen Knauft for the ethnographic information she collected with Gebusi women during 1980–82 and for her photos of Gebusi during this same period, as credited in the book's text and Web pages. I owe a special debt to my undergraduate and graduate students at Emory University. They have given me the courage not simply to teach anthropology from the heart but to go back to the field and learn it all over again.

This book is dedicated to my Gebusi friends. I care about them deeply!

Entry

IT LOOKS SO GRAND from a thousand feet up, the forest glowing deep, green, and vast. The broccoli tops of the trees form an endless carpet, an emerald skin guarding worlds of life within. You look down to see two blue-brown ribbons of water etching the forest canopy. You follow them through the window of your tiny plane as they snake toward each other and merge in gentle delight. Below, in the nestled crook of these two rivers, you look closer, to where the green shifts from dark to bright, from old forest to new growth that is repeatedly cut down but always sprouting anew. Inside this lime-green patch, you see a score of white squares arranged neatly in two rows. Ten line up evenly on one side while their partners face them across a broad lawn, metal roofs glinting in the strong sun. You recall how these structures were built as homes by early Australian patrol officers, so colonial and rugged, trekking in across the swamps and rivers. Adjacent to the houses is the rectangle they laid out, flat and long, its grass kept short and trim. Your plane will swoop down on it now, the gilded spine of that book you have come so far to read. But its content is not what you thought it would be, not a text at all. As you descend, its meaning becomes the faces that line the airstrip, bright and eager as their skin is dark. They watch expectantly as you land. You open the door to a searing blast of heat and humanity. Welcome to the Nomad Station.

Introduction

In Search of Surprise

LIKE MOST ANTHROPOLOGISTS, I was unprepared for what I would find. In 1980, I had been married for just a few months when Eileen and I flew from Michigan across the Pacific. We were going to live for two years in a remote area of the rainforest north of Australia, in the small nation of Papua New Guinea. I was twenty-six years old and had never been west of Oregon. I had no idea what changes lay in store either for us or for the people we were going to live with.

Well into the twentieth century, the large and rugged tropical island of New Guinea harbored people who had had little contact with outsiders. In the area where we were going, initial contact between some groups and Westerners had not occurred until the 1960s. The 450 people whom we encountered had a name and a language that were not yet known to anthropologists. As individuals, the Gebusi (geh-BOO-see) were amazing—at turns regal, funny, infuriating, entrancing, romantic, violent, and immersed in a world of towering trees and foliage, heat and rain, and mosquitoes and illness. Their lives were as different from ours as they could be. Practices and beliefs that were practically lore in anthropology were alive and well: ritual dancers in eye-popping costumes, entranced spirit mediums, all-night songfests and divinations, rigid separation between men and women, and striking sexual practices. A mere shadow to us at first, the dark side of Gebusi lives also became real: death inquests, sorcery accusations, village fights, and wife beating. In the past, cannibalism had been common, and we later discovered that a woman from our village had been eaten a year and a half prior to our arrival. As I gradually realized, the killing of sorcery suspects had produced one of the highest rates of homicide in the cross-cultural record.

The challenge of living and working with the Gebusi turned our own lives into something of an extreme sport. But in the crucible of personal experience, the Gebusi became not only human to us but also, despite their tragic violence, wonderful people. With wit and passion, they lived rich and festive lives. Vibrant and friendly, they turned life's cruelest ironies into their best jokes and its biggest tensions into their most elaborate fantasies. Their humor, spirituality, deep togetherness, and

3

raw pragmatism made them, for the most part, great fun to be with. I have never felt more included in a social world. And what personalities! To lump them together as simply "Gebusi" is as bland as it would be to describe Oprah Winfrey, Brad Pitt, and Bart Simpson as simply "American." The Gebusi were not simply "a society" or "a culture"; they were an incredible mix of unique individuals.

Anthropology is little if not the discovery of the human unexpected. I initially went to the Gebusi's part of the rainforest to study political decision making. Armed with tape recorder and typewriter, I wanted to document how communications with spirits during all-night séances produced concrete results—the decision to mount a hunting expedition, conduct a ritual, fight an enemy, or accuse a sorcerer. But spirit séances more closely resembled a YouTube soundtrack than a political council. The spirit medium sang of spirit women who flew about seductively and teased men in the audience. The male listeners joked back while bantering loudly with one another. In the bargain, their own social relations were intensified, patched up, and cemented. That community results could actually emerge during the night-long séance seemed almost beside the point. And yet, the results were sometimes really important, including one spiritual pronouncement that ended up forcing some villagers to leave and form a new settlement. Sorcerers could be scapegoated and threatened with death; people could be accused or found innocent of crimes. Politics, friendship, and sidesplitting humor combined with sexual teasing, spirituality, and conflict in ways that made my head spin.

You might imagine the first time I tried to translate a Gebusi spirit séance from one of my tape recordings. I sat with male informants in all seriousness as the recorder played. At first, they were astonished to hear their own voices. But they quickly shifted from amazement to howling laughter. Then they attempted, image by laborious image, line by laborious line, to explain the humor that I had committed to tape. With no reliable interpreters, I was learning their language "monolingually." As it turned out, the spiritual poetry of Gebusi séance songs bore as little relation to their normal speech as rock lyrics do to the sentences of an anthropology textbook. The Gebusi responded to my confusion by gleefully repeating the jokes that I had recorded. Although I was unable to turn nighttime humor into daytime clarity, I certainly gave the men a good laugh—and fueled my own uncertainty. Seeing our strange interaction, Eileen asked the women what was going on. She was told that many of the songs I was trying to write down were "no good" or "rotten."

For the most part, Gebusi were not only jovial but considerate, quick to apologize, and adept at making the best of difficulties. I ended up liking most of them a lot. As I came to understand their rituals, beliefs, and customs, I strongly appreciated their culture. But I remained keenly aware of my own ethical and moral values, derived from elsewhere. What was I supposed to do with my sense of morality when it collided with theirs?

Much like my own dilemma, cultural anthropology has often been driven by competing desires. Anthropologists want to appreciatively understand the cultures they study. But they also feel compelled to confront the social difficulties and injustices they observe. In Western scholarship, the goal of appreciating other cultures on their own terms was highlighted during the eighteenth and nineteenth centuries by European theorists such as Giambatista Vico and Johannes Herder. Broadly speaking, they argued that cultures should be viewed in the context of their own time and place. Later, the same principle was emphasized by the "founding father" of American anthropology, Franz Boas. Similarly, in recent decades, cultural anthropologists have been passionate to understand foreign peoples through the lens of their customs and beliefs. Why should Western ways of life be considered superior?

On the other hand, anthropologists are also mindful of problems and inequities in the societies they study. Some of these injustices have been fueled by the incursions of outsiders. During centuries of colonialism, for instance, Western powers have exploited or enslaved people from many regions, including North and South America, Oceania, most of Africa, and large parts of Asia. Such incursions have often subordinated or stigmatized large segments of indigenous populations on grounds of cultural or social difference, race, ethnicity, religion, gender, or age.

But such injustices are not always linked to external forces. Among Gebusi, the domination of women and the scapegoating of sorcerers grate roughly against the splendor of Gebusi ritual performance, spirit belief, and communal festivity. These paradoxes cannot be explained away by the impact of colonialism or Western intrusion.

This fact underscores the challenge that anthropologists face as they focus on social problems and encounter suffering caused or abetted by local customs. It is often difficult for cultural anthropologists to reconcile the wonder of cultural diversity with the difficulties that may be caused by subjugation or violence in the heart of the societies they study. In this regard, ethnographers frequently see social and political life during fieldwork through the crosshairs of local varieties of ethnocentrism, sexism, racism, ageism, religious intolerance, or other forms of scapegoatism. In the process, anthropologists often become more self-aware of the ethnical standards that they themselves hold and that they project or risk projecting onto the people they study. This was the dilemma I faced when I first began my fieldwork.

Ultimately, the Gebusi presented surprises beyond the delightful "good company" of their social life and the violence of their sorcery beliefs and gender practices. It was only later, after returning from the field, that I realized how rare it was even in New Guinea for indigenous customs to flourish with so little inhibition. But my bigger surprises came when I returned to live and work with the Gebusi in 1998 and again in 2008. I suspected that many new influences had swept through the years between these visits. On each occasion, I readied myself to find these changes and to take them at face value. But how could I know what lay in store?

By 1998, my old community had, by choice, picked up and moved from the deep forest to the outskirts of the Nomad Station, which boasts an airstrip and a government post. Previously isolated in their rainforest settlements, the Gebusi were now part of a multiethnic community in and around the station at Nomad, which includes more than a thousand persons speaking five different languages. In their new setting, my Gebusi friends were stalwart Christians worshipping at one of three local churches. Their children learned to read and write at the Nomad Community School for seven hours a day, five days a week. Gebusi men and boys organized their own rugby and soccer team, the "Gasumi Youths," which played supervised matches against rival groups each weekend on the government ballfield. On Tuesdays and Fridays, Gebusi women lugged heavy net bags of food from the forest and from their gardens to the Nomad Station market in hopes of earning a few coins. New crops such as manioc, peanuts, and pineapples sprouted in their gardens. Sweet potatoes were now a starch staple, and tubers were also grown for sale at the market.

Gebusi entertainment had also changed. On Friday and Saturday nights, young people tried to find a "party," "video night," or "disco"; dancing to cassette tapes of rock music was now the rage. Spirit séances had been replaced by modern music sung to the accompaniment of guitars and ukuleles. When children drew pictures of what they wanted to be when they grew up, their pages filled with colorful portraits of pilots, policemen, soldiers, heavy-machine operators, nurses, teachers, rock singers, and Christians in heaven. Though traditional dances still represented a kind of history or folklore, indigenous rituals were rarely staged in the villages. Without spirit mediums, Gebusi had no effective way to communicate with their traditional spirits, and sorcery inquests following death had been replaced by Christian funerals. Violence against sorcery suspects was practically nonexistent. The Gebusi themselves said that they had exchanged their old spirits for new ones associated with a more developed way of life. In the process, however, they had become subordinate to outsiders who were in charge of activities and institutions associated with the Nomad Station.

By 2008, Gebusi had changed strikingly once again. Due to logistical problems and lack of funds, the Nomad airstrip had been shut down. Government officials had left, the school, health clinic, and sports leagues were shut down, and the market was desultory. With many of their avenues to becoming modern cut off, Gebusi cultivated a remarkable resurgence of many of their traditional cultures—while also taking a much stronger role in the activities of their Catholic church. In character and emotional tone, they seemed to feel much more in charge of the life of their society.

If Gebusi were uncommonly traditional in 1980–82, they then became surprisingly modern—and since, they have more fully combined traditional elements and modern ones on their own terms. Not all peoples change so quickly, nor do they necessarily cycle between periods of less and greater traditional identity.

My fortune has been to forge a deep and lasting connection with a remote people who maintained amazingly rich traditions, sought out and developed a locally modern way of life, and then found greater solace and meaning in some of their earlier customs. The experiences of Gebusi can't, and don't, reflect those of other peoples around the world. But they do illustrate how people develop and change their lives under different conditions. The process of becoming modern while also retaining traditional identity is globally common but neither simple nor singular. Cultural change in the contemporary world is as diverse as the colors that refract through a prism. By seeing these refractions, we can understand how people in various regions share increasingly modern experiences but develop in unique traditional ways. Some peoples resist outside influences. Others blend old customs with new ones. Some agitate for their own autonomy while others accept national or international authority. Though these can be alternative processes, they are more commonly mixed within a single society. Sometimes they are combined in the motives and actions of single individuals. To study these developments is to engage an anthropology of cultural change and social transformation.

Given their distinctive path of tradition and change, the Gebusi provide an intriguing framework for viewing topics commonly covered in anthropology courses. These include the growing or gathering of food; the ways in which kin-ship organizes people into groups; patterns of social and economic exchange; features of leadership, politics, and dispute; religious beliefs and spiritual prac-tices; issues of sex and gender; the construction of ethnicity and race; the impact of colonialism and nationalism; and, through it all, the dynamics of sociocultural change. The first part of this book portrays these developments among the Gebusi in 1980–82; the second part examines them in 1998, and the third part examines them in 2008. Rather then describing the Gebusi in general terms, I present them as individuals whose lives have unfolded along with my own over the course of twenty-eight years.

My purpose in writing this book has been both simpler and more difficult than providing a general account of Gebusi culture. Rather, my goal has been to let the Gebusi as people come alive to the reader, to portray their past and their present, and to connect the dramatic changes they have undergone with those in my career and in contemporary anthropology.

PART ONE

1980–82

CHAPTER 1

The author snaps fingers in a welcoming line of adult Gebusi men. (PHOTO: Eileen Marie Knauft)

Friends in the Forest

THE BANANAS WERE ALL piled up, hot and grimy. Steam floated up from the pile—as if the air around us could have gotten any hotter. Some were stout as well as long, but most were slender, and a few were quite tiny. But their variety in dozens was a mystery to us then. All of them had been carefully scraped, but long strands of soot and globs of charcoal remained from their time in the fire.

What to do with this mound of starchy bananas, presented to us so formally in that first village? Kukudobi villagers had probably not seen a white person since 1975, five years before our arrival. At that time, the Australian patrol officers who had tramped to major settlements once a year and counted the local inhabitants suddenly left for good— along with the other Australians. Like a tempest in the forest, our arrival had certainly caused a hubbub. Children fled and men gasped with curious excitement. Emerging from under the trees, the four local men who were carrying our supplies took the lead, and we followed them ("When in Rome…") to the central longhouse. We sat down cross-legged, and a flood of villagers did likewise around us.

They must have done the cooking quickly or known about our arrival in advance, because it wasn't long before the smoldering stack of starch was brought in on a palm leaf platter and laid down with gusto in front of us. I was suddenly the focus of intense public scrutiny. Short men with bamboo tubes through their noses looked on from all around. I was too embarrassed to check with our carriers or even with Eileen about what I should do next. Everything was heat and stickiness. I took one of the sooty plantains and began to munch on it, trying to show appreciation, and Eileen did the same. The bananas were dry, but we forced ourselves to chew through one and pick up another. The people around us started to grin as we swallowed their food. Our progress was slow, however, and, judging from the size of the platter, our task was ultimately hopeless. Using my hands, I signaled that the pile of food was large, my stomach was small, and many people could certainly be fed. What a relief when they broke into pleasant conversation and stretched out their arms, sharing the bananas throughout the longhouse. We had apparently passed our first test.

11

Anthropologists often talk about "the gift," especially in Melanesia. How people put hard work and sweat, good intentions and hopes into tangible things that they give to one another speaks volumes about human connection. Gifts are at once a social economy and a materialized emotion. As Marcel Mauss suggested, gifts reflect and reinforce social bonds between givers and recipients. In American society, gifts at Christmastime are loaded with meanings that are reflected in whom we give presents to, how much thought and investment we put into each gift, and what reactions or returns we get in reciprocity.

As in many parts of New Guinea, Gebusi believed that gifts should be given to visitors who were peaceful. Their most basic gift was the fruit of their most regular work, as well as their primary source of nutrition: starchy cooked bananas. Well beyond the giving of basic food, however, material exchange was linked to human connection. Gebusi relationships were defined by the things that one gave or did not give to others. Later on, I established an "exchange name" with each man in our village—based on something that one of us had given to or shared with the other. Gusiayn was my "bird-egg," and Iwayb was my "Tahitian chestnut." Based on my own gifts, Yuway became my "fishing line," and Halowa my "salt." Whenever we saw each other, we called each other by these names, and our relationship was referred to similarly by others: "Here comes your 'bird egg;' there goes your 'salt'." To have a social identity and to have given and shared something that was memorable were one and the same.

In that first village of Kokudobi, Eileen and I were fortunate to have accepted those starchy bananas; we ate some and shared the rest with others. It was a simple act, but symbolic in ways we could not have anticipated. The patrol officers before us had also come to forest villages—once a year, to count heads for the colonial census. But they had brought along their servants or "houseboys" to cook the tins of meat and bags of rice they had hauled in. In our case, word had already spread that we were looking for a rainforest village to live in, and that we ate local food. So we received a hopeful reception of cooked bananas. The other features of traditional welcome were not yet on our horizon—the calling out of gift and kin names, the hearty snapping of fingers with each host, the dramatic sharing of smoke-filled tobacco pipes among men, the drinking of water from twelve-foot-long bamboo tubes, and the palaver that lasted until the hosts arrived with great whoops to present more food. But even in that first village, the lead card of social life, the giving of food, had been extended, and we had accepted. It was a good start.

As we soon found out, all the villages we visited wanted us to live with them. Though bossy, the Australians had provided a trickle of outside goods, and when they left, the trickle had dried up. Local people craved the trade items they now associated with us as white-skinned outsiders: cloth, salt, beads, fishing hooks, soap, and, especially, metal tools. When contrasted to a blunt stone adze, a steel ax goes through a rainforest tree like a knife through butter. Metal axes made it easy for people to clear bigger garden plots, grow more food, and build stronger houses. Metal knives and machetes found many further uses, from skinning animals to clearing weeds.

Besides stoking a passion for trade goods, the Australians left a political legacy that the Gebusi roundly appreciated: they pacified the Bedamini. More numerous and aggressive than the Gebusi or their other neighbors, the Bedamini people had traditionally sent war parties deep into neighboring areas. Their tactics were brutally efficient: surround an enemy longhouse at dawn, set it ablaze, and slaughter the inhabitants as they fled. Gebusi had been repeatedly victimized by these raids; in some cases, whole villages had been wiped out. Not infrequently, the Bedamini would cut up the bodies of those they had slain and carry them home for feasting. It is important to distinguish rumors of cannibalism from the actual practice. But its occurrence has been well documented and admitted among Bedamini—and by Gebusi themselves following the killing of sorcery suspects.

Being but 450 people against the Bedamini's 3,000, and with fewer residents in most of their settlements, Gebusi were no match for Bedamini warriors. If Australian patrol officers had not stepped in and stopped Bedamini raids, the Gebusi might have been only a remnant people by the time we arrived. As it was, thirteen years of colonial influence had gradually curtailed Bedamini expansion. In 1980, Gebusi were still visibly scared of the Bedamini, but they were seldom killed and no longer massacred by them. Despite, or perhaps because of, colonial intervention against their enemies, Gebusi themselves had rarely felt the boot of colonial domination. Australian patrol officers had been rough and bossy, but the benefits of their military intervention far outweighed the costs of their brief annual visits. Among Gebusi, the officers' main objectives were to update the local census and to lecture the villagers, via interpreters, about keeping the village clean and living in harmony with one another. The Australians viewed the Gebusi as victims rather than aggressors and as "quiet tractable people;" they seldom intervened in Gebusi affairs. Hence the irony that, even as the Bedamini were being pacified by armed patrols, the Gebusi were left alone to continue sorcery inquests, executions, and even cannibalism within their own communities. Living deep and scattered in the rainforest, they concealed their own actions from colonial interference.

Though the Gebusi in 1980 appeared to be a pristine people, in fact they were not. What we took to be "traditional" had flourished in the wake of the Australian pacification of the Bedamini and in the larger clearings, gardens, and villages that the Gebusi had produced with steel tools. Because Gebusi associated physical growth and social development with spiritual regeneration, the benefits of Bedamini pacification and of steel implements affirmed their religious values as well as their social life. Like streams that converge in the forest, material production and spiritual reproduction came increasingly together in major rituals, especially during the initiation of young people into adulthood. Gebusi lives swelled with the combined power of religious, sexual, and social force. Ironically, then, colonial intrusion gave the Gebusi the freedom to develop many of their own customs and beliefs. In some ways, Gebusi had become even more "Gebusi-like" than they had been before. Although they seemed unacculturated, Gebusi traditions underscored the importance of changes all around them. A tribal powerhouse had been laid low while the neighboring Gebusi had been left to cultivate their own customs. By the 1980s, Gebusi resented Bedamini not so much

for their former raids as for being recipients of government development projects that the Gebusi wanted for themselves.

That Gebusi combined an exuberant tradition with a desire for contact with
outsiders made them a perfect fit for us. Little wonder that we were enamored of
them or that they wanted us for themselves. At first, however, we weren't interested.

Our journey had begun with a blank spot on a map. That was where my graduate advisor and I had thought, back at the University of Michigan, that I would
find the most fascinating people. The largest scale maps then available were produced by the U.S. Army—in case even the remotest parts of the globe needed
military intervention. The map of Papua New Guinea's Western Province showed
an unknown space that stretched across a swampy rainforest north of the Tomu
River. The two of us thought that the culture of the people who lived there could
be roughly triangulated on the basis of what was known about groups that lived
twenty-five to forty miles away in different directions. There was no name for the
peoples of the Tomu River, but I talked by phone to a missionary who had completed some aerial survey work in the area. He thought that the closest people
were probably the "Kramo." Armed with this information, I obtained funding from
the U.S. National Science Foundation and the U.S. National Institutes of Health
to study political consensus formation led by spirit mediums among people called
the Kramo in a remote rainforest in Papua New Guinea's Western Province.

But there was a good reason for the blank spot on the map: no one lived
there. Eileen and I finally accepted this fact after leaving Kukudobi and trudging
for what seemed like forever to the distant village of Honabi, at the edge of the
settlements of the Honibo ethnic group. The inhabitants told us consistently, and
in as many ways as our inadequate language would allow, that there was nothing
farther ahead of us but swamp and mosquitoes, both of which we had already
endured to our limit. They also informed us that the few people, called the
Kabasi, who had previously lived in this area had deserted it and gone to live near
a crocodile skin trading post to the east. Even if we had wanted to continue our
trek into their erstwhile territory, our carriers would not agree to go with us. Our
trail had ended. In professional terms, we had traveled to Papua New Guinea on
doctoral research grants to study people whom we couldn't find or who didn't
exist (see map on page 15).

Sensing our uncertainty and perhaps our fear, the Honibo people brightly
insisted that we stay and live with them instead. Though they claimed that they
had a tradition of entranced spirit singing, their assertions were hedged with
ambivalence. When we probed deeper, they also admitted that they typically abandoned their village for several months during the dry season, split into tiny groups,
and foraged for food even deeper in the rainforest. As the evening grew longer
and the mosquitoes bit harder, the prospect of adapting to their lifestyle for two
years seemed more dreadful than admitting failure. Not knowing what else to do,
we opted to trudge back to the Nomad Station via the village that our carriers
lived in, which was not altogether out of the way. The more we found out about

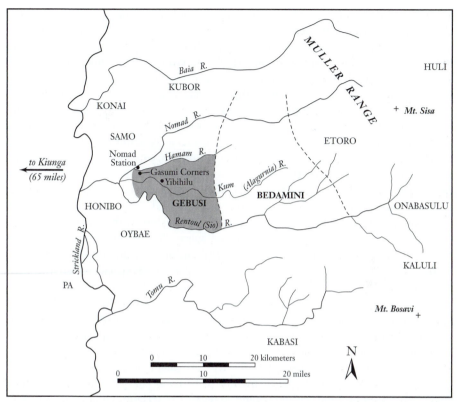

The Gebusi and nearby groups

this impending stop, the more interested we became. By this time, our carriers had become real people to us. Yuway was a wonderfully decent young man, as sensitive as he was tall, and strong for a Gebusi. He had a spontaneous sense of concern, interest, and patience even though we couldn't yet communicate verbally. He would wait to help us over slippery log bridges, and he usually volunteered to shoulder the heaviest load. Gono never said much, but he was as sinewy and dependable as a tree, and he was always alert. Hawi was our nominal interpreter, and though his translations ultimately proved more troublesome than helpful, he was socially and physically agile. Finally there was Swamin, older than his unmarried companions by half a generation but more muscled than they. He would flash a captivating smile under his impish hooked nose and pepper his remarks with articulate bursts that, given the reactions he got from the other three, convinced us that he was both very funny and very smart. As Hawi informed us, Swamin was also a spirit medium who held communal séances on a regular basis.

When we finally reached their village of Yibihilu, the "place of the deep waters," we thought we had reached the local version of paradise. We had stumbled for days through a sea of foliage, mud, and vines under a closed rainforest canopy. We felt like the miniature children in *Honey, I Shrunk the Kids!* as they navigated enormous obstacles in a galactic backyard of foliage. I yearned to look up and out, to see more than the next hidden root that could send us sprawling. The "place of the deep waters," by contrast, was perched on a forty-foot bluff overlooking a serpentine bend in the Kum River. The porch of the longhouse extended out over a canyon through which the river rushed before pooling in a serene basin some hundred yards wide and across which we could see a crocodile lazing in the sun. Farther downstream, the watercourse was calm enough to be traveled by canoe—which was far preferable to tromping through the muddy forest. At dusk, the sky above the river became a breathtaking sunset. The villagers would stop and stare. *Bubia maysum*—"The crimson is being laid down."

If the village seemed majestic, the people were yet better. Having learned more about us from our carriers in five minutes that the other villages had in five days, their kin and friends gave us the kind of warm welcome, especially in such a remote place, that made us feel on top of the world rather than at its end. As the traumas and troubles of our journey were discussed to the tiniest detail, the villagers laughed good-naturedly. That we were already trying to speak their language—however haltingly—was widely and enthusiastically noted. That we ate local food and that I had somehow carried my own backpack, which the men enjoyed trying on, were also taken as positive signs. There was also a bonus in that Eileen was present. White women had rarely been seen by the Gebusi, and probably never in Yibihilu. Eileen shared food and laughter with the women and played with the children. They were enthusiastic and responded in kind. If the men "had" me, the women took Eileen into their own world.

In remarkably short stead, our physical presence, our possessions, and our desire to speak the local tongue seemed to paint us as paragons of beneficence, a gold mine of goods, and a three-ringed circus of entertainment rolled into one. Our hands were shaken, fingers snapped, and bellies gorged with countless gifts of food. Everyone seemed quite genuinely to want our friendship. If our reception was anything less than overwhelming, we were too euphoric to notice. As if we needed further encouragement, Swamin held an all-night spirit séance. Word of our presence had drawn villagers from surrounding hamlets. Given the convergence of so many people and the surge of good feelings, a songfest of celebration was almost inevitable. The stars shone as they do only when there is no competing light for hundreds of miles. The songs of the men swelled as the silhouette of the forest canopy loomed over us in the moonlight. Beneath the glow, their deep harmonies echoed through the village as if in a wild cathedral. The music was different from and more amazing than any I had ever heard. I knew that the Gebusi believed in a whole realm of forest spirits and unseen places that come alive through the songs of the spirit medium. But as the sound washed over me, I knew almost nothing of its meaning. In the moment, this only added to the mystery and splendor of the Gebusi cosmos—a world of wonder I had come to explore.

❀   ❀   ❀

There was so much that we didn't know about the Gebusi at first—including their name. Our ethnographic maps and the missionary who had told us about the "Kramo" had placed a group called the "Bibo" at our present location. But the people of Yibihilu found this terribly funny. They brought us a large starchy banana and indicated that this was the only "bibo" in their territory—one of their three-dozen varieties of plantains. There were no people called "Bibo." They said in no uncertain terms that their own identity, and also their language, was "Gebusi."

The discoveries of fieldwork had already brought us full circle. Eileen and I had gone halfway around the world to study a Kramo people who didn't exist. We had projected their presence based on our incomplete maps and our imaginations. But the people we did find—and came to like so quickly—were, at least in academic name, an undiscovered group. As green and insecure as we were at the time, this was a comfort. In retrospect, though, our nominal "discovery" exposed as much about ourselves as it did about the people we were living with: it revealed our Western drive to label other peoples and to project onto them our own sense of discovery. Like many anthropologists, we were starting to learn new things about our own way of life at the same time, and in many respects for the very reason that we were trying to reach out and understand the lives of others.

Beyond the Gebusi's name, we also quickly encountered one of their central concepts—one that took much longer to understand. With predictable difficulty, we had been trying to explain exactly why we had come to the rainforest. Villagers were especially curious about this because we didn't fit the mold of whites they had previously encountered or heard about. Were we patrol officers who ordered people around and then disappeared for another year? No. Were we those white people they had heard about but never seen who held up a big book (the Bible) and exhorted villagers not to dance or be initiated but to sing to a new spirit instead? No, not that either. Then why had we come? We tried to communicate that we wanted to learn and speak their language, to understand their songs, to watch their dances, to join them at their feasts—in short, to be with them as they lived and learn what they were like. In a flash, they seemed to grasp our meaning: we wanted to learn their *kogwayay*. They appeared so certain of this that we had no choice or desire but to agree with them. Of course, we had no idea what *kogwayay* meant. But in truth, they were entirely correct.

Kogwayay is—or at least was in 1980–82—the single word that best describes the heart of Gebusi culture. In a way, the term even represents their concept of culture itself—the beliefs, practices, and styles of living that are special and unique to them as a people. At one level, *kogwayay* refers to customs that make the Gebusi different from others. As Gebusi themselves used the term, it refers especially to their distinctive traditions of dancing, singing, and bodily decoration. But what is the term's deeper meaning? The Gebusi were not much help here. For them, *kogwayay* was a catchall marker of cultural distinction rather than a tool for dissecting it.

When you think about it, it's not surprising that people have a hard time explaining concepts that are central to their culture. Such meanings are often seen as "beyond words." How easy would it be for your average American, Canadian, or Englishman to define and explain what "love" is to someone who had never heard of this term? In the case of *kogwayay*, we were fortunate that the word breaks down into three distinct units of meaning, what linguists call morphemes: *kog-*, *-wa-*, and *-yay*. *Kog* conveys "togetherness," "friendship," and "similarity." These meanings reflected the collective and communal nature of Gebusi life.

Gebusi almost always preferred to do things with as many other people as possible, and they hated being alone. They were the opposite of loners. The *wa* component of the word is the Gebusi root of *wa-la*, "to talk." It refers to pleasant dialogues and conversations that are roundly shared. This is what the men did in the longhouse at night—they "*wa*-la'd" by sharing news and gossip, joking, fantasizing, and telling stories around the small yellow glow of the resin lantern. This was the Gebusi equivalent of the late-night talk that echoes through the halls of a college dorm. Hour after hour and evening after evening, I came to realize how rare it was for the Gebusi to get angry with one another in these gabfests. Disagreements were tempered by friendly smiles; embarrassments were covered by jokes and shifts of conversation.

Yay supplied the exuberant conclusion to *kog-wa-yay*, its exclamation point. Particularly for men, to *yay* or to *kay* is to cheer, yell, joke, and cry out as loudly and happily as possible—and preferably in unison with other men. These yells have bodily meaning as well. When a Gebusi called out in concert with those around him, his "breath-heart" *(solof)* pushed out and mingled with that of others. To *yay* or *kay* is to send forth and unite human spiritual energy; it is a vital assertion of collective life.

Taken together, what do *kog-*, *-wa-*, and *-yay* mean? And why should we care? No single English word captures their essence—and this fact is important. As anthropologists, we are charged with learning and conveying concepts that are important to other people even and especially when they exceed our initial understanding. *Kogwayay* was clearly important to the Gebusi. The word was frequently used and talked about, it evoked strong feelings, and it was highly elaborated in central rituals and ceremonies. In Gebusi culture, *kogwayay* was what anthropologist Sherry Ortner has more generally called a "key symbol." Collectively, the three meanings of the word—togetherness, talk, and cheering—conveyed core Gebusi values of happy social unity, of living in good company with one another. And *kogwayay* permeated Gebusi social life. This was evident on a daily basis and was epitomized at important events such as feasts, dances, spirit séances, and the initiation of teenagers into adulthood.

Although *kogwayay* was a powerful and deeply held concept, it did not stand alone. It highlighted the positive side of Gebusi culture, the bright side of their moon. Most peoples try to depict themselves in a good and favorable light, and the Gebusi were no exception. If you were asked to name central values in American and other Western societies, you might mention concepts such as "freedom," "individuality," "love of country," "economic success," "love," and "family values." Of course, we all know that these are sometimes ideals more than realities. Many marriages end in divorce; families can be shackled by poverty; and discrimination based on race, ethnicity, sex, or age can be as deeply ingrained as it is illegal. A critic from another culture might argue that American society is cutthroat, egotistical, hedonistic, imperialistic, and much less equal or free than we like to believe. If culture is an assertion of ideals and values, these can sometimes serve to hide problems or difficulties. In this sense, culture is a double-edged sword of beliefs and representations. On the one hand, it emphasizes values and ideals that are often, if not typically, good and healthy. On the other hand, trumpeting these values can also downplay or deny less pleasant realities. Certainly it would be shortsighted to dismiss the importance of cultural values. Where would we be without them? So, too, it is good to appreciate the values of other peoples, including the Gebusi. But it is also important to recognize the underside of culture—realities that are neglected by cultural ideals. Both sides of this coin are important.

Where do we draw the line between an appreciative and a critical view of cultural values? Do we emphasize the fight to free the slaves during the American Civil War? Or the history of slavery that made that war necessary? Do we emphasize the human benefit of toppling a dictator like Saddam Hussein? Or the many lives that have been lost as a result? Such questions have few simple answers. But asking them makes us more aware of both the positive power of culture and the problems it can hide.

Gebusi culture can be viewed in this same light. The good company of *kogwayay* was a strong practice as well as a wonderful ideal. But *kogwayay* was also controlled and dominated by men. It was men rather than women who collectively cheered and publicly yelled. Men were the ones who gathered for public talk each evening on the large porch that overlooked the river. During this time, women were largely confined to whispered conversations in a cramped female sleeping room along one wall of the longhouse, away from the men and older boys. In terms of decision making, it was typically men who determined which settlement their respective families would live in—who would have togetherness, and with whom. Men took charge of the events most strongly associated with *kogwayay*—ritual feasts, dances, spirit séances, and initiations. At feasts, men from the host village would proudly present visitors with piles of cooked sago starch—though this food was produced by women's hard labor. In the evenings, it was men who dressed up in stunning costumes to dance. At initiations, young men were the main focus and were decorated most elaborately. As if to deny the notion of motherhood, boys were nurtured to manhood not by females but, as described in Chapter 5, by the men themselves—through the transmission of male life force from one generation to the next.

Male control was especially pronounced at spirit séances. Late in the evening, men would gather in the dark longhouse and arrange themselves around the spirit medium while he sat, smoked tobacco, and slowly went into a controlled trance. The medium's own spirit would then leave his body and be replaced by a soul from the spirit world. After a while, the new spirit's voice would start chanting through the spirit medium, first whispering and then singing in soft falsetto tones. As the words of the spirit became clearer, the men clustered around the medium and formed a chorus to echo them. Their singing encouraged the medium's spirit to sing louder and with greater confidence. Gradually, the spirit's chants became full songs, each line of which was repeated and chorused in full harmony and top voice, by a robust male chorus.

At the same time, Gebusi women were excluded from the séance, though they were exposed to its content as they sat or dozed in their cramped quarters. Meanwhile, the men shouted, joked, and laughed; the occasion was an all-night songfest of masculine bravado. Perhaps most strikingly, the primary spirits who sang were young women. And not just any women, but gorgeous young spirit women who longed to have sex and joke with Gebusi men. In effect, the men's séance singing voiced, projected, and received back their sexual fantasies of women—at the same time that real Gebusi women could be beaten by husbands or brothers for being flirtatious. By contrast, spirit women were literally embodied by the men themselves, first in the voice of the male spirit medium and then in the men's collective chorus. Spirit séances were thus, to some degree, a male fantasy that celebrated men's sexual desires at the same time that real Gebusi women were excluded, controlled, and sometimes disparaged.

Given this male bias, what were we to make of Gebusi "good company"? Was kogwayay merely a cultural value that disguised male dominance over women? This question brings us to the crux of anthropology's appreciation of cultural diversity, on the one hand, and its critique of inequality on the other. For the most part, Gebusi women accepted and appreciated the culture they lived in. At spirit séances, they sometimes took offense at male joking, but more often they indulged and genuinely enjoyed it. Women were excited and galvanized by ritual feasts and initiations, and they actively played their own roles at these events. On these and other occasions, they enjoyed interacting with women who visited from other settlements. In part, it was true that Gebusi women lived in the cultural shadow of Gebusi men. Sometimes they resisted their second-class status, but for the most part they accepted and embraced it. As Eileen found out, the women swelled with pride at their own and the men's accomplishments, even when men presented the fruits of women's work as their own. So, too, women tended to accept men's collective prerogative to take violent action against sorcery suspects and also (though not in all cases) the right of a man to beat his wife.

Just as Gebusi women reached a basic if occasionally ambivalent accommodation with Gebusi men, the same was true for Eileen and me. Anthropologists are not immune to the ethical tensions of the communities they study. Indeed, it seems impossible during the course of fieldwork *not* to be influenced by moral and ethical tensions. Admitting these tensions is important; they form part of our work and part of who we are. For our part, Eileen and I had encountered strong debates about gender relations and women's rights when we were students at the University of Michigan. Women I knew and respected, including Eileen, identified strongly with the cause of women's rights. So did I. Gender and sex were also becoming central issues of anthropological study. Hard as it may be to imagine now, the activities and opinions of women in foreign cultures had often been neglected in earlier anthropology research. To remedy this bias, it was important to actively study both women's experiences and their relations with men in ethnographic fieldwork.

In many if not most regions of the world, the activities and experiences of men and women differ significantly. Among the peoples and cultures of New Guinea, the division between male and female realms is especially marked. But the Gebusi were more complicated than this. It was obvious from the start that notions of femaleness and fantasies about women were central to the ceremonial life of men. So, too, the discrepancy between men's fantasies and the actual role of women was substantial. But just as few women would talk to me about important issues, men would not talk to Eileen about the role of women in the spirit world. The men absorbed me into their culture with gusto, including in their all-night songfests, ritual joking and smoking, feast preparations, and initiation secrets. Though women worked to enable many of these events, they stayed on the sidelines and often had little to say about the proceedings. More than women, men had an elaborate verbal culture and talked energetically with visiting outsiders. Extending this pattern, they actively cultivated my ability to speak Gebusi so that they could share information with me.

The social life of Gebusi men was, simply put, a lot of fun. I enjoyed their banter and horseplay, smoked their tobacco through big bamboo tubes, joked with them, and participated in community feasts. To her great credit, Eileen gathered a wealth of information about Gebusi women. As is common in communal but sex-segregated societies, Gebusi women had their own female-centered interactions. Their more muted style of socializing is easier to appreciate in hindsight, however, than it was for either of us at the time. The children, though, were a source of joy for us both. Eileen took a particular liking to an impish little boy named Sayu. He was four or five years old and simply the most charismatic child either of us had ever known. His mother, Boyl, was an attractive woman with a broad smile and, we thought, the strongest intellect in the village. This sealed her friendship with Eileen; theirs was a special relationship. For a while, we had Boyl cook and share food with us, with Sayu never far away. However, her husband became jealous, and this ended the arrangement.

In the beginning, we didn't know what would happen next. We knew that the people of Yibihilu were vibrant and welcoming and that their culture was alive with song and celebration. We had naiveté, energy, and trust in our purpose. And these were indispensable for fieldwork that was both deeply difficult and ultimately limitless. After several weeks of visiting, it was time for us and for the people of Yibihilu to decide if a house should be built for us at "the place of the deep waters." The villagers continued to be friendly, and some of them were becoming our personal friends. But they were also very different from us, and we felt the force of this difference.

One night, the conversation finally turned—uncertainly, via Hawi—to how long we would stay in Yibihilu. Dusk was turning into night, and the men and boys around me became silhouettes with bones in their noses and feathers in their hair. Trophy skulls of pigs and cassowaries swayed from the rafters. A chunk of resin sizzled on the stone lamp. I looked up and saw people and personalities I was beginning to know. But they also appeared alien. Some were covered head to foot with the scaly skin of ringworm. Others had streaks of soot or caked ulcers on their skin or large cracks in the thick callouses that lined their feet. Their toes splayed, as if they had been born to stride along mossy log bridges that Eileen and I inched across timidly. Even when sitting down, I towered over them. My gawky six-foot-plus white frame stood out against their dark bodies, which averaged just five feet four inches at full height. But their skill and prowess in the forest dwarfed my own. How quickly and silently they could climb a tree, club a lizard, shoot a fish, or ford a stream. I knew that until recently they had eaten the flesh of persons killed as sorcerers. Their polished arrows were propped in the corner. Many layers of their culture remained obscure to me. The joy of our beginning made me question whether my giddiness would change to disillusion-ment when the novelty of our warm welcome wore off. But the dice, it seemed, had already been rolled. After undergoing years of scholarly training, journeying halfway around the world, and enduring mosquitoes and leeches, and with my personal and professional identity on the line, how could I turn back? They asked, "How long do you think you will stay?" I heard myself say, "Two years." My head swam as I heard the hubbub around me. But in the best Gebusi tradition of "everything is going to be fine," the discussion quickly turned to where the thatched house for us should be built. On this side of the village? Or on that one? The following morning, strings were laid on the ground to mark where the walls would be. Our house was built above them.

CHAPTER 2

Men bring back bananas from gardens along the Kum River. (PHOTO: Bruce Knauft)

Rhythms of Survival

Boyl slung her load of leaves to the ground as the other women staggered into the village and followed suit. The foliage had been stripped from sago palms, folded, and then loaded onto their backs in net bags that were supported by tumplines across their foreheads. These leaves would form the bulk of our house, as they do all Gebusi dwellings. We hardly guessed that a house made mostly of leaves could provide shelter against up to fourteen feet of rainfall each year and in temperatures that top one hundred degrees. But they do. The leaves are carefully pinned to wooden strips about five feet long, from which they extend by almost a yard. Hundreds of these leaf strips are lashed like shingles to the roof beams of the house, with just an inch or so over-lap between each strip and the one above it. For the village longhouse, which measured 74 by 34 feet, the tens of thousands of leaves needed for the structure easily weighed several tons. The bulk of the dwelling was the massive roof, which peaked almost twenty-five feet high in the air and sloped over the house's windowless walls until it almost touched the ground.

We were intrigued to see our own house take shape. Yuway and the other men scampered over the frame like skilled acrobats, hoisting log supports and the heavy ridgepole. Without measuring tape, plumb line, or any materials other than wood, leaves, and vines, they built the roof and then the rest of the house with all the confidence of a first-rate construction crew. The Gebusi overcame a lack of formal training with practical ingenuity and intimate knowledge of forest materials. Their indigenous numbers are just three: "one" (*hele*), "two" (*bena*), and "two plus one" (*bene bwar hele bwar*). Anything greater than that is simply "many" (*bihina*). Counting was as irrelevant to the Gebusi as their phys-ical skills were finely honed. As ad hoc engineers, they were astounding. This is not to say that arithmetic has been undeveloped in the history of other non-Western cultures. Western counting systems are them-selves based on Arabic numerals that are mid-Eastern in origin. In New Guinea itself, some societies have developed elaborate numerologies. Like the ancient Babylonians, the Kapauku people of West New Guinea developed a base-sixty number system, which they used to count items into the thousands just for fun. But one group's chosen passion is another's apathy. Although the Gebusi shortchanged their numerals, they had a rich vocabulary for a seemingly endless variety of plants, vines, and trees, each of which had special properties and uses.

If culture humanizes the environment, the Gebusi longhouse was their biggest accomplishment of material culture. Being the main gathering place for the fifty-two residents of Yibihilu, the "house long" (*masam sak*) was their tangible sign of village cooperation, physical prowess, and collective labor. Materially minded anthropologists describe culture as "adaptive" because its creative diversity has allowed humans to survive in so many different physical environments—from the Arctic to the tropics and practically everywhere in between, for tens of thousands of years. Whereas other animals are limited largely by genetically determined or "instinctual" paths of behavior, we humans add an enormous capacity for learning and for organizing our efforts through language. As Leslie White put it, culture gives us an "extra-somatic" way to adapt to the world around us.

Given the prominence of the Gebusi longhouse, it surprised us at first that it was often almost empty. It turned out that the longhouse was the permanent residence of just two extended families, with the others living in smaller houses in the community clearing. But the longhouse had been built by the community at large and it functioned as the general evening gathering place and site of community celebrations and collective rituals. Although humming with energy when the village was full of people, the central dwelling gave way to the surrounding forest as a focus of activity during the bulk of most days. Hawi goes off with a group of young men to spear fish. Boyl and her husband depart to collect bananas from a distant garden and to see if tubers are ready to harvest. Two young girls leave with their adult sisters to forage for fresh bamboo shoots, to rummage in the nest of a wild bush hen for eggs, or to scoop for freshwater prawns under rocks in the stream. Along the way, they keep a keen eye open for a stray bush rat or snake that could be clubbed with a stick or sliced with a knife. Men carry bows and arrows and look for signs of a wild pig, a sleeping lizard, a possum on a low-lying branch, or a large, flightless cassowary bird scavenging in the brush. Even a good-sized tarantula can be seized for the cooking fire. The Gebusi eat practically anything that moves.

By late afternoon, those within a reasonable distance return to the village for an evening meal and general conversation. The atmosphere is languid as families congregate. Men sit together and share large bamboo tube pipes filled with powerful home-grown tobacco. Women chat as they stoke the hearth and cook the bananas. Back in the forest, some families find themselves too deep in the bush to return for the night; they make a temporary camp and sleep in a makeshift shelter or lean-to. Imba and his wife, Walab, walk for a day to distant clan land, accompanied by their siblings and children. The men in the group chop down and split open a stately sago palm; then the women pound the soft interior of the tree into pith. Deep in the forest, it can take women two weeks or more to process the pith and leach its pulpy fiber into heavy bundles of caked sago flour. In the meantime, the whole group lives in the forest. Imba and his male kin hunt and forage; the children play together or set off with a group of adults to gather breadfruit or Tahitian chestnuts from stands of trees. The mini-community sleeps in a temporary shelter of poles and sticks covered with sago leaf thatch to keep out the rain. When the sago palm is completely processed, the fruits of the women's labor are bundled in bark, wrapped in leaves, slung on their backs in big net bags, and hauled to the river, where the sago can be taken back to the settlement by canoe. For weeks on end, the heavy parcels will supply starchy flour that can be easily stored and then wrapped in fresh leaves and cooked directly on the fire.

Beyond its food, the rainforest is ripe with meaning. Hogayo lingers by an old settlement where his father was born; Walab stops to drink from a stream that belongs to her mother's family line. Memories are associated with each stand of trees, creek, small hillock, or patch of old garden land that has since been overgrown. For the Gebusi, to walk through the forest is to relive past experiences and to remember what the forest has provided their kin, their ancestors, and themselves. They rediscover how the trees have grown, when their fruits will be ripe, what animals have left traces nearby, and when the area can be revisited to reap one or another natural harvest. The forest is not simply "land," it is a living tableau with meaning and nuance in each nook and wrinkle. Gebusi describe their lands with fondness and nostalgia. They name individual places and luxuriate in their tranquil distinctions. When the Gebusi sing at dances and séances, many of their most haunting songs recall places in the forest.

Between daily trips and more extended ones, the residents of Yibihilu spent almost half their nights—45 percent, to be precise—in the forest or at another settlement. In earlier days, they could easily scatter to the bush if they knew or thought that enemies or foreigners were on the prowl. It is no surprise, then, that the early Australian patrol officers struggled to locate groups of Gebusi in the forest. Partly out of frustration, they labeled the local population as "nomads." Indeed, they designated the whole region as the Nomad Sub-District and named their government station the Nomad Patrol Post. In fact, though, they were mistaken. Anthropologists define nomads as people who have no permanent residence— people who shift their settlement every few weeks to hunt and or to tend their livestock. Sedentary peoples, by contrast, build durable houses and live in long-lasting settlements. Certainly, the Gebusi longhouse qualifies as a durable residence, and even in pre-colonial times, Gebusi villages lasted for at least several years. Though the Gebusi travel extensively across their lands, they identify themselves as members of a specific settlement and spend over half of their nights in their principal residence.

If the Gebusi lifestyle sometimes flirts with being semi-nomadic, it is tempered by the benefits of growing food in gardens that can be reached by an hour or two of walking from the main settlement. Notwithstanding festive attractions of communal village living, Gebusi survival depends on growing crops, especially bananas, in cleared gardens. In their part of the lowland rainforest, large game animals aren't plentiful. These are mostly wild pigs or flightless cassowaries, which look like strange, small ostriches. Though the Gebusi eat and enjoy the smaller creatures of the forest, these don't supply many calories on a daily basis. It is doubtful whether the Gebusi could survive on the basis of hunting, fishing, and gathering alone.

In a very few areas of the world, including along the coast of the northwestern United States and southwestern Canada, wild resources such as fish and nuts were plentiful enough so that indigenous peoples could form large and complex societies even without growing their own food. Along parts of the south coast of New Guinea, where the swamp is flush with both fish and sago palms, native peoples flourished and maintained large villages while foraging for these wild foods. But in the rainforest where the Gebusi live, which is two hundred miles inland, fish and sago aren't plentiful enough to provide a steady diet. So the Gebusi plant gardens, even if they do this as simply and with as little work as possible.

The biggest task, at least for the men, is the felling of trees. Though most families maintain individual gardens, large ones also may be cleared as a communal project. After several weeks at Yibihilu, we went with some villagers to see how this was done. We left in high spirits, the men whooping and the children frolicking. It was going to be a big garden. As we walked twenty minutes to the site, it felt more like a festive occasion than a work brigade.

Along with the rest of the men, I took turns chopping trees and resting by the makeshift cooking fires while chatting, munching bananas, and smoking Gebusi tobacco. To my surprise, Yuway told me not to chop any of the trees all the way through—each time I was stopped when I was only about halfway done. The other men were doing the same. Perplexed, I asked why. I became only more confused when Yuway and the other men made dramatic pantomimes of noise and crashing. After two more hours of "half-work," hardly a single tree had been felled. My companions seemed quite content and even expectant while I remained baffled. Our work pace dwindled until only a handful of men were left at one end of the large plot. There, they attacked a particularly large and majestic piece of timber—while the rest of us were waved off to the far margins of the area. Everyone took great pains to tell Eileen and me that we should not, under any circumstances, wander back into the garden area. Knowing that the Gebusi had deep spiritual ties to their land—and that many of their spirits lived in large trees—I thought that the land might now be under a spiritual taboo. Perhaps special rites or spells would be performed by the senior men to supplicate the spirits of the largest tree before felling it, so the spirits wouldn't be angry about the destruction of their "home." Maybe after that, I thought, we would finish chopping the biggest tree's smaller cousins. But I was wrong.

A few minutes later, the enormous tree began to creak and groan in response to the continuing blows of the senior men's axes. Though towering above the lesser trees, a thick skein of vines and foliage knitted it to its neighbors. Finally, it tottered and fell with an amazing crash. As it went down, its force spread to the other trees in domino fashion—through the entire acre of half-cut timber. In a flash, hefty trunks were toppled and flung in all directions—like telephone poles ripped up by a falling master pylon. It was frightful, wonderful, and awe-ful—an arboreal tornado. Then, as quickly as it started, it was over. All that remained were the whoops of the men, the blizzard of leaves that filled the sky on their way to the ground, and a garden plot strewn with fallen trees. Stunned, I had to sit down.

As I regained my bearings, my confusion persisted. The trees had been felled with remarkably little effort, to be sure. But now their massive trunks and branches smothered the garden land beneath. How could the plot be planted, much less cultivated? Yuway and the others were unconcerned. They pointed out that banana suckers and root crop seedlings had already been stuck in the ground days before. When I had arrived at the site and the trees had still been standing, I had not even noticed them. Although a few of these plantings were now crushed by the fallen limbs, most of them were merely sheltered from the blaze of the sun and the pelting of rains by the branches that now hovered just over them. Without this covering, the new seedlings would have wilted in the tropical sun or been washed away by torrential storms. As the foliage of the fallen trees decomposed above them, the crops beneath would sprout through these fertilizing remains and would then be strong enough to grow unshielded. Though the garden now looked like a chaos of fallen limbs, it was, in fact, a finely honed and ingenious means of cultivation. Anthropologist Edward Schieffelin gave the practice a fitting name: "felling the trees on top of the crop."

The main food planted in Gebusi gardens is, of course, plantains—starchy bananas. These require almost no weeding, grow quickly, and don't bear fruit until the plants have hoisted their caloric pods beyond the reach of wild pigs. As a result, Gebusi dispense with having to build fences to keep animals such as pigs away from their crops. Theoretically, the bananas could be eaten by birds and fruit bats when they ripen, but most of the plantains are starchy rather than of the sweet variety that attract flying freeloaders. In any event, villagers usually harvest the fruit before it is ripe enough for birds and bats to eat. The hard plantains are made edible by simply throwing them on the fire: as the thick banana skin is charred, the fruit inside softens and cooks. Retrieved with wooden cooking tongs, the bananas are then scraped of charcoal and eaten straightaway.

The Gebusi grow crops without laboring heavily. Because they let the land lie fallow and regenerate for many years before recutting and replanting it, their food raising qualifies as "horticulture." By contrast, anthropologists usually define "agriculture" as cultivation that requires greater effort—practices such as irrigating, fertilizing, plowing, fencing, and/or terracing. These techniques increase the quantity of crops that can be raised on a given piece of land, but they exact a heavy price in physical labor or mechanized intervention. The Gebusi stay happily at the other end of this continuum. Because they have plenty of land, they have little need to invest great effort in any one plot. Even the best garden plots are abandoned after one or two plantings. Weeds, shrubs, and then trees emerge as the rainforest reclaims its terrain. A new layer of nutrients enriches the poor clay soil. Ideally, the grandson of the man who planted the initial garden comes back to reclaim and recultivate it. In so doing, he draws upon the ancestral substance of the regenerated land as he fortifies his own essence and that of his family.

The resulting cycle of reproduction is hence spiritual and cultural as well as caloric and demographic—the rejuvenation of land, food, people, and spiritual bonds. Given that land is plentiful, it is easily lent to friends and kin. As such, the land and the energy of the spirits are a collective rather than an individual resource.

Across generations, Gebusi have maintained an ample supply of food in a part of the rainforest that is not particularly bountiful. In the process, they don't seem to have strained themselves unduly. Certainly, they endure stints of intense labor. Women carry more than their share of heavy loads through the rainforest, and they transport firewood, food, and even their babies in net bags slung on their backs. Although men can also bear these burdens, it is women who give the Gebusi their ultimate "carrying capacity." Even for women, however, many hours on most days drift by in relaxation—conversing, eating, and playing with children. And men have even more time for social pursuits than women. Their palavers extend for long hours into the evening, by which time most women are asleep. Every week and a half or so, men gather for an all-night spirit séance. After this extended songfest, they typically sleep for a good part of the following day. In addition, there are all-night ritual feasts and dances that energize the entire settlement; these occurred about once a month during 1980–82.

Marshall Sahlins has called simple human cultures "original affluent societies." Although the technology and material culture may be rudimentary, people in such societies are typically able to spend hours each day socializing or lazing around. Although obtaining food and shelter require work, this effort ebbs and flows not so much as a struggle against nature but in relaxed harmony with the environment. From the icy Arctic to the parched deserts of central Australia, simple human societies have survived with plenty of time to spare. Against this standard, the growing complexity and advanced technology of modern societies reduces rather than increases our leisure time. On most nights, the Gebusi get a good nine hours or more of sleep. Here in the United States, I am lucky to get seven. Each of our so-called labor-saving devices brings new demands for productive work.

If Gebusi lives throw the frenzied pace of modern society into relief, they also possess their own afflictions. Their deeper struggle has not been so much to acquire food as to fight off illness and, as discussed in the next chapter, to endure the human violence fueled by sickness and death. The Gebusi's biggest enemies have ultimately been very small. Mosquitoes bring the scourge of malaria. Parasitic worms cause chronic and draining illnesses. Communicable diseases such as tuberculosis and introduced influenza wreak havoc. In the hot, humid climate, cuts and scrapes easily fester and form debilitating skin ulcers. All these ailments sap energy and could be combatted by better nutrition. But Gebusi are at pains to improve their diet. Though their staples of plantains and sago brim with starch, they give little protein. Forest animals can be hunted, but they are hard to catch on a regular basis or in large numbers. Hunting more often deep in the forest would also expose Gebusi to yet more mosquitoes and malaria and would put them at greater risk of accident and injury. Malnutrition is hence a problem. Young children often have the tiny limbs and distended "sago belly" of a diet that is high in starch but low in protein. Ultimately, the "affluence" of Gebusi leisure is itself an adaptation to their environment: it is more efficient to conserve energy and relax than to work harder while only minimally improving nutrition.

The same is true of the Gebusi approach to raising pigs. Gebusi love to eat pork but don't like the work of raising many pigs. They would have to feed the pigs every day and also fence gardens nearby to keep the pigs from rooting them up. So they take the easy way out. When the opportunity arises, Gebusi capture wild piglets in the forest. They feed them leftover food, carry them around in little net bags, and, to an extent, tame them. But as the pigs start to grow, Gebusi turn them loose. The critters live in the forest on their own but still come back to their Gebusi owners for occasional handouts of food. As a novel result, the pigs are neither wild nor domestic but somewhere in between. When a major feast comes up, Gebusi use a special twist on a tactic found in the Hänsel and Gretel fairy tale. To entice their pigs back, Gebusi lure them with pieces of banana or sago left by the pig's tracks in the forest. They then extend a trail of food for the pig to follow right back to the village. Like Hänsel and Gretel in reverse, the pigs find their way unwittingly home, where they can be slaughtered fresh on the spot. Keeping their pigs semi-domesticated doesn't allow Gebusi to raise very many of them—barely one for each extended family. But it does provide a reliable source of meat for their most special occasions while avoiding the heavy work of having to feed, tend, and restrain pigs or even carry them back to the village when slaughtered.

This leads to a larger point. Though anthropologists use concepts and categories to classify societies, people like the Gebusi defy easy classification. The Gebusi are "sedentary," but their lifestyle is mobile and almost "semi-nomadic." They raise crops and are "horticulturalists," but they also hunt and forage. They are efficient at raising pigs, but the animals are only "semi-domesticated" and are few in number. Even in terms of New Guinea, the Gebusi have neither the high-intensity food production and population density of highlands dwellers nor the sago-and-fish foraging lifestyle of their lowland neighbors. Personally, I like the fact that the Gebusi are "in-betweeners." Like many peoples when considered closely, they combine or hybridize our own categories of analysis. The many ways that people accommodate their local ecologies are a testament to human creativity and to the power of culture as a means of adaptation. I am continually fascinated by how people not only survive but also find meaning and purpose across different environments in different parts of the globe. This capacity seems increasingly important today as we struggle with modern problems of pollution, global warming, depletion of fossil fuels, malnutrition, and disease. As ecological threats grow more ominous, humans need increasing resilience and creativity to pursue long-term adaptations.

If the Gebusi are hard to pigeonhole, so, too, are most other peoples. Even the small region of the South Pacific called Melanesia harbors a huge diversity of different peoples and cultures. And countries that we may think of as single units—such as China, India, Indonesia, Russia, and certainly the United States—house a complex and fascinating range of peoples, cultures, and blendings. This diversity is not only interesting but also central to the problems, challenges, and opportunities of the contemporary world.

Human diversity sparks our appreciation of alternative ways of living. But how do we keep track of this variety? It is useful to have concepts and categories that organize this diversity. But it is the complications of and exceptions to these categories that push us to new levels of understanding. People like the Gebusi, who are in-between some of these categories, help us appreciate their intersections as well as their limits. As we will see in Part Two of this book, understanding these combinations becomes increasingly important as we consider patterns of contemporary change and transformation. As our categories of understanding traverse modern time as well as ethnographic space, it becomes vital that they be flexible and accommodating of human diversity.

Amid our concepts of analytic and scientific understanding, it is also important that we not lose sight of the meanings and values that people hold in different world areas. For Gebusi as well, meanings and values form key parts of social existence and motivation as well as having intrinsic human significance. Concerning Gebusi subsistence, for instance, objective categories and concepts seldom reveal how much Gebusi enjoy their land and how much their lives echo its moods and nuances. A storm blows in suddenly and doesn't let up for hours. Rain pelts and pockmarks the village; it carves gullies and then little canyons in the central clearing. The streams swell and the rivers roil and flood. Bluffs of clay become slides of mud, and traveling anywhere becomes slippery and sloppy. Plans are cancelled. But rather than curse the weather, Gebusi simply take the day off. Toasty in their houses, men light up their pipes and chat while women play with children, put some plantains on the fire, or thread more inches on the large net bags they are making. Someone tells a story or a myth. Plans unfold for a coming feast. Those returning in the downpour make fun of how wet and muddy they got. Sometimes, as if to defy the rain, they whoop loudly and march through it proudly.

When a dry spell descends and the rivers shrink, men make plans for spearing or poisoning fish. The low, clear water exposes their prey and makes them easier to catch. Hawi was one of the best fishermen. His favorite stalking place was above the rapids in a quiet pool of the Kum River. He would swim underwater and jab at his targets with a pronged spike. One day, he speared the biggest fish of all—it must have weighed more than twenty pounds. To the people of Yibihilu, landing this giant prize was akin to winning the Super Bowl. Cries of joy and amazement filled the air. As word spread, a feast became inevitable. More than good fortune or skill, the taking of the huge fish affirmed the goodness of the village, the beneficence of the river, and the harmony of the villagers with their forest spirits. Portions of the fish were shared among each and every inhabitant of Yibihilu, the "place of the deep waters." To this day, Hawi is my "fish," my *dio*, based on the piece of fish that he shared with me that afternoon. In the evening, Swiman held one of his biggest and most dramatic séances. In song after song, his spirits described how the big fish had given itself up to Hawi's skill and the strength of his village. The lives of the fish people, their comings and goings in the river, came alive in vivid detail. The other fish were ripe for the taking, the spirits said. The men in the audience went wild.

Although the Gebusi basked in their environment, we as Westerners were hard-pressed to follow their lead. For us, daily physical maintenance was a major challenge. During the course of two years, ailments and illnesses became inevitable: the headaches and chills of malaria; digestive disorders; intestinal worms; skin lesions, boils, and rashes; and jungle rot that thrives in your body's most private parts. Our lives were made bearable by a small arsenal of medications, both for ourselves and for Gebusi. Not being doctors, it was often hard to know how we could or should try to help our friends with medicines. But the people of Yibihilu were good role models for us: they accepted infirmity when it came and made the best of life while it lasted. Tabway was afflicted with a putrefying ulcer on her thigh. Her leg would shudder in torment, but her face would stay calm or even show a soft smile. Sefomay's foot was permanently and painfully swollen to twice its normal size. She would joke that her "leg was rotting"—but her spirit was not.

Sickness and death visited Gebusi at every season of life. Malaria, pneumonia, filariasis or "elephantiasis," tuberculosis, influenza, and diarrhea were at once causal and contributing factors. Gebusi were distressed by microbes, parasites, clogged lungs, contaminated blood, and swollen spleens. By the time they reached what we would call middle age, most of them were physically wizened. Almost all adults had had at least one bout of a near-death illness. Sickness dovetailed with poor nutrition, since weaker bodies have a tougher time fighting infection. Of girls who lived to be five, only one in three survived to age forty. For boys of similar age, only about one in six lived to their fifth decade.

If Gebusi could not cheat death, they savored life while it lasted. They enjoyed simple pleasures, smiled often, laughed easily, and celebrated when they could. Notwithstanding their crusades against sorcery, there was little they could do to reduce their physical risk—either from disease or from one another. The deaths that we witnessed were met with quietude and acceptance. The warm hands of friends gave way to piercing wails only at the end.

Gebusi ailments put our own in perspective. On a daily basis, our two biggest challenges were heat and insects. Such "little" things are almost embarrassing to admit, but chronic discomforts loom as large in fieldwork as they are typically neglected in scholarly accounts. If heat and humidity turned our papers limp and our shoes green with mold, we easily felt the same way. The following extract is from my field notes:

> You can't be cool when the humidity and temperature both exceed 98.6. I sit in the shade of my house and calm myself inside and out. Mental strain fuels sweat and throbs my head. I stay absolutely still, motionless, relaxing, eyes closed. The sweat beads, then dribbles from my brow, chest, and thighs. I splash with water from my basin, but more sweat replaces it. I go to my sleeping room, a bit darker, and take off all my clothes, every stitch. I kneel on the floor beside my sleeping net. Fractions of confinement make a difference. The mesh of my sleeping net holds extra heat that radiates from my body, so I do not go inside it.
>
> The three-point stance is my naked attempt to relax in the heat. I can't lie down, since this creates hot contact between my side and whatever I am

laying on; a pool of sweat quickly appears. My best posture keeps an illusion of repose for ten minutes or so with the smallest possible part of my body touching the floor, as much as possible languid in air. The three points of contact are the tip of my big toes, kneecaps, and elbows. This reduces my surface area of contact to a few scant inches. If I get it right, I can hang my head without having to support it with my fingers (since sweat erupts wherever skin touches skin). So my head hangs limp an inch or two off the floor. My mind calms, so does my skin. The sweat still collects across my cheeks and drips from my nose. It splats onto the floor, but softly, slowly.

After ten minutes, I am as serene as I can be. Relaxation is key, since heat makes friends with anxiety and stress. Yesterday I misplaced my notebook and my frustration quickly steamed my glasses. My three-point stance won't cure the heat. But it makes it easier to live with.

For their part, the Gebusi hardly minded the temperature or the humidity. They often kept cooking fires smoldering in their houses, which have no chimneys. The added heat and smoke dispersed the mosquitoes and drove away insects that would otherwise infest the thatch and wood of the house. But it was different for us as fieldworkers. We were raised in northern areas of the United States It was hard to tolerate the added heat and smoke of a continual fire in our house. So we opted for less fire—and got more bugs. Insects were a whole separate dimension of fieldwork. I couldn't ignore them:

They are everywhere. Even sitting in a canoe in the middle of the Kum River, the creepies and crawlies land on you. Some of them are really strange looking. They sport weird colors and wild-flight torsos and ways of moving that come from another world. Magnified a thousand times, they would be perfect for the next alien thriller from Hollywood. But most of them are innocuous. You just pick or brush them off and move on.

There are several exceptions. Oversize grasshoppers give a startle when they land on you suddenly. Five-inch spiders raise my adrenaline when I find them sharing the close confines of the outhouse. Cockroaches are everywhere. Hundreds of the big ones live in our cardboard cartons and eat the labels off our precious tins of food. But the mosquitoes I hardly even count as insects because they are so insidious. Not just because there are so many of them, nor because they fly into our thatched house without pause or restriction. It's the malaria and elephantiasis they bring. They wait like cowards until dusk before taunting you with their mock fragility. They lilt in squadrons on low power but somehow float just beyond your grasp, waiting like lunar modules to hit your pay dirt. Swatting hard only flits them away to a yet choicer landing place. "One small bite for one mosquito, one giant risk for mankind."

There is a special insult to getting several bites. How many did you really receive in the dimness? Was it only two? Or four or six? Is that another new one now again, just beside the others? Did you *really* take your antimalarial pill (none of which are completely effective)? The best thing is to go inside the mosquito net—and that very quickly, because *nothing* is worse than having mosquitoes get *inside* your net. But we can't live under a mosquito net from six at night until six in the morning. We have to eat and wash, write our notes, and of course, talk with people. The evening should be one of the most enjoyable parts of the day. Wearing heavy clothes or lathering on high concentrations of DEET isn't feasible night after night. So we have no real solution, take our hits, and do the best we can. But going to the bathroom remains the worst. Mosquitoes love the bottom of the latrine pit, and they fly up in droves whenever something goes down the hole. They attack our most vulnerable parts when we are most exposed. Talk about a bite in the butt!

If heat and insects were our daily scourge, the Gebusi kept our irritations in perspective. Despite their own much graver ailments, their lives remained vibrant. This pulled us beyond the orbit of our own concerns. Call it cultural gravity— the ability of others' lives to sweep you up and draw you in to your own surprise and against all challenge. This is the deepest part of fieldwork, the part that makes you grow. We joked with the Gebusi, shared with them, took part in their activities, and became part of their world. Reciprocally, they seemed to enjoy us, accepted our idiosyncrasies, and included us in their activities as much as they could. In professional terms, this is what is often described as the primary fieldwork method in cultural anthropology: "participant observation."

Professionally, I think our biggest challenge was learning the Gebusi language. Given their remoteness, there was no way we could have done this ahead of time. We had received training in how to learn an unwritten language without the help of translators. In the field, bit by slow, painful bit, we learned to recognize and make sounds that do not exist in English. We compiled lists of Gebusi words and phrases—and puzzled over their meanings. In all of these tasks, Yuway was my most patient, insightful, and pleasant helper. Increasingly over the course of weeks and months, he and I became special friends. He even helped me tackle the complexities of Gebusi tense and grammar, and these were the worst. The Gebusi like to pile meanings into verbs while leaving out nouns and other phrases. For instance, the question "Would he have killed me?" is spoken in Gebusi as a single verb, "kill" (*golo*), which is then modified by a string of suffixes to indicate a presumed subject, a presumed object, conditional tense, causative action, and interrogative aspect. The whole sentence is one word: *golo-hi-lay-ba*. Fortunately, we knew from the start that learning the language would be our most difficult task. After a few weeks, we could make simple communications in broken Gebusi. After a few months, we began to figure out what the Gebusi were saying to one another (not in the simple, slowed-down language that they used with us, but in the idioms, quick pacing, and assumptions that they used with one another). My advisor wrote and told us not to get too discouraged. He suggested that if we focused on language learning for the first six months, we would be okay. He also said that our language abilities would continue to improve and that two-thirds of our understanding would likely emerge during the last third of our fieldwork. So we would have to be patient. He was right.

Along the way, we developed our own rhythms of daily adaptation. Fieldwork is at heart its own brand of optimal foraging. As the Gebusi shifted their activities to gain the most from their surroundings, we tried to do the same. For us, however, our desire to participate, to observe, and to record our experiences became a dance between "living with" and "writing up." Days during fieldwork blended language learning, observation, note-taking, interviews, writing, and reflection—amid the constant intensity of public social living. I was continually surprised at how long it took me to type up my notes and organize them into larger topical files. Even when not much was going on in the village, I seemed to be behind in my work. It became painfully obvious that fieldwork was not a process of quickly discovering "the truth." My learning about Gebusi emerged gradually through a blur of confusing experiences and competing interpretations. We repeatedly found that our language skills were deficient, our interpretations misleading, and our assumptions simply wrong. I remember during our first weeks pointing to various objects with my index finger and asking in simple Gebusi, "What is it?" (Ke ka-ba). But no matter what I pointed to, the answer I got was always the same, "*Dob.*" I was completely perplexed. The mystery was explained when I learned the meaning of *dob*. *Dob* was the finger I was pointing with! Understanding was always a process of learning from our mistakes. We began at the lowest rung, asking nonsensical questions like "Is your son a girl?" But just as quickly, we learned to laugh at our foibles. It helped a lot that Gebusi laughed so good-naturedly along with us, just as they did at their own mistakes and problems.

As time went on and our comprehension improved, I came to see cultural anthropology as a kind of dialogue—a conversation between Gebusi meanings and our own understandings. The trick was to have each side of this cultural equation make sense in terms of the other. This process was rooted in participation and observation, but it continued afterward in writing and reflection. Writing ethnography is almost invariably a process of trying to explain clearly events and actions that were, in fact, confusing and opaque when observed and experienced to begin with.

During fieldwork, this process linked us directly back to our relationship with the Gebusi. In our lives and our work, a balance between give-and-take was key: the ability to admit error and try yet again, to receive as well as give, to be acted upon as well as acting. In this, Gebusi were wonderful teachers. Reciprocity was at the heart of their social life: they maintained a vigilant balance between giving and getting, between acting and being acted upon. As we increasingly came to realize, balanced reciprocity pervaded many if not most aspects of Gebusi culture, including their relation to their physical environment, their distribution of food, their ritual celebrations, their marriage patterns, their connections with the spirit world, and even their patterns of death and killing. The ideal of balanced reciprocity was one of the most personally and professionally important things that I learned from the Gebusi. Apart from their gendered divisions, they were egalitarian to a fault. They reinforced this norm by constantly striving to maintain a balance between receiving and giving.

The big feast was yesterday. Today, our friends are happily eating food that the visitors brought and gave them in exchange for the lavish meal our settlement hosted. Since my household contributed fish and rice to the communal effort, people now want to repay me.

This morning, a member of each major family in the village came and presented me with a bird egg. I was deeply touched. Most memorable was five-year-old Kawe, who has become my "biscuit" exchange-name friend. I saw him coming from across the village. With the confident stride and smile of a grown-up, he looked at me from twenty yards away and walked over directly, never shifting his gaze. Stopping in front of me, he flashed his cutest tooth-missing grin and extended his little hand that held his egg. He placed the egg in my palm, turned around, and walked back proudly, never uttering a word or looking back. I will never forget it.

CHAPTER 3

A woman mourns the death of her husband. (PHOTO: Eileen Marie Knauft)

Lives of Death

IT IS HARD TO watch a baby die. Its scrawny body cries until its wails lose force and leave a ghostly little corpse. It was also hard on us that Gebusi men didn't seem to mind. During our first five weeks in the field, we saw first one baby die and then another. As the mother wailed with grief, her women-kin gathered in support. But the men continued to joke and smoke in the longhouse, and the boys played gaily in the village clearing. Only the baby's father stayed close by, and even this was with an air of detached waiting—until the small body could be summarily buried. Managing babies and managing death were both women's work; if women bore the day-to-day challenge and joy of caring for new life, they also bore the sting of its death. Along with Eileen, I visited the mother in each case to lend support. But both times I felt, as a man, that the most courteous thing I could do was to leave. As the second infant was dying, I talked with Owaya, its father. He said that the baby was dying "just because." But then he wondered whether a woman from Wasobi might have sent sorcery to kill it. As I later found out, the Gebusi attributed all natural deaths to sorcery. But they really only investigated the deaths of adults and older children.

The Gebusi don't think of infants as fully human until they are about seven months old, when their first teeth emerge. Until then, a human spirit is not thought to be completely rooted in their bodies, and they aren't even given a name. Many infants only flirt with life; a third of them die during their first year. The community in general and men in particular seem to protect themselves from identifying too closely with so many young lives that end so quickly. But this distance is not shared by the mother, red-eyed and weeping, nor by her female kin. The father, for his part, seems awkwardly in the middle, experiencing neither the women's emotion nor the other men's distance. As for us, Eileen cried with the women and deeply felt their pain. I commiserated with her in private. But the men treated me jovially, as if nothing had happened. At heart, I was confused. It was my first real lesson in the contours and confinements of Gebusi emotion.

Just three weeks after the second infant died, a third death hit the village: Dugawe killed himself. Unlike the infant deaths, which were

39

taken as "normal," this one shocked the community. No one could remember a man having killed himself. Although we didn't foresee it at the time, Dugawe's death drew us into a whirling cultural vortex. Events and experiences that we could hardly understand flew by; we struggled to piece them together. People we knew and liked suddenly did things we could not believe. In retracing this path—with its twists and turns, and my own confusions—I came to know much about the Gebusi, about the culture of life and death, and about the challenges of anthropological understanding.

At first, I didn't believe Yuway and Silap (Boyl's husband) when they came to tell me the news; they seemed so matter of fact. But within minutes, we rushed off to the forest so they could retrieve Dugawe's body. When we arrived, the dead man's wife and two other women were weeping by the corpse. Silap brushed them aside and wailed loudly by the body. Dugawe had been Silap's classificatory "brother-in-law" (gol) and "initiation-mate" (sam). Gebusi settlements coalesce by bringing men—and women—together from different family lines. Relations within the village reflect a rich and tangled web of kinship and friendship based on a wide range of family, marital, and friendly but nonkin connections. Silap and Dugawe had not been members of the same male line, but they had long lived in the same village, had become friends, had been initiated together, and were distantly related through intermarriage.

After Silap finished wailing, the women came back to resume their crying. They called to Dugawe and told him how sorry they were about his death and how much they wanted him back. Their raw emotion was thought to soothe Dugawe's lingering soul and ease its gradual passage to the land of the dead. Meanwhile, Silap smoked tobacco with Yuway and waited until other men from Yibihilu arrived. None of them seemed particularly upset as they discussed how to take Dugawe's body back to the village. Wondering why he had killed himself, I went with others to inspect his body. Dugawe had been a strong, handsome man, but now his face was pale and slack, already beginning to swell in the tropical heat. I looked for signs of foul play. Perhaps his death was a murder disguised as a suicide. But the only sign of struggle was a mark on the front of his faded T-shirt. Something had poked and scratched the fabric for a couple of inches, but the shirt was not punctured, and nothing had pierced Dugawe's skin. To the men, however, the tiny scratch revealed a larger canvas of anger and shame. As we later found out, Dugawe had fought with his wife, Sialim, before committing suicide. During the scuffle, she had held an arrow, thrust it toward him, and scratched his shirt. Their fight had been about a sexual affair that was generally acknowledged between Sialim and a young man, Sagawa. Publicly cuckolded, Dugawe had been furious; he had wanted to hunt and kill his wayward wife, her lover, or both of them. But Silap and others had discouraged him from doing this. Incensed but lacking other recourse, Dugawe had fought with his wife. But he was further shamed by her scratching his shirt, his prized possession. When she went off to fetch water, the men said, he had taken tubes of poison concocted for killing fish in the stream and, in a fit of rage, had drunk them all. Empty tubes with the smell of the potent toxin were found nearby. Dugawe had died a writhing death after poisoning himself in anger against his wife. But he was so much bigger and stronger than she. Why was his anger so self-directed?

For the moment, all I could do was try to keep up with events as the men lashed Dugawe's body to a stretcher and marched it briskly through the forest back to Yibihilu. Eventually they stopped for a smoke and a rest. They joked about the upcoming feast and ribbed me good-naturedly about how I would look if I wore a traditional Gebusi male skirt of "ass grass" for the occasion. Though we had outpaced the women, their wailing could now be heard. The men hurried to reshoulder the corpse, but the women were already arriving, including Sialim. By chance, two more women came through the forest from another direction and converged on us at the same moment. They were fictive "mothers" of Dugawe from an adjacent community who had come to view his body. Upon seeing his corpse, and also his wayward wife, they virtually exploded. Screaming, the two of them tore straight into Sialim. She turned to avoid them, but the lead woman walloped her on the back with a steel ax she was wielding, blunt side forward. She followed this with another heavy blow. Then she turned and threw herself on Dugawe's corpse, pawing and crying in great screaming sobs, as if her emotion could wake it up. Simultaneously, the second woman resumed the first one's attack, screeching at full pitch and poking and shoving Sialim with a pointed stick as if she were going to drive it right through her. Two men rushed in to hold her back while others wrestled Dugawe's closest "mother" away from his corpse. The remainder abruptly picked up the body and raced off with it down the trail. Yuway, Silap, and I followed in close pursuit while the women trailed behind.

When we finally arrived at Yibihilu, Dugawe's body was laid in state in his family house, a scant twenty-five yards from our own. A crowd of women screeched and wailed while others arrived in short order. Many of them pummeled and berated Sialim, who hunched and whimpered but could not run away without neglecting her duty to mourn her dead husband. Our neighbor, Owaya, came up and waved a firebrand in Sialim's face. He let forth with a withering diatribe, which he punctuated with shouts of "Si-nay!" As I later learned, this translates roughly as "Burn! Cook! We'll eat!" This was what the Gebusi traditionally did to persons executed as sorcerers. Owaya whacked Sialim with his burning stick and then shoved it into the net bag on her back. She gasped, whimpered, and shuffled several feet farther away.

Inside the house, we gathered with the women who had come to weep over the corpse. Like Dugawe's "mother," some of them flailed hysterically when they first arrived. After a few minutes, the atmosphere slowly calmed. But then a man painted in black suddenly lunged through the doorway. With a loud cry, he drew an arrow back in his bow and then released the bowstring with a loud snap. In my shock, I didn't realize at first that he still held the arrow with the other fingers of his shooting hand—he had snapped his bowstring without releasing the arrow. Yelling, he repeated his action and plucked his bow indiscriminately at all of us sitting in the house. In response, Silap rushed in and interposed himself. With calming words, outstretched hands, and a wan smile, he gradually placated the intruder. As Silap and the attacker moved outside, I went with them and saw that more than twenty warriors from other settlements were now massing. Almost as quickly, however, the men of Yibihilu were also gathering, not as antagonists, but as peacemakers. Armed with stoked tobacco pipes, they snapped fingers and shared smokes with each of the visitors in turn. Their action seemed to melt the tension like a cooling rain in the heat of the day. In short order, the visitors retired to the longhouse and were provided resting mats; they began to relax. Those of us from Yibihilu scurried to find and cook bananas to give by way of hospitality.

An hour or so later, a government constable arrived from the Nomad Station. Silap and some other men had taken the rare step of sending word to him about Dugawe's death—and inviting him to come to Yibihilu to investigate. Why? Apparently they were worried that the authorities might receive a different tale of Dugawe's death from some other source. After a long conversation through several interpreters, the constable finally wrote a brief entry in his police book: "Reason of death: Suicide caused by his wife fooling around." Though the constable's inquiry was completed, discussion about Sialim continued. Given the anger against her, it was decided that she should go back with the Nomad officer straightaway and stay temporarily at the Nomad Station for her own protection. The main events of the day were then over, but the piercing wails of women continued through the night.

By the following morning, Dugawe's body had bloated grotesquely. His swollen limbs oozed corpse fluid, and his skin peeled to expose putrefying red and yellow-green flesh. His belly and even his genitals had swelled with the gases of decomposition. I will never forget the stench, which burned up my nose, down my throat, and into my brain. Equally powerful was the response of Dugawe's female relatives. With unearthly sobs, they draped themselves physically over the corpse, lovingly massaged its slime, and peeled its skin. Then they rubbed their own arms and legs with the ooze of the body. Corpse fluid on one's skin is a tangible sign of grief, of physical as well as emotional connection with the deceased—making one's body akin to the corpse. Seeing this, it was said, Dugawe's departing soul would know how much they cared for him. Just a little, this would ease his pain and anger at having died.

The men of Yibihilu dug Dugawe's grave by his family house. Then the women rolled Dugawe's corpse onto Silap's back. As he strained and stood up with the weight of the body, its arms flung out dramatically to both sides. The women shrieked. Men rushed to steady the corpse and help Silap place it in the grave. Dugawe's traditional possessions—his bamboo pipe, bow and arrows, and so on—were quickly arranged in the grave by his female kin. Bark was placed over the corpse, and then the hole was filled in. Just as directly, the men retired to the longhouse to rest. The closest female relatives flung themselves on the mounded grave and wailed.

Prior to fieldwork, the only dead body I had seen was the sedate face of a friend of my parents during an open-casket funeral. Now I was shocked and repulsed by the events surrounding Dugawe's death. It seemed hideous that his corpse was allowed to decay and that our women friends wallowed in its stench before it was buried. But I also began to realize that this raw transformation—of a human being into a decomposing natural object—presented an emotionally and physically honest view of death. The reality of Dugawe's disfigurement showed me the fact of his death like nothing else could do. His demise was not hidden, not made pretty, not covered up in pallid attempts to "spare grief." Were Gebusi customs improper? Or, was it my own culture's attempt to gloss over and downplay the physical reality of death that was off kilter?

I ultimately found that the extreme behavior of Gebusi women with corpses puzzled me less than the tamer conduct of the men. As they went to the longhouse to smoke, joke, and drink bowls of local root intoxicant, the men acted as if nothing was wrong. When I heard that a visiting spirit medium would hold a public séance, I thought he would commune with Dugawe's spirit and inquire about his death. Instead, the séance was a songfest of ribald entertainment. When I asked why, the men said that Dugawe's spirit was as yet too angry to talk about his death. In the meantime, since they were all together, they thought it best to relax and have a good time.

It was all rather bewildering. Which details surrounding Dugawe's death were relevant, and which were superficial? How did Gebusi funeral practices and sorcery beliefs influence their social relationships and their emotional lives? I tried to connect the dots by writing descriptions and reflections. But even as the picture stayed fuzzy, additional questions arose. What did Dugawe's sexual and marital problems with Sialim reveal about Gebusi gender relations? And, to what extent were the circumstances of Dugawe's death exceptional or anomalous in Gebusi society? As I struggled for answers, further events both sharpened my questions and posed new ones. Gradually, the events following Dugawe's death unfolded into a sorcery investigation—an inquiry into who had "killed" him. Its twists and turns helped me answer the questions I had, but not in the ways I expected. In retrospect, I realized that this trail of discovery revealed much about the practice of ethnography as well as about the customs and beliefs of the Gebusi.

Although the big funeral feast for Dugawe took place just two days after his burial, it ended up being a sideshow to events that occurred weeks later. By the time the sorcery investigation resumed, my opinion of Sialim had changed. At first, I thought she had acted irresponsibly. She had carried on a sexual affair with a young man named Sagawa, and she had apparently shamed her husband into killing himself. But additional facts painted a different picture. As Eileen found out from the women, Dugawe had years earlier killed not only his first wife but also his own small son. These murders had been so awful that villagers had informed the police, and Dugawe had served a five-year prison term outside the Nomad Station area. To our knowledge, he was the only Gebusi to have been incarcerated in this way.

His prison term over, Dugawe had returned to the area and married Sialim, who had recently been widowed by the death of Dugawe's "brother." Gebusi widows often end up marrying a male family relative of their dead husband. Anthropologists term this "marriage by levirate." Such unions have the effect of keeping the widow's labor and children within the family line of her original husband. Knowing Dugawe's history, however, Sialim did not want to marry him. As newlyweds, they fought, and he frequently beat her. On one occasion, she finally sought recourse from the patrol officers at the Nomad Station. Given her bruises and Dugawe's violent past, the police arrested him again and held him at the local jail. It was while he was in jail that Sialim took up with Sagawa, her young lover. Perhaps she hoped that her relationship with Sagawa would become a de facto marriage before Dugawe was released from jail. But Dugawe was discharged earlier than expected. Enraged, he wanted to kill Sialim and her partner. But Silap and the other men of Yibihilu persuaded him that he would then receive an even longer prison term than the one he had already endured. In the midst of this tense situation, Dugawe took up again with Sialim. But after their fight in the forest, he committed suicide.

From a Western feminist perspective, it might be argued that Sialim could hardly be blamed. She had been saddled with an abusive marriage and a murderous spouse. She had tried to find refuge, sought solace with another partner, and then stood up for herself when Dugawe fought with her. What villagers took as a sign of travesty—her fighting with her husband and scratching his shirt with an arrow—could have been a desperate attempt at self-defense. However, Sialim was rebuked not only by the men of Yibihilu but especially by Dugawe's female kin. She had gone outside the community, gotten her husband jailed, and cheated on him. To make matters worse, her romantic affair was with a young man who had not yet been initiated.

What was I to think? I could criticize Gebusi values as condoning violent sexism. But Sialim had violated standards of marital fidelity that were deeply held by the Gebusi. I felt stuck in the middle between these viewpoints. Most importantly, though, we were concerned for Sialim's safety, fearing she could be attacked or killed. Eileen asked the police to protect her, and this dovetailed with the men's desires to forestall any more agitation. Fortunately for everyone, she was taken off to Nomad.

As I slowly came to realize, Gebusi inquests into and retributions for sorcery typically did not take place until well after the burial of the person who had died. The main exception was if the corpse itself "signaled" while lying in state that a given sorcery suspect had "killed" him or her. A sorcery suspect might be enjoined to vehemently shake the rotting corpse while wailing his or her grief. If at that unlucky moment the corpse gave a "sign"—spilling cadaveric fluid, "moaning" due to gases in its lungs, or bulging its eyes out or even opening or bursting them as a result of gas pressure from decomposition within the braincase—then the suspect could be axed to death on the spot. If the "verdict" of the corpse was clear, there would be little protest over the killing from even the closest relatives of the person executed. But this had not happened while Dugawe's corpse was starting to decompose. So the men of Yibihilu had soothed the anger of Dugawe's visiting relatives by extending hospitality—snapping fingers, sharing tobacco, giving food, and holding a séance.

The villagers felt that further inquiry should not take place in the heat of the moment but should be conducted more objectively over a longer time, somewhat like a murder investigation in Western societies. For the Gebusi, however, the purpose of the inquest was to ferret out the sorcerers who had killed Dugawe through spiritual means. In their belief, all human deaths were caused by people— either through sorcery or through violence. Even a man who had fallen out of a coconut tree and broken his back had been killed by a sorcerer: because the man had successfully climbed many coconut trees in the past, a sorcerer must have made him lose his grip. Deaths from sickness were likewise attributed to sorcery— the sorcerer had caused the lethal illness. In the case of Dugawe's death, the Gebusi took it as self-evident that sorcerers either had driven Dugawe crazy enough to kill himself or had killed him and then tampered with the evidence to make it look like suicide.

Five weeks after his funeral feast, the real investigation into Dugawe's death began. In a nod to neutrality, the inquest séances were conducted by a spirit medium who had had little personal connection with Dugawe. But when these séances were inconclusive, further investigation was led by our clever friend Swamin, the main spirit medium of Yibihilu. By this time, I had discovered that Gebusi sorcery had two main types. In one type, called *bogay*, the sorcerer was believed to secretly tie up the feces or other bodily leavings of the victim, thus causing a long, painful illness. The sorcerer then "killed" the victim by burning the fecal matter or other leavings. Anthropologists sometimes call this "imitative magic"—magical use of supernatural powers based on the principle that "like produces like." In the other variety of Gebusi sorcery, called *ogowili*, sorcerers were believed to take the form of magical warriors who attacked the victim in the forest, usually when he or she was alone. The sorcerer-warriors then killed the victim with arrows and clubs, ate out his or her insides, magically sewed him or her up, and finally cast a spell to give the person amnesia. Although the victim might amble uncertainly back to the village, he or she would die a sudden death shortly thereafter.

Bogay comes under the heading of what ethnographers call "parcel sorcery," that is, sickness sent by manipulating a parcel of the victim's leavings. By contrast, *ogowili* qualifies as "assault sorcery," a cannibal attack by magical warriors. For the Gebusi, *bogay* explained the torment of a long, lethal illness, while *ogowili* explained deaths that were relatively quick and sudden, as well as those caused by accident— and suicide. In these cases, assault sorcerers were believed to force their victims to put themselves in precarious danger. One way or the other, Gebusi believed that all deaths from sickness, accident, or suicide were caused by sorcery. In reality, we found no evidence that Gebusi actually practiced either type of sorcery—and we found much evidence to the contrary. Assault sorcery—that is, the eating and then magical sewing up of a victim to disguise a lethal attack—is simply impossible from our point of view. Although parcel sorcery is attempted quite genuinely by some peoples in Melanesia and elsewhere, our investigations among Gebusi suggested consistently that their accusations of parcel sorcery were trumped-up charges against unfortunate suspects. But Gebusi continued to have unshakable belief in parcel sorcery. Gebusi men staunchly committed themselves to exposing *bogay* sorcerers and taking action against them, including within their own community.

In Dugawe's case, death was believed to be caused by assault sorcery (*ogowili*). Although the *ogowili* is thought to be a man who takes the form of a magical warrior, he may be manipulated to do this by a malicious woman. Possibly, then, Sialim could be found guilty of Dugawe's death if she had had sex with an *ogowili* and induced him to drive her husband crazy. For the Gebusi, this was plausible since Sialim was known to have had a sexual affair with Sagawa.

In his séances, however, Swamin's spirits suggested a different scenario. Rather than accuse Sialim, the spirits described how *ogowili* warriors had descended on Dugawe from a distant settlement while Sialim was away fetching water. Though the assault sorcerers had disguised the evidence and covered their tracks, Swamin's spirits assured the assembled men that signs of their attack could still be found in the forest near where Dugawe's death had occurred. Further, the *ogowili* might then be tracked back to their own settlement, where they could, at least in principle, be attacked in their human form to avenge the killing of Dugawe. To track assault sorcerers through the forest, however, the Gebusi needed spiritual help to guide them.

As Swamin's séance ended, at about five o'clock in the morning, the men of Yibihilu got ready to search for the assault sorcerers responsible for Dugawe's death. Uncertain what was going to happen next, I pulled on my boots and grabbed my flashlight in the predawn darkness. The men were carrying bows and arrows, and some had painted their faces black, like warriors. Eventually, we approached Abwiswimaym, the forest plot where Dugawe had drunk poison. The mood became tense as we anticipated the ghostly form of an assault sorcerer ahead. Quietly and anxiously, men sought cover, pointed their arrows, and advanced warily on their spectral enemy. I pinched my arm to remind myself that we were not likely to find an actual person but rather the evidence of a magical attack by spiritual warriors lurking nearby. But after a while, the area was declared safe.

Next, we searched upstream for the *buluf*—the magically transformed remains of Dugawe after his insides had ostensibly been eaten by sorcerers. With Swamin's spirits guiding us, we found an odd-looking stick that was said to be the "knife" that the sorcerers had used to cut Dugawe open. An indentation in the ground was the "footprint" of an *ogowili*. A discolored patch of dirt was Dugawe's "blood," which they said had poured out during the attack. As incredulous as I was of these associations, the Gebusi around me were convinced. But then again, the very power of assault sorcerers rests in their ability to disguise their attacks and make the results look almost normal. After searching a nearby stream for Dugawe's "skin" and "bones," we followed the water upstream in the general direction of a distant community. But Swamin's spirits then lost the trail of the assailants and could not find it again. Ultimately, then, we could not track the assault sorcerers to their homes or identify them by name. To the men, however, the investigation validated the information given by Swamin's spirits during his séance. Dugawe had been killed by an assault sorcerer from a distant village, but the identity of the person was impossible to determine and no further action could be feasibly taken.

Though I thought this would be the end of Dugawe's story, its final twists did not unfold for another seven months. During this time, Sialim spent more and more time with Swamin's household. Eventually, she willingly consented to marry him—over the entreaties and objections of her young lover, Sagawa. Strong and robust for a middle-aged man, Swamin had been a widower. During our final year of fieldwork, he and Sialim seemed to be happily married.

Though this would have been a good Hollywood ending, it was not the one we ultimately came away with. It turned out that three years previously, Swamin had killed Sialim's own mother. The old woman, named Mokoyl, had been named as the parcel sorcerer responsible for the death of Swamin's first wife. Mokoyl had tried to prove her innocence by conducting a bird egg divination—cooking eggs that were placed inside a mound of damp and uncooked sago starch. Unfortunately, the eggs had been badly undercooked. When Mokoyl had given Swamin one of the eggs to eat—as she was expected to do as part of the divination—he had promptly vomited. This had been taken as a sign that Swamin's dead wife was clutching his throat, refusing Mokoyl's food, and confirming Mokoyl's guilt. A few weeks later (about a year before we arrived in New Guinea), Swamin had attacked Mokoyl while she was alone in the forest with Boyl (the woman who ended up being Eileen's best friend). As Boyl told Eileen, she herself had tried to run away when Swamin approached. But he had demanded that she stay as a witness, lest he chase her down as well. Petrified, Boyl had watched as Swamin extracted an ostensible confession from Mokoyl and then spilt her skull with his bush knife. He left her dead in the forest as Boyl ran off. Given the spiritual evidence that had seemed to confirm Mokoyl's guilt, most of the community agreed that Mokoyl was guilty and had deserved to die. Her body had been summarily buried in the forest. But villagers from an adjacent settlement, knowing that Mokoyl had been a robust older woman with ample flesh, had dug up her body and eaten parts of it before it decomposed. In so doing, they had also indicated their support for the killing. Government officers never found out about the incident.

🌿   🌿   🌿

If we add this last episode to the chain of events surrounding Dugawe's death, what conclusions can we draw? With the benefit of hindsight, reflection, and analysis, anthropologists are charged with making sense of diverse societies and cultures—and with their own. Experience becomes fieldwork, and fieldwork becomes ethnographic writing. But how does this transition occur? For me in the field, it was challenging. No Gebusi ever gave us a full narrative of Dugawe's death, its aftermath, and the events that preceded it. Rather, the story emerged from our observations over time, casual conversations, transcriptions of spirit séances, event calendars, and structured interviews with individual Gebusi concerning life histories, kinship, and mortality. Also important were oral accounts and cross-checking concerning events that predated our arrival, such as the killing of Dugawe's first wife and of Sialim's mother. This information was written up in daily entries and in reflections on what we thought was happening. Within a few days (while the information was still fresh), we typed these up as field notes and analyzed them in relation to other information we were gathering. Even with events that I witnessed and experienced myself, my awareness was often dim and partial at first—strong in emotion but weak in understanding. An initial event like Dugawe's death, dramatic as it was, became but one end of a tangled web. It sucked me into a thicket of crisscrossed meanings and histories. Village life was a continuing stream of dramas that linked people together while exposing their differences. Even in the few weeks between Dugawe's burial and the inquest séances for his death, the villagers undertook spiritual investigations for seven other sicknesses, including my own, when I was stricken with my first serious bout of malaria. We found ourselves living in an intricate soap opera—truth more surprising than fiction. Lovers, killers, spouses, co-residents, friends, and relatives all played their parts in concocting a strong and sometimes toxic brew. No wonder that coming together in collective good company was so important to Gebusi—or that it was such an accomplishment!

What is "participant observation" in such a world? In the present case, I observed and, to some extent, participated in the retrieval of Dugawe's body, his funeral and burial, and the spirit séances and sorcery investigations that followed. However, I did not want to participate in any attack on a suspected sorcerer. Eileen helped facilitate Sialim's departure to a safer place when sentiments against her were highest. This said, we worried that more severe violence might occur. Later in our fieldwork, when our understanding was better, an older woman in the village was accused of being a parcel sorcerer. In this case, we were able to act like kin supporters and side with the woman's family when she was forced to test her innocence by cooking a divination sago. Fortunately, no violent action was taken against her, but she nonetheless had to move out of the village with her closest kin. As this episode clearly indicates, cultural anthropologists often court risk and uncertainty as they decide what to observe and how and when to participate in the "participant observation" of fieldwork.

Between events we observed, those we were able to reliably reconstruct, and those we were able to participate in with good conscience, what larger patterns emerge concerning Dugawe's death, its precedents, and its legacy? We can review. My account began with a description of Dugawe's suicide, the attacks on Sialim, and the mourning and burial of Dugawe's body. Then came the surprisingly festive events of the funeral feast held to commemorate him. These were followed by a month of waiting. Then, after other aborted attempts, Swamin, the community's principal spirit medium, conducted a death inquest séance for Dugawe. Surprisingly, his spirits recast the death as an attack by male assault sorcerers from a distant settlement. A hunt in the forest for the sorcerers was inconclusive. Eventually, Dugawe's spirit was declared appeased and his widow, Sialim, was exonerated. Several months later, Sialim and Swamin were married. Rounding out this history were events that occurred prior to our fieldwork. These included Dugawe's killing of his first wife and son; Swamin's killing of Sialim's mother, the jailing of Dugawe for having beaten Sialim; and Sialim's sexual affair with Sagawa.

This web of incidents shows how major events among the Gebusi, such as Dugawe's death, are rarely isolated phenomena. Their causes and conditions link backward and forward through time. In viewing the larger picture, many topics that might seem disparate—sickness and death, marriage, sex, sorcery, homicide, and suicide—come into interconnected focus. In addition, a single event, such as Dugawe's death, can expose a host of broader issues: emotional dynamics among Gebusi, relations between men and women, the importance of spirits and spirit mediums, the impact of government incarceration, and even the role of subsistence practices such as fish poisoning. Far from being separate, these features resonate and twine together.

So what does Dugawe's story tell us about the Gebusi? Concerning Gebusi sorcery and gender relations, the events surrounding Dugawe's death illustrate the following:

1. Gebusi women take primary responsibility for mourning and for emotionally identifying with the person who has died. Men investigate the death and take action against those deemed responsible as sorcerers.

2. Gebusi visitors' burials and funeral feasts express antagonism, but this aggression is undercut by the hosts' hospitality. Deeper anger is usually not expressed until proper inquests and divinations have been arranged.

3. The Gebusi believe that all adult deaths from sickness, accident, or suicide are caused by either male assault sorcerers (*ogowili*) or by male or female parcel sorcerers (*bogay*). Of the two, suspects for parcel sorcery (such as Sialim's mother) are more likely to be executed.

4. There is virtually no objective evidence that the Gebusi actually practice sorcery, but they firmly believe in its existence. In this sense, Gebusi sorcery is a form of scapegoating. The Gebusi "confirm" the identity of sorcerers through an elaborate variety of spiritual inquests and divinations.

5. Male spirit mediums play a key role in Gebusi sorcery accusations. The opinion of their spirits during all-night séances is highly influential, and they can direct the finding and interpretation of "evidence" that is used to validate an accusation.

6. Though spirit mediums should be neutral parties, the outcome of the sorcery inquest may end up benefiting the spirit medium who conducts them. In Dugawe's case, Swamin's spirits directed antagonism away from Sialim, whom he ended up marrying a few months later.

7. After sorcery inquests are completed, social relations are often re-established between the families involved—even if an accused sorcerer has been attacked or killed. After Sialim's mother was executed, her relatives made peace with the killers. Sialim herself continued to live in the Yibihilu community after both her mother's killing and her husband's suicide. Indeed, she ended up marrying her mother's killer.

8. Sickness, death, sorcery, and marriage often link in a cycle of reciprocity or balance over time. Events that seem spontaneous, idiosyncratic, or even bizarre may end up illustrating deeper cultural continuities. In Dugawe's

case, Sialim was attacked in reciprocity for his suicide. The earlier death of Swamin's wife was balanced by Swamin's killing of Mokoyl and then by the "replacing" of his deceased wife by his marriage to Mokoly's daughter, Sialim.

The practices and beliefs described above were confirmed by the rest of my fieldwork with the Gebusi in 1980–82 as distinctive to Gebusi religion, politics, and social relations. In much ethnographic writing, one finds similar remarks to the effect that "People X do or believe Y under condition Z." It should be noted, however, that in most, if not all, cases, these summary statements collapse and compress a tangle of ethnographic experiences and information. Such statements are generalizations; they bleach out the complexities of human experience and imply that behaviors and customs continually repeat themselves rather than having the potential to change over time. If their limitations are admitted and understood, however, such thumbnail statements can serve as useful guides for generalization and cross-cultural comparison.

During our fieldwork, features of Gebusi life gradually became both more meaningful and more comparable or contrastive to our understanding of customs in other societies, including our own. This increased awareness sharpens our final lingering question above concerning Dugawe's death: How typical were the events surrounding it in Gebusi culture? This question looms large for ethnography. How do we know if we are observing events that are widespread or "normal" in a given society? Are we paying too much attention to some practices or beliefs at the expense of others? And what patterns of change have emerged to change the relationship between some practices and others over time?

In some ways, the events surrounding Dugawe's death were both normal *and* exceptional, both traditional *and* new for the Gebusi. On the one hand, the burial practices, antagonistic displays, sorcery inquests, and spiritual divinations that surrounded his death were "typical" for many Gebusi during the 1970s and 1980s. On the other hand, certain features of Dugawe's case were exceptional, even unique. His was the only male suicide in almost four hundred adult Gebusi deaths that I was able to document and cross-check through genealogical investigation. He was also the only Gebusi who had killed his wife or his child. Not coincidentally, he was the only Gebusi we knew of from that period who had served a lengthy prison term. Quite possibly, Dugawe's experiences in prison and then at the Nomad jail increased his stress upon being released. That is, his unique experience of confinement and stigmatization may have contributed to his ultimate suicide.

Sialim's actions were also unique; I know of no Gebusi woman before or since who managed to have her husband jailed for having beaten her. She was also exceptional in conducting an open sexual affair while her husband was still alive. These features—Dugawe's unusual violence and Sialim's forceful response—heightened or exaggerated features of male-female opposition in Gebusi culture. Their particular result relates as well to the legacy of Australian colonialism and the presence of Papua New Guinean constables at the Nomad Station. Without these influences, Dugawe would not have been imprisoned in the first place or jailed for beating Sialim.

And yet, these new developments blended as if seamlessly with general patterns of Gebusi culture. This included the subsequent marriage of Sialim to Swamin, which completed a cycle of balanced exchange both in death and in life: the death of Swamin's first wife was avenged by the killing of Sialim's mother and then structurally "replaced" by Swamin's marriage to Sialim herself. Sialim willingly accepted and in some ways pursued this resolution. Did she really care for Swamin? Was she grateful to his spirits for their help in saving her? Or was he simply a convenient protector? Did Sialim dispute the execution of her own mother, or did she accept this killing as legitimate—as some Gebusi do when their relatives are killed as sorcerers? It was hard for us to tell. Perhaps all of these were true for Sialim to some extent. Though it may seem odd or even shocking that a woman could marry her mother's killer, it is not uncommon in cultures around the world for people to live with those who have harmed them or their close relatives. In Western countries, including the United States, this pattern is common in cases of child abuse or spousal abuse; the victim may accept and even defend the family member who perpetrates domestic violence.

Events such as Dugawe's death and its aftermath challenged us to the hilt. They also yielded insights that were crucial to our understanding of death and dying, gender relations, scapegoating, and the power of human affiliation in the face of violence and suffering. Most ethnographers strive to find generalities while valuing the uniqueness of the people and events they study. They seek to appreciate cultures while exposing their ideologies and inequities. And they try to balance participant observation with the importance of their own feelings and values. Like most ethnographers, we both succeeded and failed in all these respects. But the attempt was well worth the effort.

Antagonists make peace by sharing a tobacco pipe over the grave of the deceased. (PHOTO: Eileen Marie Knauft)

Getting Along
with Kin and Killers

To FOLLOW THE PLAY, you have to know the characters. If the play is in sports, you need to know what team the players are on, what sport they are playing, and what the rules are. For me, lives in Yibihilu seemed halfway between a dramatic play and an intense sport. The sport analogy may be stretching things, because the "game" was to manage one's relationship to others in the community, not to defeat a rival team. Indeed, when men and boys in the village played soccer (which government officers had introduced), they preferred the game to end in a tie rather than having one team win and the other lose. But in daily life, people *were* organized into groups. And we had to know the groups and their rules of relationship to know what was going on. Suddenly, a dispute would break out. All at once, one group would be swinging clubs against another, which retaliated in like fashion—while a third group stood as peacekeepers in the middle, trying to break things up. It all happened spontaneously, and we couldn't tell why people divided as they did. The same was true more generally—groups of people would casually depart to forage in the forest, give and receive gifts of food at feasts, or present costume decorations to initiates. Why did some people act together as a group as opposed to others? And why had some people been killed within the community while most others remained friends?

In societies like that of the Gebusi, principles of cooperation and division stem from patterns of kinship and marriage. Anthropologists have long emphasized the importance of kinship, especially in non-Western cultures. In fact, if there is one topic that is specific to anthropology but largely unconsidered by the other social sciences, it is the social organization of kin and relatives. On the surface, kinship is a simple concept. Each of us has a family and relatives, and it seems natural to think that we know about relations between kin. We know about parenthood and about our brothers and sisters; we know what marriage is, who our cousins are, and so on. But things are less obvious when we consider other cultures—or even when we consider our own more closely.

In Gebusi society and many other societies, if you ask someone what group he or she belongs to, the person will tell you the name of his or her clan. A clan is a permanent social group whose members pass down membership through descent from one generation to the next. Members of a clan generally believe that they should not marry one another and that they derive from a common ancestor. We say "believe" because all members of a clan may not, in fact, be able to trace links through a male or female line to an ancestor who they identify as having in common. Among the Gebusi, clan membership is passed down through the male line—a bit like the way last names in most Western societies have historically been passed down. So we can call the Gebusi descent groups "patriclans." By contrast, however, most people in countries like the United States do not belong to clans—or even to any descent group at all. They typically belong to "families" but not to larger, permanent named groups defined through descent and which possess special rights and duties. Among Gebusi, all members of a named patriclan call one another "brother," "sister," "father," "father's sister," "grandparent," and so on—even though most of them are what Americans and other Westerners would call "cousins," "uncles," "aunts," and "grand-aunts and -uncles."

Sometimes, the extended ties of descent groups can be quite strong. Take an example relating to marriage. When Saliam's first husband died, she was expected to marry the deceased man's patriclan "brother," Daguwa, who was a widower at the time. This "marriage by levirate" had the effect of keeping Saliam—and her daughter from this previous marriage—within a close branch of her dead husband's patriclan. This was true even through Daguwa was not the true brother but rather what we would call a cousin of Saliam's first husband. We can graphically show the family relationship that emerged between Saliam and her two husbands, in turn, by the standard symbols that anthropologists use to show kinship: a triangle for a man, a circle for a woman, an equal sign for marriage, a slash to indicate someone who has died, a vertical line for descent, a horizontal line for siblingship, and a slash across a horizontal line to indicate that descent or clanship cannot be demonstrated by actual kinship (see figures 4.1 and 4.2).

If we want to be yet more complete, we can add in Daguwa's first marriage and the children of the two marriages. Because this involves persons who died from homicide, we can indicate these persons with an "X" rather than a slash. Likewise, we can indicate the order of each person's marriages with numerals in boxes (see figure 4.3).

Though kinship diagrams take some getting used to, they are important ways for anthropologists to keep track of social relations among people in small-scale communities. And they can alert us to things we might otherwise miss. For instance, figure 4.3 reminds us that the marriage between Saliam and Daguwa was actually the second one for each of them. It also shows that Saliam had a surviving daughter from her first marriage, that Daguwa's first wife and son were killed and that Saliam and Daguwa's own marriage did not produce any children. Finally, it shows that, despite Daguwa's violence, the clanship between Daguwa and Saliam's first husband helped him maintain his claim to her.

Figure 4.1
Key to kinship terms

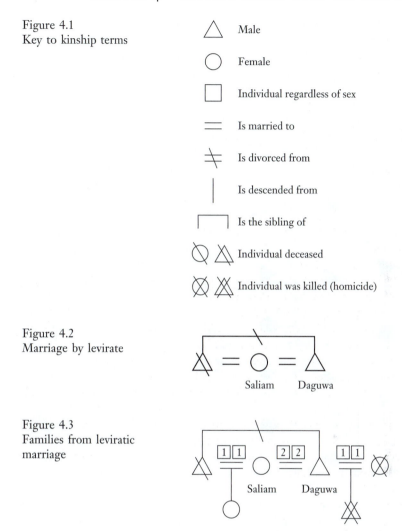

Figure 4.2
Marriage by levirate

Figure 4.3
Families from leviratic
marriage

What about the power of "sisterhood" between women as opposed to the bond of "brotherhood" between men? Because the Gebusi trace descent through the male line, connections of "brotherhood" and "sisterhood" pertain only as long as the links between generations go through fathers (see figure 4.4). Generational ties don't turn Gebusi into members of the same clan if they are traced through mothers. For many of us born and raised in Western countries, the people we consider "cousins" can be related to us on either our mother's or our father's side. But for Gebusi, a first cousin on the father's side is either a "brother" or a "sister," whereas a first cousin on the mother's side is almost never a member of one's clan at all.

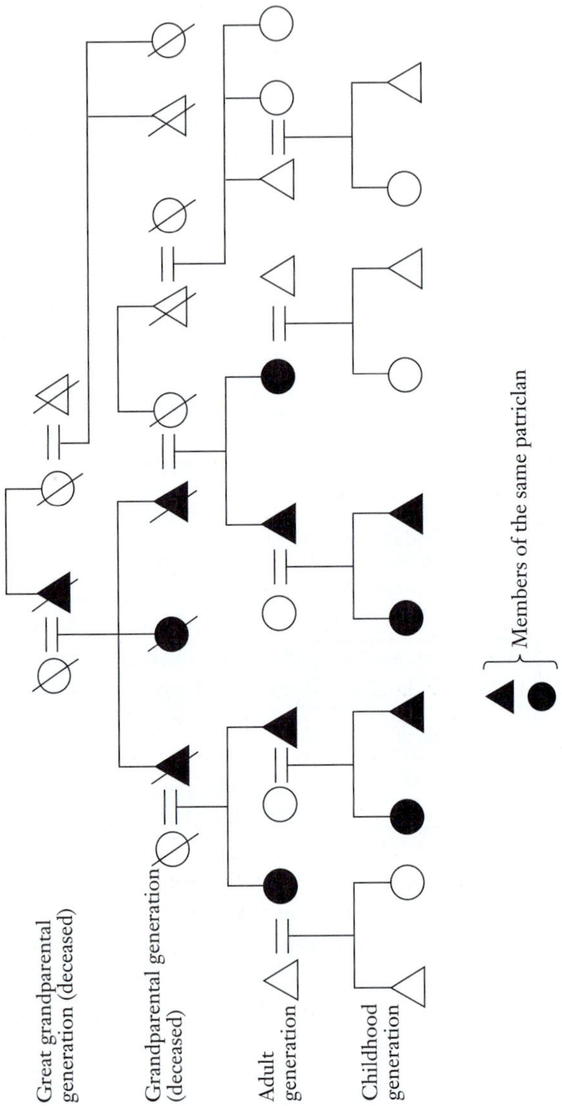

Figure 4.4
Gebusi clanship

Members of the same patriclan

Great grandparental generation (deceased)

Grandparental generation (deceased)

Adult generation

Childhood generation

Does this all seem complicated? It certainly was for me. Truth be told, kinship is just about the driest and most boring part of cultural anthropology, at least for most students. When I was in college, I felt about kinship the way I felt about calculus: I knew it must be important, but I couldn't really see the point—and I didn't seem to be very good at it.

Looking at kinship across cultures, it becomes clear there are hundreds of ways that cultures group relatives together, decide who is "really" related to whom, establish rules and patterns of intermarriage, structure alliances and divisions between groups of kin, and so on. When I started reading about this before going to graduate school, I thought I would go crazy! But then I started doing fieldwork. Learning kinship in the abstract is, well, abstract. But when your friends are dating, marrying, fighting, giving gifts to one another, and all the rest, you often can't figure out who is doing what to whom and why *except* through kinship. And then kinship becomes not just important but a fascinating human puzzle.

In addition to kinship, marriage among the Gebusi is also very important. But Gebusi practice "preferential sister-exchange." When a woman marries into a given clan, a "sister" of the husband should also marry a "brother" of the bride. As such, the marriage of a woman into her husband's clan should be matched by a balancing marriage of a woman from this second clan into her own—so neither patriclan "loses" a woman without gaining one back. This may sound like a strange way of getting married, as if women were pawns exchanged between groups of men. We may like to think that women and men should get married because they want to, not because they feel obligated. But among groups like the Gebusi, sister-exchange is more interesting and surprising than either of these alternatives.

First, the Gebusi ideal of marital balance is taken loosely and can be extended. Because Gebusi have complicated ways of extending "siblingship" beyond even the patriclan, they can sometimes find creative ways to "define" a woman as a kind of "sister." Second, the bride-to-be has a degree of veto power in marriage. If a Gebusi woman really objects to marrying a given man, her wishes may hold sway. As Eileen found, this was also true in the distant past. Some of the oldest Gebusi women had bluntly refused a proposed marriage and hence had thwarted a sister-exchange.

Alternatively, a teenage girl and a young man could become romantically attracted even though there was little chance that a "sister" of the young man would marry a "brother" of the young woman. Such "unreciprocated" marriages drew strong objections from the young woman's fathers and brothers. But the young couple could prevail if the woman was strong willed or ran away with her new husband. Though the parents or brothers of the woman could object mightily, and though they could beat her if they found her, many of these romantic unions persisted and were ultimately accepted as marriages.

Marriage between certain kinds of Gebusi relatives was considered impossible and was completely prohibited. All human cultures put a taboo on some kinds of marriages, such as that between a woman and her own true son. But other rules concerning who can or cannot marry vary widely from one society to another. In some cultures, a person is restricted to finding a partner in one-half, one-quarter, or even only one-eighth of the available descent groups. Western societies tend toward the other extreme: the only marriages that are completely prohibited are usually those within the nuclear family and sometimes between very close cousins. This leaves almost the whole rest of society as an open field from which you can find a marriage partner.

The Gebusi are somewhere between these extremes. They generally prohibit marriage within the clan, which averages eighteen persons in size. In anthropological terms, this means that Gebusi clans are "exogamous"—their members have to marry outside the clan. For any individual, one or two additional clans may be considered a "brother" clan, based on vague ancestral ties. Marriage between such brother clans is frowned upon but not completely prohibited. Other restrictions are less widespread. A Gebusi shouldn't marry the child of a paternal aunt or a maternal uncle. (After all, these persons are "mothers" and "children" to each other!) But more distant relatives on the mother's side can be married. In a village like Yibihilu, an unmarried young person finds that about two-thirds of the appropriately aged persons of the opposite sex are marriageable. Most Gebusi find their marriage partners within their village or among those who live in smaller hamlets within an hour's walk of the main settlement. As such, we can say that Gebusi communities are largely endogamous.

On some occasions, a Gebusi woman actively wants to complete a sister-exchange. If a young woman likes her own brother and his new wife—not to mention the new wife's brother, her own potential spouse—then she looks forward to completing the matrimonial exchange. The two couples will typically live together as a joint family, and such family units tend to be strong and cooperative among Gebusi.

Ultimately, then, the notion that Gebusi sister-exchange is "preferential" means just that: sister-exchange is preferred "if possible." But if not, that's life. In actuality, just over half of all first Gebusi marriages (52 percent) were sister-exchanges. Most of the remainder were what we liked to call "romantic unions" that did not follow the rules of sister-exchange. Despite the pronouncements of Gebusi men that "we exchange women," women and men who wanted to marry without exchange often found a way to do so. Various features of Gebusi social organization helped them out. Within each Gebusi patriclan are smaller sub-groups whose members *can* trace an actual linkage to one another via male descent. In anthropological terms, these small groups are "lineages." More specifically, because Gebusi lineages are traced through the male line, we call them "patrilineages."

In the case of the Gebusi, patrilineages represent very tight and very small atoms of kinship defined through male descent. Overwhelmingly, their members live together in the same settlement. Given their small size, a Gebusi patrilineage might include only one young unmarried woman—or maybe none at all. *Yet it is within the patrilineage rather than the larger clan that a young man's claim to use his "sister" for exchange in marriage remains strong.* Members of the larger patriclan, by contrast, do not necessarily live together and often have little ability to actively pressure a distant clan "sister" to complete a sister-exchange marriage.

If Gebusi patrilineages are small, and if members of the larger clan often do not live with one another, then who else do people live with? Typically, they live with other close kin related to them by marriage or via their mothers. For instance, more than 80 percent of men who have a living mother's brother live in the same settlement as this man. Seventy percent of men who have a true brother-in-law reside in the same village as this man. From a woman's point of view, this is good: it means that residing with her husband does not generally distance her from her own brother. And when she gets older, she is apt to live in the same village as both her son and her brother. In the mix, she usually resides as well with a range of close female kin on whom she can rely and with whom she can perform collective tasks.

Taken as a whole, Gebusi villages bubble with kinship relations that are variously traced through mothers, fathers, classificatory brother- and sisterhood, and intermarriage. The fifty-two residents of Yibihilu identified with thirteen different clans. The men of the village belonged to seven different clans and eleven different patrilineages. As many as one-third of them were totally unrelated to one another. As such, Gebusi villages are multiclan settlements rather than clustered around the men of a single patriclan. This helps explain why Gebusi place such a high value on collective good company across diverse lines of kinship and friendship; it helps keep their villages integrated and cooperative.

Having reviewed Gebusi social organization, we can now put the pieces together. In particular, we can ask what portrait emerges from Gebusi kinship and residence patterns that combine very small lineages, preferential marriage by sister-exchange, and village residence based on diverse ties of kinship, intermarriage, and friendship. As we have seen, only about half of first Gebusi marriages are balanced through sister-exchange. And this creates a problem, because the Gebusi lack any effective way to recompense an extended family or patrilineage that loses a sister or daughter in marriage. In some parts of Melanesia, Africa, and Asia, a woman's marriage can be "paid for" by valuable gifts given by the groom and his kin group to the close relatives of the bride. These payments are sometimes called "bride-price." Many anthropologists prefer the term "bride-wealth," however, because the transaction is not a human purchase but the opening round of wealth exchanges that may last for years between the closest kin of the groom and the bride.

Among the Gebusi, however, bride-wealth or bride-price is rudimentary. A groom might give a few gifts to the mother or brothers of his bride, but these presents are typically small and are not considered an exchange for the woman herself. Instead of material compensation, the Gebusi have practiced a direct or person-for-person form of reciprocity. The ideal, of course, is sister-exchange marriage. But when there is no return marriage, there is also no payment to mollify the bride's kin for her loss to their group. So what happens? Although this causes resentment, the Gebusi tend to sweep it under their cultural rug. Most in-laws claim that they accept marital imbalance and get along well. Indeed, in-laws co-reside just as often when the marriage that links them is unreciprocated as when it is balanced through sister-exchange. Given their strong cultural emphasis on good company, it is not easy for Gebusi to admit or address tensions between in-laws.

Here is where issues of kinship, residence, and social etiquette link to Gebusi politics and disputes. And at least to me, this is where the discussion gets really interesting. It's one thing to know about the kinship and residential makeup of a society. But it's more significant to use this knowledge to understand important and otherwise hard-to-explain trends. For the Gebusi, these have included a very high rate of violence and killing associated with sorcery accusations. Why has the Gebusi rate of killing been so high, and who stands the greatest chance of being killed?

One of the most important facts here is that Gebusi sorcery accusations are especially likely between members of patrilineages that are linked by a marriage that has not been reciprocated. At this point, I should emphasize that the Gebusi themselves do not say this. As we have seen, Gebusi men have a profound ability to emphasize good company and to suppress or dissociate from their anger. Even during a spirit séance when a community member is accused of being a sorcerer, the clan and lineage relatives of the accused usually say nothing at all. They may even continue joking so as not to lose public face. Gebusi believe that sorcery accusations should be proved by tangible evidence. As described in Chapter 3, these clues take a variety of forms, including a "sign" by the corpse, a packet of "skin and blood" identified by a spirit medium, leavings from the victim that have been "burned" by the sorcerer, or divination food that has been undercooked by an accused sorcerer. To Gebusi, these findings represent tangible physical evidence—as real as fingerprints on a smoking gun. Why was the sorcerer accused or attacked? Because, Gebusi say, the objective evidence shows him or her to be guilty! This evidence typically is convincing to a wide range of people and tends to be supported rather than opposed by men from the many clans in the settlement.

Given this context, how can I suggest that unacknowledged tensions related to marriage and sister-exchange inform sorcery accusations between Gebusi patrilineages? Here, we must shift gears. Gebusi's own explanations are crucial, but they do not tell the whole story. Beyond what people think and say, it's important to focus on what they actually do. And especially in small-scale societies, these actions often link to patterns of kinship and residence.

We all know that people often say one thing and do another. In American society, we may promise to marry someone "til death do us part." But between 40 and 50 percent of marriages in the United States end in divorce. As an anthropologist, it is important—indeed, key—to consider the gap between ideals and actions. In making this move, however, we create more distance between our perspective and those of the people we are studying. To say that many Americans who marry get divorced captures neither the joy of a good marriage nor the pain of a bad one. It is a statistical assessment, not an emotional or humanistic one; it pulls us away from understanding human lives.

Anthropologists have often debated which is better—a close-up portrait that is rich with people's experiences, or a more detached view that is systematic and encompassing. Is a statistical depiction more scientific or more dehumanizing? My own opinion is that both views are needed—and that they need to be combined. Like using the zoom function on a camera, the anthropologist should sometimes focus on the details of individual lives and experiences. But she or he should also draw back—as in the present chapter—and look more dispassionately at the larger picture, statistics and all.

For the Gebusi, I tried to gain a society-wide view by collecting census material, residence histories, and kinship information. By charting the genealogies of eighteen clans—as far back as Gebusi could remember—I documented the cause and circumstances of death for each deceased person. Then I double-checked each account with someone from a different clan, to make sure the information was accurate. This was a tedious task, as you might imagine. But the Gebusi were interested in the details, and I think they were proud to present them correctly. And when they didn't, they quickly realized that I could uncover their "embellishments" by obtaining a more accurate story from someone else.

To make a long process short, we can return to the question raised previously: How do we know that Gebusi who are related via unreciprocated marriage do, in fact, accuse one another of sorcery even though the Gebusi don't make this statement themselves—any more than Americans at weddings announce that the marriage may fail? Within the Gebusi community, statistics reveal that persons related by marriage are more than three times more likely to accuse one another of sorcery than would be expected by chance. In father-in-law/son-in-law relations, the rate of sorcery accusations is a whopping fifteen times greater than would be expected by chance. In more than 70 percent of cases in which a relative via marriage is accused, the marriage that links the patrilineages of the accuser and the victim has not been reciprocated. Viewed broadly, this makes sense. Gebusi marriage is based on "person-for-person" exchange. So is Gebusi killing: the life of the sorcerer is taken "in exchange" for the death of the person who died of sickness. These aspects of positive and negative exchange link together. If there is no exchange for a woman in life, it increases the chances of violent revenge between the two patrilineages when a person dies from an illness.

Killings of the Gebusi were remarkably frequent. Of all adult deaths, almost one-third were homicides (129 of 394, or 32.7 percent). This rate of violence is even greater than that of the Yanomami, the so-called fierce people of the Amazon rainforest. Per person, this rate of killing equals the carnage of the bloodiest war in world history, World War II in Europe—including the Holocaust. Not all Gebusi killings were individual executions of sorcery suspects, but the majority were—61 percent. Another 21 percent were the result of Bedamini raids, in which large numbers of Gebusi could be killed simultaneously. (These raids were also linked to sorcery in that most of them were instigated by disgruntled Gebusi who contracted Bedamini to venture into Gebusi territory and attack one of their villages that was thought to be harboring sorcerers.) Only 5.5 percent of violent Gebusi deaths resulted from battles or fights between massed groups of Gebusi warriors.

Gebusi adults of both sexes and almost all age categories could be killed as sorcerers. In relative terms, however, the persons most likely to be accused and executed were senior adults—which for the Gebusi means anyone in their thirties or older. Although I don't have the numbers to prove it, I think there are several reasons for this. As they live longer, the Gebusi accumulate more disputes and resentments, including via nonreciprocal marriages. When someone dies of sickness, there is a greater chance that one of these past disputes may consciously or unconsciously inform an inquest that finds the other party guilty of sorcery. In addition, older persons can become increasingly concerned with and angry about their own growing list of friends and relatives who have died. They can also be thought to be angry enough over these deaths to themselves direct spiritual malevolence against others. By contrast, children are never accused of sorcery; in Gebusi belief, they are not old enough to know how to perform it.

Between the extremes of older persons and children, young men may sometimes be accused of sorcery and executed. In the more distant past (the 1950s and 1960s), late adolescent males were commonly targeted as sorcerers. But one category of adults has been almost completely immune from Gebusi sorcery accusation: young women. In their midteens and into their twenties, Gebusi women were virtually never accused or attacked as sorcerers. From a society-wide standpoint, this is significant. Young women are crucial to a society's reproductive and demographic survival. As unconscionable as it is in moral and ethical terms, the killing of older persons has less impact on reproduction. Few Gebusi women seem to give birth beyond their early thirties. Men are even more "dispensable" in demographic terms because a relatively small number of men may impregnate a larger number of women to repopulate the society. Enormous numbers of European men were killed during World War I, but the population replenished itself quickly because so many young women were available for childbearing. In the case of the Gebusi, the relative immunity of young women from sorcery execution meant that the internal homicide rate, high as it was, did not preclude their collective survival. People lived in good company even as they killed those they suspected of breaking this rule, especially as they got older. A greater survival threat was posed by the Gebusi's neighbors, the Bedamini, who would indiscriminately kill Gebusi women and children as well as men during their fearsome raids.

What has happened to the Gebusi rate of violent death over time? As Australian colonial officers suppressed Bedamini raiding, from 1963 to 1975, the Gebusi who died of homicide declined from a whopping 39 percent of all adult deaths (97 killings out of 249 deaths) to 23.3 percent (24 killings out of 103 deaths). This decline continued during the first seven years of national independence: from 1975 until our departure in 1982, 19 percent of adults died from homicide (8 of 42 deaths). Despite this general improvement, those killings that did occur were targeted increasingly against women. Prior to pacification, the rate of homicide had been 26.4 percent higher for men than that for women. This balance then shifted: between 1975 and 1982, women were killed more than twice as often as men. Why? There are several reasons. First, the Gebusi became increasingly reluctant to kill people whose murder might come to the attention of police at the Nomad Station. Although officers seldom knew what went on in the villages, they might have learned about a killing from angry relatives of the slain person. In practical fact, the killing of a woman—particularly if she was an elderly widow—was not as likely to generate an outpouring of anger as when violence was directed against an adult male. Old widows are sometimes perceived as a drain on the community because they have a declining ability to work, and their childbearing years are over. They may be seen as irritable, uncooperative, and apt to use spiritual power to compensate for their own physical decline. Reciprocally, if older widows do not have grown sons to support them, they can be relatively easy targets of sorcery accusation. And if they are killed in the forest, away from the main settlement, as was the case with Saliam's mother, chances are good that their deaths will not be reported to the authorities.

In some ways, Gebusi violence against sorcerers has gradually become more similar to that in Western history. From the late-fifteenth through the late-eighteenth centuries, some historians estimate that the Christian church killed approximately 300,000 women as witches. Fear of largely female witchcraft was found in significant parts of Europe and America during the 1600s and early 1700s,

including in the famous witch trials at Salem in 1692. Among the Gebusi, however, sorcery is tied less to waves of community hysteria than to resentment over
high rates of death due to sickness and to marital imbalances that fester between
in-laws. These tensions ultimately find expression in sorcery inquests, divinations,
and accusations.

How have the Gebusi themselves viewed their killing? This question is
poignant because their violence has so frequently been directed against those who
are supposed to be friendly acquaintances within the community. To a surprising
degree, Gebusi have rationalized these discrepancies away. For them, it is not
murder to kill a sorcerer. Rather, it is a legitimate and proper way to dispense
with someone who has him- or herself committed a terrible killing. In Gebusi
belief, these lethal sorcerers must be eliminated to keep the death toll due to sickness from climbing even higher. It may be hard for us to appreciate the degree
to which the Gebusi have believed in their sorcery divinations and inquests.
Outside the narrow context of sorcery inquests, most Gebusi were good-natured
and friendly, not angry or violent. In contrast to males in some other parts of
Melanesia, Gebusi men were self-effacing in public and more likely to minimize
than to magnify their aggression. When the death of a close relative or spouse
was followed by a verified sorcery accusation, however, even the most mild-
mannered man could become a killer. When an ambush and a killing were finally
arranged, the accuser was often aided by others who wanted to rid the community of someone considered to be a public menace.

In the aftermath of a sorcery execution, the killer and his supporters were
rarely attacked. Instead, the community tended to close ranks behind them. In
the same way that accusations needed to have "objective" confirmation and support from different clans in the village, so, too, the person who killed a publicly
accused sorcerer could generally count on the support of the community to protect him. Faced with this reality, the relatives of the person who had been killed
typically had little choice but to accept the death and either stay in the community or move on to another settlement. Even when they wanted revenge, the men
of the sorcerer's patrilineage were few in number—not numerous enough to prevail against the rest of the community.

Beyond our concern for the people who were themselves attacked or killed,
why should we care about Gebusi sorcery and violence? One reason is that their
accusations reveal the influence of culture in creating stigma. Cultural beliefs
can powerfully validate discrimination—as if discrimination was "objective" and
"true." Scapegoating of innocent people can be abetted by structural tensions of
social organization, kinship, and demography that may lay outside the daily
awareness of those involved. Given this, a scientific understanding of social organization is particularly important to complement our awareness of people's stated
motives and lived experiences. In American society, for example, tensions in family structure that result from class inequality, unemployment, racism, and gendered inequality clearly inform patterns of violence and domestic abuse.

By understanding how inequality works among peoples such as the Gebusi,
we may see more clearly how larger patterns of discrimination operate in other
societies. For instance, Western cultural values of equality concerning race,

gender, ethnicity, nationality, and religion are strongly assumed in discourses of human rights, freedom, and democracy. Amid this positive emphasis, however, it would be easy to overlook patterns of inequality and discrimination that persist in fact. As with the Gebusi, we may confuse how we would *like* society to function with how it actually operates. Just as we may believe in marriage despite a significant rate of divorce, we may believe in sexual, racial, and cultural equality and yet find that women are not paid as much as men for doing similar work or that foreigners or racial or ethnic minorities are relegated disproportionately to low levels of income and status. In this regard, it is also easy to neglect patterns of kinship and social organization that are important to ethnic or foreign-born minorities even though their networks of affiliation remain outside legal recognition or mainstream cultural understanding. This is not to say that social inequities are necessarily due to willful malevolence. It is rather to underscore how culturally constructed beliefs—and their discrepancy from actual behavior—can be as strong in our own society as we may discover them to be in others. Cultural anthropology often looks to other cultures to rediscover our own beliefs and actions. Beyond their intrinsic value, features of social structure, kinship, and community organization help us understand much about the human condition at home as well as abroad.

CHAPTER 5

A Gebusi dancer embodies spirits at a ritual feast. (PHOTO: Bruce Knauft)

Spirits, Sex, and Celebration

GENDER, SEX, AND SPIRITUALITY among Gebusi differ greatly from Western practices; they stretch our envelope of understanding. Among these differences, Gebusi admit alternative expressions of sexuality, particularly for men. This is not to suggest that Gebusi practices are a model of sexual tolerance much less of gendered equality. But neither is it to say that they have nothing to teach us. Notwithstanding its tensions and challenges, exposure to Gebusi sexual culture was a rich part of my fieldwork. Although I thought I was tolerant to begin with, I came away with a greater understanding of and respect for sexual diversity than I could ever have imagined. I also became more aware of gendered discrimination than I had been previously. I am grateful that my Gebusi friends let me know about the sexual side of their culture. If sex is often a delicate topic, it is also an important one, and one that needs to be studied with special sensitivity.

My awareness of Gebusi sexual culture began with the male joking that laced events such as ritual feasts and dances, storytelling, and spirit séances. Here is an example of Gebusi male joking:

YABA [TO DOGON]: *Go over there and sleep with the women. Build your "fire" over there.* [Go over and have sex with them.]

SWAMIN [TO YABA]: *If he goes over there and lies down, where are* you [Yaba] *going to put your "forehead"* [phallus] *to sleep?! You'll just have to go over and lay your "forehead" on his* [Dogon's] *grass skirt!!*

YABA [TO DOGON]: *You're wearing a big grass skirt* [for me to lie on].

DOGON [TO YABA]: [You do and] *I'll pull off your loincloth!!*

YABA [TO DOGON]: *And you'll sleep there* [in my crotch]*!!*

[Whooping and laughter from the other men.]

DOGON [TO YABA]: *No! I'll give your loincloth to the women and take off their clothes for you* [so you can take the female role]*!!*

[More laughter from the men.]

SWAMIN: *The younger men must be getting tired from ladling out all their "kava"* *[semen]! I'll ladle out mine with a thrust!!* [Kicks out his foot.]

[General laughter.]

DOGON [TO YABA]:   *Can you give some to me??*

YABA [TO DOGON]:   *We'll have to lay down "forehead" [phallus] as a gift-exchange name!*

YABA AND DOGON [LEANING THEIR HEADS TOGETHER]:   *YAY!!*

[Laughter and yelling.]

Simmering in everyday life, male joking found its greatest outlet on festive occasions and during celebrations. Jokesters didn't have to be related to each other; in fact, it was best if they were not. Dogon and Yaba were unrelated and didn't live in the same community; not being otherwise connected, they were all the more in "good company" for being able to joke together. These connections were made easier by men who were related to both jokesters. In the present case, this role was taken by Swamin, who was a community co-resident and distant in-law of Yaba's and a maternal relative of but not co-resident with Dogon. At the time, all three men were widowers in their early thirties. What about the content of their bawdy jibes? Were Yaba and Dogon really apt to have sexual relations or to use "phallus" as a gift-exchange name between them? No; their joking signaled nonsexual friendship. Much sexual joking, some of it quite physical, flirts with possibilities that aren't consummated. Thinking back, the same was true of the locker-room pranks played by members of my high school soccer team in Connecticut. In a similar way, much Gebusi horseplay is what could be called "homosocial" rather than "homosexual." Its humor derives from threatening but not actually engaging in sex.

At first, I wasn't sure if Gebusi males engaged each other sexually at all. Groups to the east of the Gebusi were known to practice male-male sexuality, but peoples farther to their west did not. I thought that my Gebusi friends were more likely to be in the former camp than the latter, but how could I know? Their interactions were certainly full of suggestive jokes. A young man might shout in jest, "Friend, your phallus was stroked, and it came up!" But beneath the surface, how much was orgasmic fire and how much was playful smoke? I suspected that male trysts took place near the outhouse at night during séances and festive dances. To find out if this was true, I found myself sitting near the appropriate longhouse exit during these events so I could see who went out and if they "hooked up." I felt very uncomfortable as I did so—as if I was snooping around or being a voyeur. At the same time, I needed to find out. I didn't want to "project" sex between men onto the Gebusi if it wasn't documented—and other anthropologists would want to know one way or the other. Imagine how bad it would be to write about Gebusi "homosexuality" only to later discover that, in fact, the practice was rare or absent. Unfortunately, my Gebusi friends seemed unable to talk about the subject in a serious way. Any sober query was quickly turned into a joke. At several feasts, I ultimately did see pairs of males slip out toward the outhouse, cavort with each other in the night shadows, and return a few minutes later. But these pairings were not between the principal joking partners. Rather, they tended to be between a teenage boy and a young initiated man.

Hawi later verified for me the substance of these sexual practices: the teenager manipulates the phallus of his elder counterpart and then orally consumes the semen. As was also the case with groups farther east, this insemination had an important cultural function: it supplied the uninitiated bachelor with male life force for his masculine development. Unlike girls, who were believed to reach maturity without intervention, boys were helped to grow and become stronger by receiving masculine life force in the form of semen. Hawi also verified that, as a rule, men who had been married for a significant time—like Swamin, Yaba, and Dogon—did not engage in trysts with other males even though they might joke about it quite realistically. In effect, they relived their earlier experiences through their sexual banter.

Armed with this knowledge, and being married myself, I felt increasingly comfortable with my own place in the Gebusi sexual scheme of things. I learned to accept male joking, including with me, and to reciprocate in like fashion. On one occasion, I went with the men to a séance held by Swamin at a small bush hamlet. As chance would have it, Eileen had lost a filling and had to take a plane from the Nomad Station airstrip to find a dentist in the country's distant capital. So I was temporarily living alone. Swamin's singing warmed up and even exceeded its normal heated pitch. In his songs, a spirit woman boldly told the men that she was hovering on top of the house in which we were singing—and that she was longing to have sex. Pandemonium broke out as men yelled about how they wanted to satisfy her desire. One of the upcoming initiates, Doliay, straddled a housepost and yanked it back and forth until the whole building shook. Hawi bellowed that he couldn't wait any longer; he wanted to shoot his arrow up into the spirit woman. As the men doubled with laughter, he grabbed his bow, drew back an arrow, and shot it right through the thatched roof. Egged on by the spirit woman, the younger men and teenage boys started pairing up and leaving for sexual trysts in the darkness outside the longhouse.

It was then that Mora stroked my arm, leaned his head close to me, and said, "Why don't we go off together?" He rubbed one of his fists up and down over the index finger of his other hand, and he motioned that I would be the one satisfied. I shouldn't have been surprised. Gebusi men had become open with me about their sexuality—and Eileen was away. After my initial shock, I thought I recovered rather well. I smiled back at Mora: "I'm really sorry, but you know, I'm already married. So I can't go off with you; it would be taboo for me." But I was as unprepared for his reply as I had been for his overture: "Don't worry. Didn't anyone tell you? We break those rules all the time. Let's go!"

I broke out in a sweat. I was not about to join Mora for a sexual tryst. But what would happen to the men's trust in me and their willingness to include me in their social and ceremonial life? Would Mora be angry and insulted? Would I compromise my status as a welcome observer? The men were already gearing up for the elaborate rituals and secret practices that would initiate the next cohort of teenage boys into adulthood. Would I be excluded from learning the keystone customs of Gebusi male culture? I already knew that insemination had cosmic and spiritual significance for Gebusi men as well as being important for the growth of teenage boys. The Gebusi word for initiation, *wa kawala*, meant literally, "child become big." This "bigness" was promoted by ingesting male semen.

As I answered Mora, I tried to suppress my anxiety. I told him that going off with a young man for sex simply wasn't my custom, my personal *kogwayay*. I said that, back where I came from, some men did have sexual trysts with young men like him, but others did not—and I happened to be in the latter group. So, I apologized, I could not go off with him.

Anthropologists are sometimes chided for generalizing about the people they study—for instance, that "the Gebusi practice sister-exchange marriage" or that "Gebusi men practice ritual homosexuality." Such sweeping generalizations can cover up much about personal variation. When Mora replied to me, he seemed to underscore this point. "That's okay," he said. "Some of us have sex a lot, but others don't do it so much." And with that, the séance went on as before. Relieved, I continued my role as observer and shadow participant—singing intermittently, asking questions, tape recording the proceedings, and joking, if anything even more good-naturedly than before.

As it turned out, Mora's reply was truer than I first realized. Though Gebusi teenagers do, in principle, complete their growth by receiving and retaining male semen, their own emerging sexuality is not so easily bottled up. Not uncommonly, the initiates-to-be found sexual release with each other. This was particularly true of Hawi and Doliay. We have encountered Hawi before—my initial helper and uncertain translator, accomplished fisherman, and energetic young bachelor. Among the cohort of soon-to-be-initiated young men, Doliay was his closest comrade. If Hawi was one of the oldest new initiates, Doliay was the youngest, perhaps sixteen years of age. He was also the shortest of the initiates, topping out at just four feet ten inches. But Doliay was a vacuum-packed firecracker. He was intense, funny, industrious, smart, and completely undaunted by the social and physical world around him. He was also remarkably robust for someone so small, as if his lesser stature had been compacted into strength.

During the months leading up to the initiation, Hawi and Doliay became a hilarious pair. At séances, they would rush out together and then saunter back a few minutes later, happily spent. Reclaiming their energy, they would then stand together and jibe. One of their favorite jokes was to reach suddenly with one hand as if to grab at the other's crotch—while holding the other hand back to guard against a similar riposte. Despite such jests, neither they nor the other men or boys made public displays of nudity or sexuality. This helped maintain the good-natured tone of collective joking, including among the senior men, whose verbal antics far outweighed their sexual encounters. However, initiates-to-be like Hawi and Doliay made no secret of the fact that they consorted with each other sexually. Swelling with bravado, they even told me one day that they would never get married to women because they had each other as sexual partners.

According to academic views of the ritual homosexuality or boy insemination that has occurred in some parts of Melanesia, young males who received semen were thought to be discouraged or prohibited from having sexual release prior to initiation—lest they deplete the male essence contained in semen that they were accumulating. Rituals that led up to manhood were supposed to be trials of discipline punctuated by acts of sexual or social subservience to men who had already been initiated. Those awaiting initiation were supposed to pursue sexual release after the rites, but not beforehand. But the Gebusi defied these assumptions.

As if to confound my expectations yet further, Hawi and especially Doliay were interested in Gebusi women as well as in each other. A few weeks after my encounter with Mora, Doliay was caught alone with Nolop in the women's sleeping section of her family house. The escapade occurred in the middle of the night while a ritual feast and dance were taking place in the longhouse. Claiming that she was not feeling well, Nolop had retired alone to her smaller house across the village while others enjoyed the festivities. During the night, Wosip, her husband, needed more tobacco and so went to retrieve some from their family house. As he stepped inside, he saw a shadowy figure bolt from his wife's sleeping quarters, leap out a side door, and dash into the night. Sounding the alarm, Wosip found his guilty wife alone in the chamber. As everyone came running, Doliay was conspicuously unaccounted for.

The implications were scandalous. A teenager and not yet initiated, Doliay was some fifteen years younger than Nolop, whose oldest child was already about twelve years old. Their encounter had probably been as brief and perhaps as opportunistic as it had been illicit. But clan genealogies were dotted with cases in which an unguarded widow or middle-aged woman had become pregnant from a younger man. Fortunately (as far as we were concerned), Wosip was probably the most mild-mannered man in the settlement. He beat Nolop, though not as severely as most men would have done. Saddled with skin bruises and a scalp laceration, Nolop cried and whimpered, sat in public, and refused Eileen's entreaties to wash off the blood that caked her skin. She recovered and reentered village life without further incident, apparently having paid her price through the beating itself.

For his part, Doliay fled to another settlement and stayed there until tempers cooled. Upon his return, he was not beaten—the Gebusi double standard remained in effect—but he was chastised so severely that it appeared he might not be initiated. Denying initiation is a severe sanction for young men who flout the rules against having sex with women. Sagawa had already been precluded from initiation because of his affair with Saliam and her husband's subsequent suicide. Our silent friend Gono, who accompanied us on our initial journey through the rainforest, had also been excluded. Gono would have been the oldest of the initiates, but he had gone ahead and married a widow several years older than himself rather than waiting for the ritual promotion to manhood. If it was possible for teenage boys to have sex with each other and sometimes, illicitly, with women, it was also possible for them to forego initiation altogether and still become full adult men.

It was ultimately not surprising that men's fantasies of illicit sex with women sometimes came to fruition: cultures often fuel the same desires that they forbid. Among the Gebusi, this tension was epitomized in the folktales that men told during the months before the initiation rites. These stories, called *gisagum*, portrayed escapades in the forest between a handsome unmarried bachelor and a gorgeous young maiden. The young couple was typically described as being brought together by forces outside their control (such as the death of their parents) that forced them to stay together and cooperate even though they were unrelated and not married. The seductive behavior and subsequent restraint of the young couple provided the dramatic centerpiece of the story. Although the male audience was sometimes led to believe that the young couple had sex, the continuing strength of the young man in the tale, as he overcame trials and defeated adversaries, showed that he had not weakened himself by forsaking his chastity. Most of the stories ended happily with the glorious initiation of the chaste young man and his subsequent marriage to the young woman. As icing on the cake, her relatives were so impressed with the young man that they typically made no requests for marital reciprocity. At one level, these *gisagum* were morality tales. The hero maintained his virtue, attracted supporters, got initiated, and—most importantly— married the woman he desired. As support to this Hollywood ending, the tales also included villainous adversaries who were vanquished by the young hero's amazing feats of strength and fortitude.

To the Gebusi male audience, however, the tales were anything but heroic or restraining. Instead, the erotic attraction between the young maiden and the hero served as a foil for the men's jokes about sexual arousal. Listeners would proclaim loudly that if *they* had been the young man in the story, the tale would have ended much differently: "If it had been me, I would have had sex with her again and again!" "I'd have failed every trial and would be dead before I could be initiated!" "I'm so pent up that I could die!" And storytellers fueled rather than dampened such banter. Indeed, the tension between the hero's exemplary actions and the contrary declarations of the male audience was the centerpiece of the story's humor. Morality tales on the surface, the stories were also a mandate for men's assertions of sexual desire that playfully broke the rules.

Ultimately, then, the surface meaning of such stories and their practical impact diverged widely. In literal terms, the stories suggested that spending one's "seed" prior to initiation imperiled one's manhood. In some Melanesian cultures, such possibilities are not a joke but have been taken very seriously. Men from the Hua and some other societies in the eastern highlands of Papua New Guinea believed that sexual exposure to women could make men not just weak but physically pregnant. In many highland societies, sex with women was said to be as quick and perfunctory as possible—to avoid the debilitating effects of literally losing one's hardness as the result of intercourse with a woman. Among the Enga of the central New Guinea highlands, men resorted to chants or magical spells to minimize their ejaculation during sexual intercourse, so as not to forfeit their strength. Though these attitudes seem extreme, they echo beliefs found in many regions concerning the depleting effects of semen loss and the polluting effects of sexual intercourse. Among the Gebusi, however, the seductive force of women was at least as much of an attraction for men as it was something to fear. Women's menstrual blood was considered noxious and contaminating to men in a general way, and women were supposed to confine themselves to a section of the women's sleeping area during the peak of their monthly period. But there seemed little interest among either men or women in severely enforcing this stricture, and men did not, in fact, seem to fear intimate contact with women. Indeed, bawdy epithets concerning female genitalia were a standard part of men's and even women's exclamations and joking. Some young men, like Doliay, were quite willing to risk having sex with women prior to their initiation. Others, like Gono and Sagawa, rejected initiation altogether by establishing or trying to establish an early marriage.

What about Gebusi women? Wives seemed to care little if their husbands had sex with a new cohort of teenage boys, or even with young initiated men. But they were furious if their husbands showed interest in other women. For themselves, as Eileen found out, women and teenage girls were far more attracted to men than they were repulsed by them. During spirit séances and storytellings, the women listened to the men's antics from their side of the sago leaf wall that separated them from the men's quarters. Sometimes, they responded with their own smiles and suppressed joking. Many young women were said to be so consumed with romantic longing for young men that they were unreliable workers. As their mothers described them, their heads were "spinning" and their ears were "blocked" from hearing the prudent advice of their mothers and other close relatives. Although adult females got angry if men fantasized about nubile girls who were too young to have sex, they were not puritanical in general. As Eileen wrote, "Gebusi women regard sexuality as a positive force in the formation of marriage— as long as such relationships are based on reciprocal sexual longing."

Given the general Gebusi emphasis on sexual desire—both heterosexual and homosexual among men—did Gebusi women have their own lesbian relations? Though older and younger women are known to have had sexual relations among the Kamula, a group to the southeast of the Gebusi, there is little comparable evidence from any other society in New Guinea. Is sex between women rare in this part of the world? Or has it merely been underreported by male anthropologists, from whom it has been kept hidden? With tactful diplomacy and in private, Eileen asked women whom she knew and trusted if Gebusi women had sex with one another. Their responses were uniformly negative, and they ranged from incredulity to disgust: "No." "Certainly not." "How could that be possible?" "How would we even go about it?" "That would be incredible, unbelievable." "Is that really something that women do where you come from?"

In men's fantasies as well as women's realities, female sexuality among the Gebusi seemed unmistakably directed toward men. During men's séances, spirit women would get pouty and even angry if Gebusi men did not become aroused and joke with them. Fickle and capricious, a spirit woman could leave the body of the Gebusi spirit medium if she felt unappreciated by the male audience. This would force the medium's own spirit to come back to his body, thus ending the séance in the middle of the night. Such a premature conclusion would preclude the instrumental goal of the occasion—for instance, to ask the spirits about sickness or sorcery, or the location of lost pigs. In short, spirit women had to be kept happy and interested by Gebusi men in order for the séance to be successful. Contrary to what I had initially thought, the "functional" and the "entertainment" sides of Gebusi spirit séances were directly linked rather than being opposed.

For Gebusi men, spirit women were highly desirable, but because they stayed in the spirit world, ordinary men could not have sex with them. The main exception here was the spirit medium. In his dreams and at séances, the medium's own spirit lived "for real" the life of the spirit world. This process began when an existing spirit medium encouraged a promising young séance singer to go into trance and sing his own songs. Over time, the senior spirit medium would narrate how a young spirit woman was drawn to the new spirit medium and wanted to marry him. This human-spirit marriage gave the new medium broad access to the spirit world while not preventing him from also having a real-world Gebusi wife and family. The brothers and sisters of the medium's spirit wife became his in-laws and supporters in the spirit world. These spirit persons were friendly and helpful, especially during spirit séances. Correspondingly, the unmarried friends of the medium's spirit wife would accompany her to the séance, sing through the medium's body, and joke salaciously with the Gebusi men. The spirit woman herself would eventually bear the medium spirit children, including his all-important spirit sons. These helpful boys or young men would come to the medium and provide key information at critical points during the séance. The bulk of the medium's songs, however, were sassy tales sung by the spirit women. During the night, their blurred identities became a perfect image of unbridled female sexuality. This proved endlessly provocative to the Gebusi audience.

Having come full circle—from men's relations with each other back to their heterosexual desires—we can better understand male Gebusi bisexuality. In recent years, anthropologists such as Gilbert Herdt and others have been documenting the full range of human sexuality diversity across different world regions, including same-sex, cross-sex, and bisexual practices and orientations. Sometimes a given sexual practice is specific to a given life stage and changes thereafter; sometimes sexual orientations are enduring or permanent. And sometimes societies tolerate, encourage, or even mandate forms of alternative sexuality, while at the same time stigmatizing others. This range of variation is amazing, and it helps us put into context and appreciate the distinctive features and limitations of sexual orientation in a given instance, whether among the Gebusi or in our own society.

Among Gebusi, men often joked that their unsatisfied desire for women was so strong that, in the absence of an available woman, they would find sexual release with a man or teenage boy instead. This was the gist of the joking sequence between Swamin, Yaba, and Dogon presented early in this chapter. This redirection of heterosexual desire back onto other males pervades Gebusi séances, stories, and ritual feasts and dances. At séances, the seductive spirit woman is impersonated by the spirit medium himself. At ritual dances, men also impersonate seductive spirit women. The dance centers on one or more beautifully costumed men who dance all night long in slow, hopping steps to the beat of long drums that they hold.

In 1912, Émile Durkheim suggested that humans project the features of their particular societies onto the worlds of their respective spirits. This notion is consistent with Gebusi spirituality at ritual dances. In broad and generic terms, the dancer's costume embraces the entire Gebusi cosmos. The upper body of the dancer is graced with feathers from birds and the fur of treetop animals, which are associated with the upper-spirit world (see the photo at the beginning of this chapter). By contrast, the dancer's lower body is festooned with images of lower-world spirits such as fish, freshwater shrimp, and crocodiles. Just as the dancer embodies the social and aesthetic harmony of the spirit world, so, too, Gebusi hosts and visitors come together harmoniously at the event itself. Reciprocally, the spirits are believed to hold a spirit world dance even as the Gebusi dance is taking place.

At the same time, in more specific sexual terms, Gebusi dances are rife with erotic elements. The dominant features of the male dancer—including his red body paint, feathers, black eye-banding, and hopping dance steps—are strongly associated with the red bird of paradise, which is the preeminent form taken by young spirit women. Men in the audience refer to and joke about the male dancer as the red bird-of-paradise woman. In essence, the dancer impersonates a seductive spirit woman to whom the men in the audience say they are erotically drawn. In much the same way, in spirit séances, the spirit medium impersonates the female spirits. But at ritual dances, this imagery is also accentuated by Gebusi women themselves. The women sit offstage and sing haunting songs of loneliness and sexual desire as the male dances. As the men look at the dancer, hear the women's singing, and pine for the beautiful spirit woman, they joke about having sex with women—at the same time that they redirect their arousal as homoerotic horseplay. Just as the "woman" whom they are visually attracted to in the dance is actually a man, so, too, their heterosexual desire is most immediately retargeted onto the men sitting nearby. Not coincidentally, ritual dances are also occasions at which young men and teenage boys can pair up for sexual trysts outside the longhouse. As such, male sexual desire for women is both genuinely heightened and selectively redirected among males.

The connection between same-sex and cross-sex desire, and between sexual frustration and redirected sexual aggression, is highlighted in the Gebusi notion of "longing," *fafadagim-da*. This is the men's most common refrain at dances and séances. To cry out, "*Ay fafadagim-da!*" is at one and the same time to declare, "I'm lonely," "I have sexual desire," "I'm strong," "I'm aggressive," "I'm angry," and "I want sexual release one way or another!" That erotic arousal implies aggression and even anger may run counter to Western sensibilities. But it makes perfect sense to Gebusi. The spirit woman is alone in the forest; she wants a man but cannot be approached by most Gebusi men. So, too, the dancer at feasts and the young maiden in Gebusi narratives are beautiful but unreachable, alluring but frustrating. This makes men angry as well as playful and assertive in their joking. During the dance itself, the erotic and more humorous aspects of this aggressiveness are brought to center stage. But in spirit séances for sorcery, the rough edge of masculine frustration can galvanize a more sinister anger as well: the rage of loneliness and loss that is caused by death from sickness in the community. This is also described as *fafadagim-da*. Hence, it is no contradiction that Gebusi spirit séances arouse sexual desire at the same time that they can promote severe violence against suspected sorcerers. Connections between sex and violence that seemed so completely strange to me when I was first with the Gebusi now made complete cultural sense.

In a parallel but somewhat different fashion, ritual feasts also draw upon the aggressive side of male passion. When they enter a host village for a feast, male visitors typically act angry or belligerent. Displays of aggression are particularly dramatic at funeral feasts, where the anger of loss runs very high. These displays are then overcome by the hosts' hospitality of smoke, food, and drink. At most feasts, this hospitality is punctuated by dancing or singing, joking, and, ultimately, the camaraderie of mutual seduction during the night. In their festive gatherings, then, Gebusi men enact and celebrate their ability to convert the threat of violence into a deep assertion of good company—staying together, talking, and joking. This illustrates how the use of sexual imagery may be used in ways that encourage collective as well as individual ties.

What do the sexual practices of the Gebusi tell us about human sexuality more generally? First, Gebusi customs underscore the degree to which sexuality and gender roles differ across cultures. Among Gebusi, men exhibited cross-sex fantasies, intentionally heightened heterosexual frustration, and bonding through same-sex relations. Women easily accepted men's sexual relations with each other but found the idea of sex between women literally unbelievable. Gebusi women valued their sexual relations with men, and infidelity in marriage was strongly discouraged, especially for women.

If we consider the distinctiveness of the Gebusi on a scale of global diversity, we can begin to appreciate how rich, variable, and often paradoxical human expressions of sexuality can be. Even among the few million inhabitants of indigenous Melanesia, sexual customs have ranged from prolonged male chastity and beliefs in women's strength-sapping impact on men to fervent love magic and serial sexual intercourse—both heterosexual and homosexual among men—to collect or ingest sexual fluids for a variety of ritual and magical purposes. In many if not most of these same societies, monogamous marriage remained the norm for the majority of adults.

Even along the lines of its own codes of behavior, Gebusi sexual culture admits much variation among individuals. This was evident in the actions of initiates like Doliay and Hawi, and in Mora's overtures and subsequent replies to me. This underscores the degree to which sexual diversity includes both personal tendencies among individuals and collective differences between cultures. If cultural proclivities are variable, individual ones can be even more so.

Cultures are also diverse in their types and degrees of sexual tolerance. Some societies are more accepting of a range of sexual behaviors; others are less so. Despite their emphasis on marriage and marital fidelity, the Gebusi were relaxed concerning sexual relations among teenage boys and young married men. In this respect, Gebusi practices have blurred the lines between what we might consider homosexual, bisexual, and heterosexual behavior. In many Western societies, these orientations are categorically distinguished—and bisexuality or homosexuality can be highly stigmatized. In one study in the United States, 29 percent of teenagers who identified themselves as gay or lesbian had attempted suicide.

Of course, Gebusi enacted their own constraints on sexual expression, including the beating of women suspected of infidelity or flirtatious misconduct. The way that cultures differently emphasize and tolerate sexual and gendered diversity underscores the degree to which our own sexuality is influenced by both cultural and personal orientations. In this respect, the anthropology of gender and sexuality can have significant personal value as well as broadening our understanding of a key feature of human and cultural diversity.

CHAPTER 6

A male initiate (Yuway) in full costume. (PHOTO: Eileen Marie Knauft)

Ultimate Splendor

GEBUSI CELEBRATION OF LIFE, spirituality, and sexuality came together most fully and completely in the climactic events of the male initiation—the biggest and most elaborate spectacle in Gebusi society. Typically occurring just once in the lifetime of each major settlement, the initiation cycle began, in a sense, with the building of the village's central longhouse. The dwelling provided enough space to house relatives, friends, and visitors from the surrounding settlements during the initiation itself. At Yibihilu, the longhouse was built by six extended families from four different clans whose young men lived in the village and were initiated there. These six young men, one from each family group, ranged from about sixteen to twenty years of age. Their names were Hawi, Doliay, Yuway, Haymp, Momiay, and Hiali (who was the younger brother of Salip).

After the investigation into Dugawe's death was finally put to rest in the fall of 1980, our friends in Yibihilu began to prepare in earnest for their initiation. During the next six months, much and then almost all activity in the village—and in surrounding settlements—focused on the upcoming celebration. Beyond representing a passage to manhood, the initiation brought together the grandest features of Gebusi society and culture. For such a small and isolated group, the scale, effort, and energy that informed these events were amazing. In October and November, villagers spent several weeks amassing huge piles of firewood to be used to cook immense quantities of feast food. In December, January, and part of February, families went deep into the forest to cut and process sago palms. After the sago was pounded and processed into sago flour by the women, families put the heavy starch into large net bags and hefted them in human caravans back to the village. In late February and early March, the men of Yibihilu dispersed into the forest to hunt and then smoke game, especially wild pigs and cassowaries. At the same time, women went off separately to process yet more sago.

Finally, it was time for everyone to reassemble in the village. The large pigs of the settlement—one for each of the six initiates—were tracked down, lured back to the village, penned in wooden cages, and fed to fatten them further. By mid-to-late March, the village was again a beehive of activity. Enormous piles of leaves and cooking stones were stacked next to the firewood. Food piles grew larger, including coconuts, greens, nuts, bamboo shoots, pit-pit, kava roots, and dried tobacco leaves. By the end of March, when everything was finally ready, the people of Yibihilu had worked and prepared for half a year. During this time, they had amassed enough food to feed virtually all of the more than four hundred Gebusi.

If food represented the initiation's material foundation, the costumes of the initiates were its artistic centerpiece. As previously mentioned, the overall term for initiation is *wa kawala,* "child become big." This refers simultaneously to the growth of the initiates and the process of getting dressed up in their elaborate costumes at the initiation itself. The costumes accrued from a far-flung network that spanned the entire tribe. People were mobilized from diverse settlements to obtain materials and construct the twenty different costume elements that made up each initiate's final outfit. The individuals who constructed these articles were linked to the initiates in a variety of ways—as a lineage or clan brother, a maternal relative, an in-law by virtue of previous marriage, or simply an unrelated friend. During the months and weeks leading up to the initiation, these many sponsors of the young men painstakingly constructed armbands, leg bands, waist bands, chest bands, feathered headdresses, shell necklaces, looped earrings, and other body decorations—all for the particular young man whom they had agreed to help initiate. In addition, each initiate ultimately received approximately a half dozen carved hardwood bows. Each bow was accompanied by a large sheaf of exquisitely carved arrows, and each arrow sported a decorated bamboo shaft and an intricately carved and painted tip of bone or hardwood. Some of the arrowheads had holes bored all the way through them; others were carved with delicate frets along the tip. Rounding out the initiation gifts were spare costume decorations and even newly made household items such as large woven net bags and woven sago pouches for the initiates. But none of the items could be publicly displayed or brought together until the final celebration.

During the weeks and months leading up to the initiation, all this effort grew toward its final climax. But how? The Gebusi have little in the way of leadership. Part of the answer lies in tradition. Based on past experience, families and household heads knew the sequence of preparations and the time needed for each. Just as importantly, they also knew how other families and even those in other settlements would respond to the delays and complications that invariably arose during the months of preparation. Collective planning increased when people came back from the forest and met each other in Yibihilu. Although each extended family was ultimately autonomous, they were eager to trade information, strategize plans and contingencies, and keep intimate track of each other's progress. The people of Yibihilu had already worked together to build their big longhouse. Now their task was to bring their human and spiritual vitality to fruition.

For purposes of organization as well as encouragement, the spirits of the Gebusi world were enthusiastically consulted. At each stage of planning, Swamin or another spirit medium held a lively séance. The hurdles of preparation were addressed, and positive resolutions charted. As Swamin described it, the spirits were planning to hold their own initiation at the same time that villagers would be holding theirs. Predictably, then, the spirits were generous with advice and support. Armed with otherwordly confidence, our friends at Yibihilu found a full complement of sponsors for each of the six initiates.

During the months of preparation, the villagers overcame periods of poor hunting, cured persons who were sick, endured two additional deaths and their associated funerals and sorcery inquests, and managed to find and retrieve their semi-domesticated pigs, which had wandered deep into the forest. Despite these obstacles, the villagers' enthusiasm stoked a rising tide of good company. I had never experienced such a frenzy of friendship, laughter, and enjoyment along with plain old hard work. Everyone—women, children, men, and, of course, the initiates themselves—were swept up in the happy maelstrom. And just when we thought the level of camaraderie was about to level off, it would ratchet up to yet a higher level. The Gebusi continued to surprise us.

As we gradually came to realize, the festivities that led up to the initiation mirrored the basic structure of hosting and celebrating with which we had already become familiar. Elaborately decorated visitors would descend on the village in a show of force or aggression. They would then be appeased by gifts from the hosts—the smoking of tobacco, the drinking of water and kava, and the consumption of large quantities of food. Hosts and visitors alike would stay awake through the night while eating, talking, and generally having a good time. If the occasion was particularly festive, one or more of the visiting men would dance in costume as women sang and men joked lustily. At dawn, when everyone was tired and happy, outstanding issues of political contention or dispute would finally be addressed. With so many people from so many kin groups feeling so good, amicable resolutions were all but assured. The visitors would then return home, weary but happy, while the hosts retired for a daytime sleep. In the months prior to the initiation, this same basic pattern of hosting and feasting was used to dedicate floorboards that extended and finished the longhouse, to commemorate a cohort of younger boys who got their ears pierced, and to observe other celebratory occasions.

By mid-March, preparations for the initiation reached fever pitch. Strangely enough, the feast that inaugurated the initiation centered on a thin forest vine named *siay*. The name of the feast was *siay sagra*—literally, to "straighten the *siay*." Hundreds of strips of the sturdy fiber would later be wrapped around the wide bark waistbands that the initiates wore as part of their final costumes. In olden days, this strong waistband was like a piece of midriff armor that protected them from enemy arrows. The presentation of the *siay* by their primary sponsors to the initiates marked a formal announcement of the initiation to come. It also established quite clearly which young men would be initiated and who from other settlements would be primarily responsible for supplying their costume parts, bows and arrows, and other gifts.

In planning for the *siay sagra*, for almost a month ahead of time, the men and boys of Yibihilu accumulated dried meat from hunted animals to give to the initiates' primary sponsors. Meanwhile, the women and older girls processed yet more sago. To only a slightly lesser extent, the sponsors also had been occupied with these same tasks—the hunting of game and the processing of sago—to give to the initiate they were sponsoring. When all was ready, each initiate traveled to the settlement of his preeminent sponsor, his *tor*, and invited him to the *siay sagra* feast at Yibihilu the following evening. In response, the young man's *tor* presented him with a large roll of cooked sago, which the initiate carried back to Yibihilu. In economic and political terms, the *siay sagra* "sealed the deal in advance of the show." In social and emotional terms, it created a sense of good company among the wide range of settlements that would celebrate the forthcoming initiation.

Two weeks later came the ultimate festivities. These began with what anthropologists call a transitional or "liminal" period for the initiates. As proposed by sociologist Arnold van Genep and later by anthropologist Victor Turner, major life cycle rituals are in many societies preceded by an "in-between" period that registers ambiguity between the person's previous position and the new one he or she will occupy. For instance, rituals of status elevation are often prefaced by rites of humility, submission, or teasing before the aspirant assumes his or her new role. For the prospective Gebusi initiates, their in-between status was signified by bold stripes of yellow ocher, painted on them from head to foot. The Gebusi word for yellow, *bebagum*, itself means "in the middle of" or "wedged in between." Along with the stripes of yellow paint, each of the initiates was festooned with a fringed headband, yellow forearm bands, a yellow-painted waist band, a nose plug, a woven throat band, and a single long egret feather, which was stuck in his hair. Perhaps most striking, apart from the initiates' yellow body paint, was a broad white leaf that was attached to the inside front of their waistbands so that it hung down almost to their knees like a large penis. A topic of lewd joking and teasing by the men, the phallic leaf was a public and obvious symbol of the initiates' pent-up sexuality. Each of them was costumed identically, down to the smallest detail. As they lined up and stood with proper humility, it seemed as though their individual identities had merged into a beautiful and yet humble collective whole.

The initiates' biggest trial was to wear the new wigs that their sponsors now came to give them. The climactic festivities would shortly follow this ritual of "tying the bark wigs" (*uga togra*). But first, its painful prologue had to be endured. Wig wearing may not sound traumatic, but the adornment was made from large wads of sodden yellow bark. Tied in bulky bundles to narrow strands of each initiate's hair, the wig pulled down mightily on the initiate's scalp. In fact, the wet bark was so heavy—I estimated eighty pounds for each initiate—that after it was tied to the initiates' hair it had to be supported with a pole held by two helpers, who strained to raise it as each of the young victims, in turn, was ordered to stand up. All the while, the surrounding men crowded around the poor initiates, whooping and joking with abandon. The prime sponsor of each young man then trimmed off the wig's long trailing streamers, which reduced its weight to perhaps "only" twenty-five pounds.

Fighting back tears, the silent initiates were ordered to line up and listen to their elders. The senior sponsor of each initiate then came forward and lectured him on Gebusi values of generosity and virtue: "Always be generous with your kinsmen and in-laws, however long they live." "Don't be stingy with your food. Always give yourself the least." "When you come across your uncle's garden and see he has some nice food, never just take it." "If you ever steal, you will be rotten and no one will like you." "Whenever guests come, you must always snap their fingers firmly and warmly." "Never hide your tobacco away, always share your smoke with anyone who visits." Predictably, the greatest admonitions concerned sex: "You can never, ever chase after another man's wife." "Never flirt with your uncle's woman." "When you see a female 'bird' alone in the forest, you can't just go and 'shoot' it because you think you are 'hungry.'" "Don't you ever pry open the 'cooking tongs' [legs] of a village woman."

Although the sponsors started out serious, their diatribes quickly lost steam; after a few minutes, their speeches labored to maintain an air of stern invective. As the sponsors finally got to their warnings about sex, the men and even the uninitiated boys could barely suppress their smiles and chuckles. Then, with loud cries of "SUI-SUI-SUI," the sponsors shooed the initiates outside to fetch water from the spring, a ten-minute walk away. Amid whoops and hollers, the men and even the boys accompanied the initiates, who carried water tubes and labored to walk while burdened with their wigs.

The initiates' trip to the watering hole turned out to be the prime occasion for revealing male secrets. In some New Guinea societies, elaborate restrictions surround the transmission of sacred male knowledge. In some cases, this information is doled out piecemeal over months or even years. Measured against such standards, the Gebusi were amazingly carefree. As we approached the spring, the men spoke in only slightly lowered tones about the various foods that the new men, once initiated, would not be allowed to eat. Red pandanus could not be eaten because it formed a red paste, like menstrual blood. Slimy forest greens could not be eaten because, when they were cooked, they oozed like a woman's genitalia. River lobsters couldn't be eaten because they once pinched a woman in her upper thigh, which made them turn red. On and on went the list—until I tallied twenty-three food items that would now be taboo to the initiates. In each case, the "rationale" for the prohibition was the same: the food had some association, however circuitous, with women's primary sexual organs. As I later found out, initiated men were not supposed to eat these foods until their first or second child was born. But most of the taboos were observed only loosely in practice. I was told that a hungry man might easily break his food taboos when out in the forest, especially if experience had taught him that there was little harm in doing so. And although the list of dietary proscriptions seemed long, almost none of the items were frequent sources of protein.

As for additional male knowledge, there seemed to be none. For a while, I thought that Gebusi men simply had to have deeper mysteries for me to discover. But I gradually came to recognize that the best-kept secret was the one I had overlooked: Gebusi men had few initiation secrets to reveal. Male sexual encounters with other men had not been hidden from women, and even the initiates had taken no pains to hide their trysts. As for the telling of food taboos at the watering hole, the reactions of the younger boys were quite revealing. Although the men urged the boys to stay away and to cover their ears—lest premature knowledge stunt their growth—most of them edged closer. Some even cupped their hands behind their ears rather than over them, the better to hear the secrets. The men seemed unconcerned. In actuality, the telling of "secrets" was mostly an occasion of laughter and male bravado. Some of the men proclaimed that they would gladly die from breaking food taboos and by exposing themselves more fully to women's sexuality. Like their myths and séances, Gebusi male secrets were at least as much a source of ribaldry as they were sober declarations. Ultimately, the same was also true of the initiates' biggest trauma—the wearing of their bark wigs. Although the wigs were painful, the initiates quickly learned to manage them by hunching forward and shifting the weight onto their shoulders. By two o'clock in the afternoon, Hawi had cut off his own wig entirely. When I asked him why, he claimed that it prevented him from preparing sago for the upcoming feast. By evening, only Yuway and Doliay still wore their wigs, and both of these were gone by the following morning.

In some Melanesian societies, traditional rites of manhood were genuinely brutal. And they sometimes began when boys were only six or seven years of age. Ordeals sometimes included nose bleeding, penis bleeding, tongue bleeding, cane swallowing and vomiting, body scarification, and being beaten, berated, rubbed with stinging nettles, and forced to live in seclusion, in their own excrement, without food or water. In some societies, new initiates were threatened with violent punishment, including death, if they violated male taboos or revealed men's secrets to women. In contrast to these extremes, the Gebusi initiation was thankfully tame. Older men said that their rites of manhood had always been this way—more a celebration than a trial of pain or suffering. The same was true of some other groups in Papua New Guinea, including the Purari peoples of the south coast who, as it happened, were also vigilant headhunters. Again, the diversity of cultures in Melanesia was remarkable.

After wearing their bark wigs, our young friends enjoyed one last night of sleep—as much as they could get, amid their excitement—for several days to come. The following morning, after being repainted in yellow ocher (but without their bark wigs), they left to revisit their main sponsors in their respective villages. I decided to go with Hawi to Swamin's little hamlet at Sowabihilu. We found ourselves crammed into a mini-longhouse with fifty other people who had come there from settlements farther afield. A similar gathering was held simultaneously at the settlement of each initiate's primary sponsor. In the process, people coalesced at a variety of staging points the night before coming together at Yibihilu for the climactic festivities.

As the sun rose the next morning, smoke from a score of blazing cook fires fingered up to greet the morning and shred the fog. The whoops of those stoking the fires and cooking the food soon mingled with the squeals of dying pigs, which stood in their cages as they were shot full of arrows by gleeful men. Singed and splayed to cook on top of the sago, the six large pigs—one for each initiate—would provide the most lavish meal since the last initiation, which had taken place in a neighboring community several years before. By mid-afternoon, the six initiates were finally ready to become truly "big"—to don their crowning costumes. We thronged around them and escorted them from the village a short way into the forest, where they could be dressed. The atmosphere was too festive to be exclusive, and in addition to the young boys who joined us, Eileen was welcomed to come and take photos. Some of the women who had woven parts of the initiation costumes also came along.

Thoroughly cleansed of any lingering yellow paint, each initiate stood up to be painstakingly dressed as an electrifying red bird of paradise. The sponsors and helpers of each initiate took primary charge. They painted with meticulous precision. Then they took the ever-so-carefully-made gifts of feathered headdresses, waist bands, shells, armbands, leg bands, woven chest bands, nose plugs, looped earrings, and more from net bags. All were scrupulously arranged and adjusted on the initiates' bodies. The closest parallel, it seemed to me, although I had never actually witnessed it, was the careful dressing of a traditional American bride prior to her wedding. The analogy wasn't completely far-fetched in that the initiation served, in its way, as a kind of male wedding. Each young man would now be suddenly and imminently marriageable. All but one of the initiates would, in fact, be married within a few months. Some of the initiation gifts they received were practically a trousseau to begin domestic life. In contrast to the initiation itself, the marriages that would follow—to women whose identity was not yet known—were strikingly unceremonial. As we later discovered, these unions were tense affairs characterized by worried courtship and adult irritation, and they were devoid of festive gift giving, costumed dancing, or public celebration. It was initiation, not marriage, that involved the cooking and distribution of the village pigs, on the one hand, and the public celebration of virile adulthood, on the other.

If the initiation was like a marriage without women, the initiates themselves were almost like brides. The bright red paint that graced them from head to toe was the ultimate feminine color. Its association with crimson menstrual blood grew deeper as the many food taboos were retold to the initiates while they were being painted and decorated. In the process, a large new phallic leaf was attached to hang down between their legs. Even more than the standard dance outfit (which also included images of other spirits), the initiation costume was a pure expression of the beauty, allure, and sexuality of the red bird of paradise. But before they could be formally displayed and celebrated, the initiates had to be completely costumed and publicly paraded back to the village. Given the importance of this task, the initiates' sponsors refused to hurry despite the beginnings of an afternoon drizzle. Huddled under trees and with bystanders holding palm fronds and our umbrellas overhead to protect them, the initiates gradually emerged in final splendor. Each painted stripe, leg band, armband, and headdress feather was perfectly aligned and exactly identical on each of the initiates. I was deeply moved to see my young friends—Yuway, Hawi, Doliay, and the rest, whom I had come to know so well—so wonderfully transformed. Their beauty was truly spectacular.

Against this aesthetic aura, the rain fell harder. The costuming was now complete, but a grand procession back to the village had become impossible. So we retired with the initiates to their family houses on the periphery of the village and waited for the storm to pass. Unfortunately, it did not. Instead, the rain grew stronger and stronger. We sat and sat as minutes became hours, from late afternoon into evening, and from evening into the night. It was an incredible, pelting rain, and it was completely unpredicted. Even as dawn broke, the water continued to thunder. The smooth village clearing had become a torrent of gullies.

There were plenty of ironies. If the storm had held off for just another fifteen minutes (or if the sponsors had been a touch quicker with their decorations), the triumphal procession could have quickly taken place. Then we all would have been happily under the roof of the main longhouse. The visitors would have come with great cries to "confront" the initiates and have had their "anger" dispelled by the silent beauty of their immovable presence. The food would then have been served and eaten, and dances by the visiting men would have continued until morning. In short, everything would have gone according to plan. Now, however, the initiates, their sponsors, and the rest of us had stayed up all night waiting for the rain to stop. Things were even worse for the throngs of visitors. Festooned for their own grand entrances, they had been forced to retreat to the forest and huddle in makeshift lean-tos in a futile attempt to keep dry. Neither they nor we had had anything to eat. Everyone was very tired and very hungry.

Why couldn't the initiates simply be led under cover to the longhouse so the visitors could enter and the food be served? The answer was consistent: "Because the initiates' red paint would run down their bodies." Beyond the importance of having a triumphant procession, it was unthinkable to the men that the beautiful red of the initiates, the congealed symbol of femininity that framed their masculinity, could be at risk of dissolving in the pouring rain. Against the proud and fixed control of the feminine represented on their skin, the specter of red liquid oozing down their carefully appointed bodies was tantamount to male menstruation—the destruction of masculinity rather than its crowning achievement. So we continued to wait for the rain to end.

To my amazement, almost no one got visibly upset. The principal exception was Silap, who cursed angrily and chastised whatever ghost was raining so literally on his parade. Almost everyone else eased into a kind of meditative doze, neither anxious nor despondent, but serene and trusting that all would work out. Despite the months of preparation and the sheer scale of the event—its social, spiritual, and material significance—the response to the storm was vintage Gebusi: quiet acceptance in the face of frustration. When the rain finally broke, in midmorning, my compatriots managed a few whoops of relief and anticipation. Cooking fires were now restoked and foods reheated. I went to check our rain gauge. It was filled to ninety-three millimeters—a bit shy of four inches of rain. This ended up being the fourth-biggest rainfall during our entire two-year stay—and the biggest within a month on either side of the initiation. Villagers shrugged it off as part of their unpredictable weather: "That's just the way it is" (*"mo ene dasum"*).

The six initiates finally lined up by the central longhouse. Standing shoulder to shoulder, they were individually brilliant but yet more spellbinding as a collective whole. Uniting the aesthetic and the material, they literally embodied the full power of Gebusi kinship and friendship, the breadth of their social connections across space, and the fullness of their spiritual identifications over time. Together, the initiates crystallized the beauty, growth, gift giving, and forbearance of the Gebusi as a whole. Into this electrifying vista, visiting men now rushed with abandon—a human stampede of celebratory aggression. Painted warriors bellowed, screamed, and sprinted through the mud as they plucked their bows. Their spiraling circle closed ever more tightly around the initiates in happy displays of mock antagonism—wave after wave, group after group. One man was carried in naked and covered head to foot in mud. His tongue hung out, and a huge mock phallus was tied to his waist. At least for the moment, he was a bloated corpse covered in cadaveric fluid—and indicting everyone around him as a sorcerer. But as might have been guessed, even this gruesome display did not unsettle the initiates, who stood their ground with serenity. Meanwhile, children scattered with ambivalent screams while adults said through their broad smiles that they, too, were scared of the "corpse."

Eventually, the attacks subsided, and the feasting and celebration began in earnest. Predictably, the festivities started with seemingly endless rounds of finger snapping, smoke sharing, kava drinking, and, especially, food giving. With thunderous whoops and hollers, the identity of an initiate's sponsor or other recipient was shouted. A representative from each of the six initiates' families then rushed to press a mound of food upon the pleased but besieged recipient. Special pleasure was taken in "force feeding" the important visitors with great gobs of dripping pig fat—pushing it in their faces until they had taken at least one or two gooey bites.

By mid-afternoon, it was time for the visitors to reciprocate and give additional gifts to the initiates—especially the prized hardwood bows and sheaves of elaborate arrows. Many of the men plucked the bows dramatically before handing them to the initiates—to show how strong the weapons were. Previously allowed to use only unpainted arrows for hunting, the initiates could now use painted and people-killing arrows in ritual display and, as need be, in warfare. Exhausted as they were, however, the initiates could hardly do more than stand. Even that became difficult, and by evening, they resorted to propping themselves up while sitting lest they topple over in sleep and smear their costumes. As part of their proud ordeal, they had not talked, eaten, or slept for two days.

Seemingly oblivious to their plight, everyone else was now revved up for a full night of partying—eating additional food, smoking more tobacco, and drinking numerous bowls of kava root liquor. Jokes flew as thick and fast as rain had fallen the previous night. By now, the longhouse was packed with people wall to wall, leaving just a small space in the center for the dancers. The yellow light of resin lanterns and bamboo torches cast a golden glow across each face and costume. The outfits of the male visitors were as spectacular and creative as they were plentiful. They included large headdresses of bird-of-paradise and cassowary feathers; red, black, and white face and body painting in innumerable patterns and combinations; bone and bamboo nose plugs and beads; leaf wreathes; and woven chest bands and armbands. Women were festooned as well: almost all of them had fresh grass skirts, bead or seed necklaces, and woven chest bands and armbands. Many also wore headdresses of fringed fiber strips and long egret feathers in their hair.

In addition to the usual male dancing, there was a special dance involving a few young women with their own red body paint, black eye banding, and red bird-of-paradise headdresses. During the plaintive songs of the women's chorus, the female dancers bounced up and down directly across from their male counterparts. Each of the young women held a long, thin rattle that she thrust up and down in front of her as she hopped opposite a male dancer—who was also pulsing up and down to the pounding beat of his drum. The sexual charge of this arrangement was impossible to miss. The men in the audience went wild, and the women also joked and laughed from their sitting places along the side of the dancing area. To cap it off, a few women could be seen joking and flirting directly with men. It was as if, for a single night, the erotic mirth of the spirit woman had become acceptable for Gebusi women as well as for men, at least in the realm of public joking. The night swept up everyone in joyful abandon. We will always remember its intensity.

🌿 🌿 🌿

The morning after was just that. As the visitors left, those from the host village crashed and slept, and so did we. While Gebusi had been busy partying, we had undergone our own initiation. Pumped by adrenalin and coffee, we had primed ourselves to observe and record what we had waited for months to see—and what we knew we might not see again. Unlike the Gebusi, we didn't know what was going to happen next or when or how it would unfold. We worried that we would miss important events. I remembered the story of a well-known anthropologist who, working alone, fell asleep from fatigue at the height of a male initiation rite and missed a key sequence of color-coded costumes that he could never reconstruct. But we were lucky because we had each other. And we had become an integral part of the action. When men gave the initiates bows and arrows, we gave each of them several shotgun cartridges—"Western arrows," as they called them—for hunting with the shotgun we had given the people of Yibihilu. When initiates received their costume elements, we gave them each a pair of bright blue satin gym trunks that we had bought for them during a field break. These gifts were wildly popular and widely talked about, the more so because it was so difficult for the Gebusi to obtain such items deep in the rainforest. In return, the families of the initiates gave us pork and sago. To this day, the surviving initiates still address us as "initiate sponsor" (*tor*).

That morning, however, all we could think of was sleep. But just when we thought the initiation was over, an additional climax occurred. In early afternoon, we awoke to a loud commotion and stumbled out of bed to see what was going on. The initiates had been herded out of the village, their costumes retouched, and then paraded back in. This time, though, they were joined by two unmarried women who stood alongside them in costumes that were, in body paint and feathers, virtually identical to their own. Together, the six young men and two young women linked fingers and stood in a single line. They bobbed up and down in unison as Tosi, the senior woman of the community, came forth to address them. Going down their line, she gently hit each of them with a sheaf of special leaves and chanted that they would henceforth be strong in heart, in breath, and in spirit. She said to each that he or she would have the inner energy of a buzzing hornet. Then she told them to be kind to and protective of others in the village. Finally, she declared for each of them the name of a young child to whom they were unrelated but whom they were charged to help and protect. With that, she turned and walked away. The initiation was over.

Thinking that we had seen everything the night before, we wrestled anew to make sense of this wonderful ending. Although women had been off-stage for many of the initiation's formal events, a senior woman had now become the center of the final ceremony. Young women had dressed up and danced as part of the previous night's festivities. Now, two women, dressed similarly to the initiates, linked themselves physically to the initiates. The male bird of paradise—the woman who had ultimately been a man—had finally expanded to include real Gebusi women. This was implicit in the night of dancing and joking, but now it was formally proclaimed in a beautiful display of true womanhood—in costumes like those of the young men. Among the Gebusi themselves, the ideal of the beautiful spirit woman had finally and truly embraced women as well as men. What had seemed like—and in many ways was—a male initiation rite was also a huge ritual celebration of male *and* female fertility, including the sexual coming-of-age for selected Gebusi women. The boundless sexual imagery of spirit women that had been so dominantly appropriated by men in other contexts was here finally accorded to and publicly acclaimed for real Gebusi women as well. It was almost as if, in its moment of final ritual celebration, Gebusi culture was able to transcend some of its own deepest divisions between women and men.

This theme grew deeper that same night. Although the initiation was over, the young men and women were now adults—and free to dance on their own. Still dressed in their red initiation costumes, the male initiates added the feathered halo of the standard dance costume and danced for the first time with drums. Moreover, they danced in pairs with the young women who had stood alongside them at the initiation's benediction. Like their linkage earlier in the day, their ritual union encompassed the male-female beauty of the Gebusi as a whole.

Given these final images, how much did we need to rethink our initial understanding of the whole celebration? Was this a male initiation? Or not? As was often the case, the intricacies of Gebusi culture made our simple question deliciously difficult. On the one hand, young Gebusi women were painted up similarly to the young men, lined up with them, danced with them, and were charged along with them during the final ceremony to protect a young child. The maturity and sexuality of the young women were obviously on display alongside the young men. In social terms, their costume elements, though not as elaborate or copious as the young men's, linked the young women to those in the community who had given or loaned these items.

On the other hand, in contrast to their male counterparts, the young women were not inseminated or otherwise sexually initiated. They were not subject to painful trials testing their stamina and did not receive bows and arrows or other stocks of possessions and costume elements. They did not have pigs killed for them, did not have important gifts of food given in their name, and were not enjoined to observe special food taboos. They did not establish lifelong relations of initiation-mate and initiate-sponsor with others in the community. In contrast to the young men, the question of whether a given young woman would get dressed up in a red bird-of-paradise costume had been uncertain; it was answered only at the last minute by the young women themselves. Some of them had been shy and decided against it. As opposed to this, the planning and gift giving of the occasion had been orchestrated around the known identity of the male initiates, and this had been central to the scale and scope of the festivities.

In some ways, then, the inclusion of women as active but secondary actors paralleled other aspects of Gebusi ceremonial life. However, the participation of young women in the final ceremony not just symbolized but embodied the central importance of Gebusi women's as well as Gebusi men's fertility. If the initiation presented the acme of the Gebusi male culture, it also extolled women and Gebusi as a whole. Spirituality, sexuality, materiality, kinship, friendship, and gender: they all came together in joy and happiness. Against all odds and impediments, against all sicknesses, deaths, and frustrations, the Gebusi somehow came together to celebrate their collective good company. It was a unity I had never seen or felt.

During our waning time of fieldwork with Gebusi after the festivities were over, I began to reflect more deeply on the strength of their culture. For all of the differences and extremes of Gebusi ways of life, I had learned from them positive human values and even joy in ways that were entirely unprecedented and uplifting for me. As much as I wanted and needed to return to the United States, it was hard to contemplate leaving my Gebusi friends and their culture. I knew that adapting once again to the more scheduled and atomized features of life in America would be difficult. And that I would deeply miss the friends and the way of life I was leaving behind.

If the avenues of modern life easily disperse into separate domains—the economic, the political, the professional, the domestic, the religious, and so on—here was a so-called simple society that managed to bring these aspects of life together in full celebration. To me, it was a testament to the human spirit that the Gebusi could create so much that was positive, beautiful, fun, and meaningful amid lives that were so difficult and tenuous. This is the way I like to remember them from that period: triumphantly asserting the richness and joyfulness of their humanity.

PART TWO
1998

CHAPTER 7

People of Gasumi Corners with the author after a Sunday church service, 1998.
(PHOTO: Bruce Knauft [self-timed])

Reentry

I feel like a neophyte all over again. Though at best not humiliating, fieldwork is always a humbling experience, and in a good sort of way. Arrows recently barbed at anthropology cast its knowledge as imperialist, gained at the expense rather than for the benefit of other people. But the gawky interloper is usually cut well down to size by the time he or she gets beyond the confines of the hotels, the taxis, and the urban elite to the place in question. Human leveling is ethnography's strength.

— Field Notes, June 1998

Leave in 1982, come back in 1998—experience culture as a time machine to the future. Sixteen years is a long time for the Gebusi. So, too, for me, and also for cultural anthropology. While a whole generation of Gebusi were getting older and producing children, I went from young adulthood to middle age in Atlanta. My son, Eric, went from conception to high school. During the 1980s and 1990s, the world also changed. Market economies, transnational influences, and national agendas spread to the farthest nooks of the globe. Cultural anthropology changed as well. If the late 1970s represented the tail end of anthropology's original interest in remote and so-called primitive societies, the 1980s and 1990s represented the head of its mushrooming interest in social change and transformation. During this time, the field's traditional interests in kinship, social organization, ritual, and exchange broadened to include a full range of contemporary practices and institutions—markets, churches, schools, governments, nongovernmental organizations, and the mosaic of social and cultural influences that tie people to their region, to their nation, and to the world at large. More than ever, the diversity of the contemporary world became anthropology's concern.

As anthropologists appreciate new worlds of experience, they also find troubling inequalities. These include the unequal distribution of wealth brought by national and international influence, by the global market economy, and by powerful institutions that interact with local types of domination. These patterns are hardly new. State empires, commercial entities, and other wielders of power have crisscrossed the world for millennia. For more than five centuries, commerce has girded the globe. During the nineteenth and twentieth centuries, sections of the east half of the island of New Guinea were variously owned and colonized by the Germans, the British, and the Australians—until the country of Papua New Guinea became independent in 1975. In remote areas including those inhabited by the Gebusi, these changes appeared in some ways to have had minimal impact. But items such as steel tools and intrusions such as colonial pacification had enormous effects. And in recent years, the flow and significance of outside influences has mushroomed. By 1998 these external forces were not just present but increasingly central, including in the Gebusi's portion of the New Guinea rainforest.

Though my fieldwork was limited in scope by its focus on a small and remote group of people, I hardly regret its results. Ethnography is as real and important as the lives it encounters, regardless of where or how numerous these are. Anthropology will be poorer if it gives up on the full range of human culture—from the most remote outpost to the most cosmopolitan city. By the mid-1990s, however, I felt strongly that my initial work with the Gebusi needed updating. Along with the geographic remoteness of the Gebusi, my family and university commitments had kept me from returning. But I had a nagging sense that my work was becoming removed from the people I had known. I needed to get back in the field. I missed my Gebusi friends and wondered what had happened to them; a reunion was long overdue. I suspected that their traditional ways of life were in tension with their present conditions, and I was deeply excited at the prospect of reengaging Gebusi in their contemporary lives.

During our first fieldwork, of course, external changes had already come to the Gebusi. In addition to steel tools and pacification of the Bedamini were cloth and occasional clothing, salt, soap, and matches, the yearly patrols of government officials, and the presence of the Nomad police when the Gebusi themselves called them. Subtler changes had also taken place. Even by 1980, most Gebusi had given up the traditional custom of tying their hair in dreadlocks in favor of cutting it short. A few men had even sported carefully shaved sideburns— recalling the hairstyle of the Australian patrol officers during the 1970s. And yet, many of the major changes that often impact peoples like the Gebusi, including missionization, wage-labor, out-migration, mining, logging, and roads to other locations—had not affected them significantly by 1980–82. But what had happened between the early 1980s and the late 1990s? Only snippets of information had reached me, and none of it was very revealing. Some colleagues suggested that modern developments—Christianization, education, migration, and economic development—would have brought major changes to the Gebusi. But others emphasized that cultural values would keep many things the same.

Even concerning violence, alternative outcomes were possible. By 1982, I knew that violent death among Gebusi had declined to about half of its precolonial level. But Gebusi had continued to scapegoat and sometimes to kill one another as sorcerers without much government awareness or intervention. What had happened since 1982 remained a mystery to me. Given the continuing absence of Australian officers, and the reluctance of national police to patrol in the rainforest, some colleagues thought that armed conflict among Gebusi would have increased. Violence had reemerged dramatically in many parts of Papua New Guinea, including in highland areas just seventy-five miles to the northeast of the Gebusi. The missionary who lived among the neighboring Bedamini people in 1980–82 said that tribal violence had increased and would continue to do so. But the increasing association of the Gebusi with activities in and around the Nomad Station, where the police were quartered, could offset this trend. So I was uncertain what I would find.

Added to my uncertainties about the Gebusi were ones about myself. In 1980, I was a fledgling twenty-six-year-old anthropologist—a researcher on a shoestring— with little to lose and everything to prove. I also had the hubris of youthful ignorance and an unbridled faith in intercultural understanding. These had galvanized the optimism that is essential not only to succeed but also to keep one from considering too concretely the true difficulty of the task ahead!

Eighteen years later, my hopes and expectations for renewing fieldwork with the Gebusi were peppered with anxieties. I was both more knowledgeable and more worried than before. Though I was going back to be with people I had known and liked, I also knew how tough it was to live in the rainforest. And the rainforest knows that a body at age forty-four is not what it was at twenty-six. In the United States, I had become a professor and the author of several books; I busied myself with the life of an academic. In contrast to my growing confidence as a scholar, I knew all too well that fieldwork would again be a humbling experience. I wondered if my sense of being a successful anthropologist would fall like a house of cards. Furthermore, I was concerned about the burden of my absence at home, and the problems that would arise if anything should happen to me.

My uncertainty was also intellectual. A middle-aged outlook often lacks the openness of a younger mind. How would I reconcile my expectation of change among the Gebusi with my appreciation of their cultural past? Anthropology crackles with debates between researchers who focus on global change and those who stress cultural continuity. Are societies more strongly informed by historical values or by recent transformations? Amid such questions, my desire to return to the Gebusi grew stronger in spite of the difficulties it posed. Their very remoteness became a reason to return—to study changes that impact people in so many parts of the world.

As I prepared to leave, I tried (even though I knew it was in fact impossible) to wipe my slate clean of expectations. I told myself to take whatever I found among the Gebusi at face value. I was going back after sixteen years, and I was going solo. After months of finding funding, navigating bureaucracy, obtaining visa permits, buying equipment, reviewing old field notes, and shedding tears of good-bye, I left for Papua New Guinea. After two weeks in the capital of Port Moresby and several days in the district capital of Kiunga, I finally took the small plane to the Nomad Station. I landed for a half-year of fieldwork on June 25, 1998. That night, I wrote the following:

Tonight, this first evening back, I sit here with Sayu and Howe, who smile brightly as I type on this keyboard. We have just looked at the screen saver, which has amazed them totally. I am caught in a time warp between the pidgin English called *tok pisin*, Gebusi language, heat, fatigue, and my wonder and amazement.

First touchdown was a rush. Hawi—with a gaunt face and a much receding hairline but still strong and energetic—was the airline agent who met me at the airstrip!! We hugged, shook hands, and snapped fingers about a dozen times. He told me he lives right at the Nomad Station—and that he has three sons and a baby daughter! Then he had to give his attention to the paperwork of the flight while my things were unloaded. When I turned around, I had the wonder of seeing age jump right before my eyes. One after another Gebusi whom I had known came up to greet me. The grown children were the most incredible. There was Sayu, our little friend about whom Eileen had joked that she would adopt and bring back to the States. He is strong, handsome, and smart! He has already become my closest companion and helper among the younger men. He combines his father's quickness and his mother's intelligence, perceptiveness, and friendship—or at least so it seems on my first impression.

Most striking among my adult friends are their hollow faces, withered bodies, and wrinkled skin that I remember as smooth. But my happiness in human connection transcends space and time. We embraced and snapped fingers mightily, including the women. Gazing into the eyes of those whom you know with fond memories from sixteen years ago, and who suddenly live again in the present, is totally thrilling and completely unforgettable. In Gebusi legends, reunions and welcomes are so warm and numerous that people's hands are worn bare by snapping fingers heartily and repeatedly. Today, I allowed myself the hubris of feeling the same way. My middle fingers are really sore from the finger snapping that I could not keep myself from continuing even if I had wanted to stop. It is like on my wedding day, when the joy of the event caused an actual soreness of smile muscles that were so irrepressibly stretched that they could not help but turn anything in the world to their overpowering good feeling.

Feelings notwithstanding, the day has been hot, and I have a mountain of decisions to make quickly. How many nights will I stay in this unpleasant little house at the Nomad Station? Where will I live after that? How can I build on today's rush of positive feeling? How should I reestablish reciprocity with my Gebusi friends? How will I cook? How many boxes should I unpack? Where are the specific parcels of utensils, sleeping equipment, cloths, toiletries, and so on that I need for this first night? (As expected, there are no real stores at Nomad, so I am glad that I have brought everything with me.) And yet, I simply must take time tonight to write the events of this astonishing day.

Amid the constant stream of visitors whom I did not want to stop, I somehow greeted everyone and found that virtually the entire generation of surviving Gebusi from Yibihilu now live in a "corner" of Nomad just across the Hamam River, about 20 or 25 minutes' walk from the Nomad Station. This is absolutely perfect, my ideal residential scenario! I should have easy access to the Nomad Station and its nationalizing influence while also being able to go with Gebusi back to the forest. Having stowed my things in the government house by about one o'clock, I couldn't resist the temptation to go to this corner settlement and see for myself the lovely place where I will likely be living. It is all simply wonderful.

Within minutes, the Gebusi astounded me. Meeting me at the Nomad Station airstrip, the descendants of Yibihilu boasted a new flock of youngsters and of children-become-adults. Within a few days, however, I found that few men of my own age or older were still alive. Most of those whom I had known as adults had died, including Silap, Boyl, Swamin, Sialim, Sagawa, Tosi, Wosop, and Imba. Of the six young men we helped initiate, only three—Hawi, Doliay, and Yuway— were still living. I mourned the passing of many friends even as I saw their personalities, amazingly, in their children, now pushing toward their own adulthood. In demographic terms, Gebusi were a new people and more numerous than before—up from 450 individuals to about 615.

Change and turnover notwithstanding, and despite the heat and mosquitoes, it felt wonderful to be back. I was remembered fondly and welcomed joyously. Two children had been named after me during my absence. Once worn, the glove of friendship always seems to fit. Within one day of my arrival, Gwabi, who had been about twelve years old in 1982, insisted that I occupy the new thatched house that he had just happened to finish building beside his older dwelling in Gasumi Corners. With this as my base of operations, I quickly found myself immersed in Gebusi life, going both to Nomad and to the forest, and rediscovering the joys and trials of life in the field. I had worried about my ability to speak Gebusi after so many years, but this came back to me faster than I expected.

My physical setup was largely as it had been in 1980–82 except that now I lived nominally alone—with Gwabi's family in their weathered house just eight feet away. Logistically, the biggest change involved my laptop and microcomputers, which greatly enhanced my work. Now I could easily write up, revise, and organize my notes—and even make entries on my microcomputer while interviewing people in their homes. No more spiral notebooks, typewriter, or carbon copies laced with correction fluid! Instead of columned paper, I used my spreadsheet programs to enter and update census, kinship, and other tables of information. But my computers also posed a constant complication: having to fiddle with the solar panels and manage my battery power, on which they were totally dependent. When a pig tore off the wires running from my battery to the solar panels, I almost blew a fuse of my own in frustration and anxiety. Fortunately, I found a way to splice the ends that were left.

In short order, I discovered that the 122 descendants of Yibihilu and its surrounding hamlets had fashioned not just a new settlement but a new way of life. Now they were living on the outskirts of the Nomad Station, just a short walk from its airstrip, school, churches, market, ball field, and government offices. In

Gasumi Corners, Gebusi family houses were scattered like islands in an archipel-
ago across three hillocks and a stream. No longer was there a central longhouse to
serve as a focus of activity. And the settlement was no longer nestled in the full
rainforest. Rather, it was sandwiched between the cleared areas that fanned out from
the Nomad Station and the primary timberland that the Gebusi used to inhabit.

From their vantage point at Gasumi Corners, my friends could still walk to
their traditional lands in the deep forest, but their lives increasingly revolved
around the institutions and activities of the Nomad Station. The result was what
might be called a new structure of feeling in Gebusi culture. Within this new
world, the social life of the primary forest, including our previous settlement of
Yibihilu, was gone. Internally, the new community still retained its kinship connections, including its links via marriage and maternal ties, as well as through
clanship. But extended families and even nuclear families now lived separately in
small individual houses; there was no central dwelling place to bring people
together. As a consequence, the traditional sense of good company—the togetherness, talk, and whooping/joking of Gebusi *kogwayay*—was greatly muted. In terms
of material goods, life was much as it had been before. Families had only a few more
manufactured items than they did in 1980–82—perhaps an extra knife, a larger metal
pot, or a shovel. The biggest visible change was the increased wearing of Western
clothes. Unlike before, village women never walked around bare-breasted; they
always covered themselves, if only with a ripped blouse. Even the men invariably
wore a shirt with their shorts (however stained or torn) when they went to Nomad.
Unlike other items, used clothes were occasionally flown in by the baleful and
quickly sold at low prices for a profit by an itinerant trader or local official.

With their new interest in activities and organizations at Nomad, Gebusi
seemed more punctual and disciplined than previously. The Sunday after my
arrival, I got my first taste of what this meant. Sayu had said that the church service would begin when the sun was "so much above the treetops." Gebusi sense
of daily time had always been as vague as the morning mists, and events invariably began later than anticipated. Mornings for Gebusi had been a relaxed time,
with important affairs left to the late afternoon or evening—when the day was
cooling off and people were well fed. That Sunday morning, I left a little ahead
of time and figured I would arrive before most of the others. But the houses along
the way were curiously empty. What was up? When I got close enough to hear
hymn singing, I realized I was late. Late! The very concept had once seemed alien
to the Gebusi. But the clock-watching pastor had rung the metal chime first in
warning and then five minutes before the service was to start. Though I had
missed the signals in the distance, everyone else was on time. On time—another
new idea for the Gebusi. In the relaxed world of the rainforest, the rhythms of
life had their own languid pace. People could simply not have been hurried. There
had been little attempt to mark specific times of day, and there were no words
for the days of the week, the months, or even the seasons; activities blended seamlessly from one day to the next. We had easily lost track of the days if we forgot

to tick them off on our calendar. Now, however, Gebusi days and even minutes were marked and measured.

Beyond church services on Sunday morning, the new weekly schedule included schooling for local children from Monday through Friday. Classes at the Nomad Community School began promptly at 8:00 A.M. and lasted until 3:30 P.M. Mindful of the time, the children of Gasumi Corners usually left for school before 7:00 A.M.—and got home after 4:00 in the afternoon. The school day itself was divided into sixteen periods, some as short as fifteen minutes. These transitions were frequently marked by the ringing of the school bell. For adults, and especially for women, Tuesdays and Fridays from 8:00–10:00 A.M. were market days. Weekend afternoons were slated for rugby and soccer on the government ball field, particularly for the men and older boys. They arrived early so they wouldn't miss their starting time. The matches were timed and refereed by government timekeepers who sounded a large horn to mark the end of the half and the end of the game. Though most Gebusi could not tell time, all the men seemed to want wristwatches—so they could ask someone else the time or at least appear to be acting based on knowledge of the hour.

If time for the Gebusi was increasingly marked against a daily and hourly clock, its passage now reflected Gebusi hopes for—and failures of—progress and improvement. Tests on Fridays gauged the learning that students had accomplished each week. Unfortunately, few children from Gasumi Corners were on track to finish elementary school—and none were slated to go on to the secondary school in Kiunga. In church, villagers were told that Judgment Day could come at any time—maybe tomorrow, maybe next week, maybe next month. If they waited to repent their sins, it might be too late—they could burn in hell. At the twice-weekly Nomad market, if food wasn't sold by the end of the session, it had to be taken home or given away. In sports, the Gebusi traditionally had played until the score was tied or until everyone had lost track. Now, by contrast, they played on the government ballfield, kept careful track of the score, and played to win by the final horn. In short, the strivings and shortcomings of the Gebusi's lifestyle were now measured against a timeline of hoped-for success.

Running out of time had not been a problem in 1980–82; the past and the future simply cycled into each other. The Gebusi word for "tomorrow," *oil*, was the same as the word for "yesterday." The word for "day after tomorrow" was the same as the one for "day before yesterday" (*bihar*). And the same was true of the word for "three days after" and "three days before" the present (*ehwar*). In terms of generations, Gebusi had used the same word for both their grandparents and their grandchildren (*owa*). And an adult man often referred to his own son as his "father" (*mam*). In the cycling of gardens and fallow land, a boy would ideally grow up to cultivate the lands of his father or grandfather and to eat of the sago palms and nuts trees planted for him there. Life had represented a spiritual and social circle. Even male life force had been physically recycled from one generation to the next. The ideal had been for things to repeat over time rather than to change. Against this background, it was hard to avoid the sense that time for the Gebusi had shifted from a circle of repetition to an arrow of anticipated progress, aimed toward a different and, they hoped, better future.

That our lives should get better over time—and that there is something wrong or unfortunate if they do not—may seem second nature in Western cultures. But for many non-Western peoples, including the Gebusi, this was a new and foreign notion. According to Reinhart Koselleck and other intellectual historians, a new notion of time that stressed the importance of attaining future progress was a key development of Euro-American cultures in the late eighteenth century—a defining feature of what we now call being or becoming modern. In this newly modern view, it was the possibilities of an unknown but hopeful future that became the guiding light of human meaning and potential rather than the glories or mysteries of a mythic past. Now, in their own fashion, Gebusi also seemed to have adopted the hopes of a "new time," including its expectation of economic, social, and moral improvement at the Nomad market, the Nomad school, and the local church. Accordingly, the people of Gasumi Corners not just wanted but expected to get bigger and better houses, more clothes and commodities, better education, increased opportunities to work for wages, and more money.

Realities, however, lagged far behind. The Nomad Sub-District where the Gebusi live still had no roads to other towns or parts of the country. Supplies were still flown in, which was very expensive. In their remote corner of the rainforest, the Gebusi still had no resources or commodities of value to outsiders. Even their hardwood trees were not plentiful enough to attract logging companies. (From an environmental perspective, however, this has been extremely fortunate.) The nearest town, Kiunga, lies eighty miles away, across foreign territory, swampland, and rivers. The trek there is dangerous and had been completed by only a few of the most intrepid young men. By air, the trip takes only an hour from Nomad. But the airfare is far too expensive for Gebusi to afford. As a result, the Gebusi have nowhere near the opportunities they would like for jobs, money, commodities, and travel. The little local economy of the Nomad Station depends primarily on the modest salaries of the few government workers who come from other parts of the country to live there. Villagers rarely gain access to regular earnings.

None of this stemmed the tide of Gebusi hopes. Sayu wanted a new boom-box and the batteries to power it. Didiga wanted a new shotgun—to replace the one I gave his father in 1981. Everyone wanted more frequent meals of store-bought food, especially tinned fish and rice, plus new sets of clothes to wear to church and school and around the village. The sports team wanted uniforms and sports shoes. But to little avail.

In such an out-of-the-way place, where did these desires come from? Since the 1960s, the Gebusi have known about airplanes, metal tools, clothes, Western-style houses, and commodities like lanterns, shoes, pots and pans, sheets, radios, and boxes with locks—and the money that buys things to put in them. Until 1975, however, these goods were associated with Australian patrol officers, whose way of life was separate, removed, and almost mystically different from their own. During the subsequent years of postcolonial government, however, Papua New Guineans who are recognizably similar to Gebusi came to live and take charge at the Nomad Station. Like the patrol officers before them, they have had conveniences, commodities, and appliances like refrigerators and VCRs that run off the station's power generator. Government officials earn money, wear nice clothes, travel by air to towns and cities, and bring back new goods plus wonderful and sometimes fantastic stories about modern ways of life.

As an anthropologist in the field, it is hard to live outside these changes. Though we lived as simply as we could, Eileen and I had certainly been magnets of material curiosity for Gebusi in 1980–82. Villagers had been fascinated and sometimes amazed by our metal boxes, tape recorder, camera, clothes, and supplies, and even the color of our skin and the texture of our hair. Although our purpose was to live with Gebusi rather than to change their lives, we also wanted to help them in whatever way we could. So our gifts provided them a small but steady stream of coveted goods—fishing hooks, salt, soap, matches, medicine, clothes, metal knives, and axes. None of these, however, seemed to have had a lasting impact on Gebusi culture as far as I know.

In 1998, I developed a similar pattern of material exchange in Gasumi Corners. But the scale of goods and desires had increased. Villagers wanted flashlights and batteries, cassette players, wristwatches, colorful shirts, and sunglasses. To help satisfy these and other desires, Gwabi and the other villagers decided that, instead of my paying rent for my house, I should visit Kiunga and bring back a planeload of goods that they could collectively own and sell for profit from a little house that they had already built as a community store. With the proceeds, they reasoned they could buy more supplies to restock the store, use some of the profits to buy what they wanted, and draw in increasing numbers of buyers from surrounding areas. At least during the time that I lived in Gasumi Corners, we were all pleased at how well this arrangement developed. When I completed my fieldwork, I paid for plane tickets for Sayu and Didiga to fly back with me to Kiunga. I showed them how to purchase goods and fly with them back to Nomad themselves—that is, how to resupply the community store on their own. (There is no way to order items at Kiunga except in person.) Such small commercial outlets are common in countries like Papua New Guinea. Over time, however, they rarely increase the overall level of village income. Especially in rural areas, such enterprises frequently fail due to problems of transportation and supply, unanticipated costs, and disputes over money.

Notwithstanding difficulties, lack of opportunity, and the bitterness of failure, the allure of material goods and of "new time"—a more modern way of life—act like tidal forces on places like Nomad. By the late 1980s, the attractions of the Nomad Station had become strong enough that virtually the entire community of Yibihilu had picked up and moved—lock, stock, and barrel—to the small portion of Gebusi land that abuts the government station and its airstrip. Back in the rainforest, the village of Yibihilu had been completely abandoned.

Modern wants are hardly unique to the Gebusi; if anything, they are global. Not just tiny stations like Nomad but towns and cities the world over attract people who hope for economic gain and modern ways of life. But for many migrants, as well as for the Gebusi, the road to economic development is very rough if not effectively blocked, no matter how hard or creatively one tries. So what happens?

The Gebusi developed a lifestyle that seemed more modern socially and culturally even if it was not much different from what it was previously in economic terms. At Nomad, these changes included regular participation in the local churches, school, market, sports leagues, and government-sponsored events and programs. These may not yield much in the way of money. Indeed, they can be costly. School requires an annual supply fee for each student, the churches collect weekly offerings, and the sports league requires dues paid to the officials who organize the games. The market could generate income for sellers, but, as we shall see, the proceeds were few. Nonetheless, these activities have afforded a strong sense of participating in and being part of a lifestyle associated with outside success. In the Nomad area, being on time, waiting patiently for instruction, and being respectful of outsiders who are in charge—at school, in church, at the market, in government projects, and on the ball field—have all been part of this modern package.

Given this, I should not have been surprised on that first Sunday. Neither at the fact that everyone was on time nor, more amazing to me, that they sat so quietly and listened so patiently as the service dragged on and the day grew hotter. In 1980–82, the Gebusi had been like branches in the wind—jostling, joking, palavering, going this way and that to their heart's content. Even senior men had rarely tried to give orders. And when they did, it was as difficult to get people to comply as it would have been to herd a bunch of cats. But here was the Christian pastor, a man from a different part of the country. He spoke *tok pisin*, the national language. He harangued parishioners at length, preaching that they must try harder to be good, that it was difficult to get into heaven, and that those who continued to sin would be rejected by God. The people of Gasumi Corners stayed, remained still, and listened. They followed the pastor as he sang hymns and worshiped this stern God. And they did this every week.

When I went to the Nomad Community School, I was struck by a similar dynamic. Rows upon rows of students listened patiently to the provincial instructor, hour after hour. As in church, participation was "call and response" in form. The instructor would read a line or give an answer, and his students would repeat in unison what he had said. The hours were long, but the students persisted. Even in the first grade alone, forty-nine pupils sat cross-legged on the hardwood floor almost all day long.

There are many other sides to Gebusi lives, of course. And during my new time in the field, I richly experienced and enjoyed these. In their new setting at Gasumi Corners, though, the questions of change that struck me during the first days of my return became increasingly important as the months went by. How was it that the Gebusi had adopted hopes, values, and activities associated with a new way of life? How did their present practices relate to their previous ones— and why did Gebusi persist in their efforts despite economic and material frustration? What explanation did the Gebusi themselves offer for why they had given up their old lives in exchange for new ones? And why do some people accept, and even willingly submit to, the authority of national or other outsiders?

This last question was especially relevant in the case of the Gebusi. The historical spread of so-called modern influences has often been associated with military, economic, or political force, including through colonialism, trade, and capitalism. This was true in some ways for Gebusi as well: Australian patrol officers introduced clothes, steel axes, and other commodities, and they pacified the neighboring Bedamini. But the Gebusi had continued to live on their own. Their way of life had been mostly on their own terms after the period of colonialism had ended. With the departure of the Australians, even the annual government patrol to the bush had ceased. The Gebusi had been safe in the rainforest. Yet, some six years after I had left, the people of Yibihilu moved to the outskirts of the Nomad Station. The government of Papua New Guinea had become a newly important force, including especially its government officers, police, and teachers. They were new role models for Gebusi, along with the Papua New Guinea church pastors who came to Nomad from other towns and cities. In response, the entire Gebusi community of Yibihilu moved to the outskirts of the Nomad Station. They moved of their own choice; no one coerced them.

In moving to the periphery of Nomad, Gebusi responded to the gap between life in the rainforest and attractions they saw in a more modern way of life. People in different cultures respond differently to the lag between their realities and the fortunes they seek. Some, like the Gebusi, strongly embrace change—they actively and fervently seek it out. Others accept new influences or ways of life only ambivalently or grudgingly. Still others actively oppose or resist external influences; they emphasize the value and the integrity of their customs. In actuality, however, these three alternatives are not mutually exclusive. In the crucible of today's world, many if not most non-Western peoples adopt all three responses to various degrees, in different contexts, and in different stages of their lives. Given this, what made the Gebusi of Gasumi Corners so quickly prominent at the "change" end of the continuum? What informed their willingness to give up relative autonomy and embrace alterations that do not, in fact, afford that much chance of material success?

One important answer lies in history. Different cultures have had different relationships with—and degrees of subordination to—Western-style colonialism, trade, and capitalism. In the current era, they also have different relationships with their own national governments. In interior New Guinea, colonialism came very late. Even then, the Gebusi were fortunate to be spared the brunt of "pacification"— and they benefited enormously when the raids of the Bedamini were stopped by colonial officers. As far as I knew, no Gebusi had ever been wounded or killed by a bullet. In economic terms, their primary complaint has not been that they have been subject to outside intrusion, but that they haven't received enough. Given this history, it is little wonder that Gebusi have welcomed rather than rejected powerful outsiders—first the Australians and then the national officials of Papua New Guinea.

Notwithstanding their history, the Gebusi's new lives still left me feeling as if I was in the midst of a split-brain experiment. On the one hand, my friends still pursued their activities in the forest—gardening, hunting, fishing, foraging, and cutting down and processing sago palms. They had their own houses in the dispersed settlement of Gasumi Corners. On the other hand, they were now willing and largely passive subjects—parishioners, pupils, wishful sellers in the market, and obedient participants in government initiatives. These institutions and activities were not merely tolerated but were actively sought out, day after day, week after week. Life in Gasumi Corners and in the rainforest was correspondingly affected. People no longer participated collectively but rather individually or as small families in activities at Nomad; each household made its own choices and commitments. Collective life in the settlement declined. In their gardens, Gebusi increasingly grew foods preferred by government officers—so they would have a chance to sell them at the Nomad market. Accordingly, they regularly hauled provisions from the rainforest to the market in hopes of making a sale. These initiatives continued week after week even though market prices were very low and most of their food did not sell.

Although the Gebusi seemed to pass easily between their old and new worlds, my own experience was disconnected. One day, I would bask in the timeless wonder of the rainforest. The next, I would sit through a two-hour church service, a long government meeting, a protracted market session, an extended lesson in arithmetic at school, or multiple games of rugby and soccer on the Nomad ball field. These newfangled institutions and activities were not, somehow, what I had thought I would be studying. But for the Gebusi, these were important activities—the cutting edge of a vibrant, modern style of life. If I was going to really take their lives at current face value, to appreciate the Gebusi in their own present, I had to both hunker down and lighten up. I needed to experience Gebusi more fully and genuinely in their own new world. I remembered how difficult and confusing my first experiences with them had been in 1980–82. And I realized that the same kind of challenge—and the same potential for discovery—awaited me again.

Church poster: the "good heart of man," open to the "good news" and closed to pagan spirits. (PHOTO: Bruce Knauft)

Yuway's Sacred Decision

Yuway's eyes simply sparkled. *"Koya, koya!"*—"Friend, friend!" We must have gazed into each other's eyes, snapped fingers, and joked heartily at least a dozen times. I came to his house, a mere five-minute walk from my own, having heard that he had finally come back from the forest, where he had been a few days earlier when I first arrived. Yuway had been my most helpful friend in 1980–82. He was an all-around good person and the tallest of the young men we had helped initiate. Shortly after the initiation, he had become a moon-eyed romantic with his fetching wife-to-be, Warbwi, and we had given him gifts to help with his marriage. That had been seventeen years ago. And here he was again, in the flesh! It was so good to see him. Every few sentences, we would smile and clasp each other again, as if to reassure ourselves that our reunion was real. We quickly brought each other up to date. He was touched to hear that I now had a son who was full grown and even taller than I. With subdued pride, Yuway told me that he and Warbwi now had four children: an adolescent boy and girl plus two younger sons. I joked with him that he must have been "busier" than I had been; we both broke into laughter.

As a few minutes passed, word spread that we two senior men were having a good jokefest together, and we ended up attracting a score of amused spectators from surrounding houses. Good-natured as he was, I realized that Yuway was slowly getting embarrassed by our traditional joking. Although I had taken our jests for granted, he started to suppress his grins. From the reactions of others around us, I could sense that old-time joking, though tolerated from me as a middle-aged man who knew their traditions, was funny in part because it was now a bit anachronistic, a touch out of place.

As if to punctuate my perception, Yuway finally told me with a smile that he was an SDA—a member of the Seventh Day Adventist Church. This was the most stringent Christian denomination in the Nomad area. I was naturally intrigued, and this led us to a thoughtful discussion of changes in Gebusi religion. Yuway said that he had come to Gasumi Corners from Yibihilu with the others some ten years earlier. Like most of them, he had also joined the Catholic Church soon after. The

Catholic pastor had been solicitous of the Gebusi and had even visited some of their settlements in the bush. Because the new church was between the new settlement near Nomad and the Nomad Station itself, the villagers thought that joining it would be a good way to help establish their new lives. As the people of Gasumi Corners got used to singing in church, Yuway said, they sang less with their own spirit mediums. The community's major shaman, Swamin, started going to church himself and then stopped singing to the traditional spirits entirely. So, too, with the other spirit mediums; they found themselves part of a community that was now singing to a new spirit, to a singular God. When the Gebusi go to church, they say literally, "We go to sing" (*gio dula*). Within a few years, the spirit séances that had galvanized Gebusi social life—and that had been such a large focus of my own work—had become history, a thing of the past.

Without spirit mediums, as Yuway explained, people in Gasumi Corners had no real way to communicate with their traditional spirits; their path of connection was "cut" (*gisaym-da*). No longer could they joke with the spirits, ask their advice about sickness or sorcery, or enlist their support for or opinions about fish poisoning and other activities. To my great surprise, the traditional world of Gebusi spirits had withered away. And with their departure, Gebusi social life had also changed. No longer were male sexual joking and camaraderie a focal source of excitement. The people of Gasumi Corners sang to their new God not in the dead of night but in the brightness of the morning, not with humor but with solemnity, not in a lively conversation with the spirits but, instead, with a subservient voice. Apparently the preacher and his God had simply been more powerful than the old ones. Together, they had the prestige and wonder of coming from afar, of being associated with the wealth, success, and accomplishments of a wider world. Although the lay pastor lived not far from Gasumi Corners, he was supported by the Catholic Church and flew regularly back to Kiunga and occasionally to his own home in one of the country's mountain districts. He was literate and well educated, wore nice clothes, had a house stocked with supplies, was able to call Kiunga on his own two-way radio, and was bent on presenting his way of life and his God as a model for the Gebusi to follow. They willingly agreed.

Yuway told me that he himself had been one of the Gasumi leaders in the Nomad Catholic Church from 1992 to 1995. (I pinched myself to note how the Gebusi now kept track of years.) But after that, he felt more distant from the parish.

"Why did you join the Seventh Day Adventists?" I asked.

"Well, the Catholic Church is kind of 'soft'; I wanted a church that was 'hard.'"

"How's that?" By this point, I was remembering that the Gebusi word for "hard" (*gof*) also means "strong," "righteous," "angry," and "potentially violent"— as well as "difficult."

"If you are really going to worship God, it shouldn't be a small thing. It should be a big thing. You should really work hard to please God. The Catholics make you work only a little hard. They let people keep lots of customs that God doesn't like—like dancing and smoking tobacco. The SDA Church knows that God doesn't like these and that they are wrong. They make their religion really hard by telling us we can't eat certain things that we like. They make us work a lot in the church yard, and they make us come for Bible learning as well as going to the long service on Saturday morning. They have pictures that show exactly what will happen to you if you have sin—you will burn in hell. With SDA, I know I am really a Christian and that I can go to heaven."

I paused to collect my thoughts. Yuway and my other friends had been so thoroughly "Gebusi" in spiritual outlook back in 1982. Yet his answer revealed not just the onus but the attraction of a fundamentalist Christian faith. Yuway's comment also pointed up the key distinction that the Gebusi make among the three local churches. Catholicism was seen as the "easiest" faith because it had the fewest taboos. Catholics were told to attend church regularly, to worship God rather than other spirits, to avoid fighting, and to not drink kava—their lightly intoxicating drink made from roots. As long as these criteria were followed for a year or two— with some allowance made for backsliding—a Gebusi could be baptized as a Catholic by the priest or bishop on one of his sporadic visits to Catholic parishes in the province.

In many parts of the world, conversion to or intensification of world religions— including Islam, Hinduism, and Judaism, in addition to numerous forms of Christianity—has been increasing. On the other hand, the particular way that a world religion is locally interpreted and expressed can be highly variable. In and around the Nomad Station, including at Gasumi Corners, the Christian churches were developed and run by relatively fundamentalist Papua New Guineans who had come to proselytize the area from other parts of the country. This gave all the local forms of Christianity a distinctive aura of Papua New Guinean fundamentalism, though, as Yuway noted, some churches were perceived, at least by the local population, to be "easier" than others.

Although about 60 percent of those in Gasumi Corners ended up becoming members of the Catholic Church, approximately one-fifth (22 percent) belonged to the Evangelical Church of Papua New Guinea. In addition to the Catholics' strictures, Evangelicals had a strong taboo against smoking tobacco and restrictions on participating in non-Christian rituals. The SDA rules were even stricter. In fact, Yuway's family was the only one in Gasumi Corners to have joined their church. In addition to bans on smoking, drinking, dancing, and observing traditional rituals, the SDAs prohibited the eating of smooth-skinned fish and any kind of pork. This last was particularly significant, because eating pigs was still a prime feature of Gebusi festivities on special occasions. SDA adherents were told that each Saturday was a day for worshiping God in church; all other work or gardening, as well as forms of public entertainment—playing ball, attending feasts, or going to disco—were condemned as irreligious.

Because I knew Yuway to be a caring person, I wondered how his personal beliefs meshed with the SDA reputation for intolerance. He said with all earnestness that he had no anger against those who went to other churches or even those who went to none at all—which included a few in Gasumi Corners. I decided to push him a little: "If someone who is a good person goes to the Catholic Church or to the Evangelical Church instead of SDA, do you think that person can go to heaven when he or she dies? Or not?"

Yuway thought for a minute, but not too long: "I don't know. Only God knows these things. But for me, I think that someone who is good inside can go to heaven, and it shouldn't matter if they go to one church or another."

"What if they don't go to any church at all?"

"Well, if they are given the chance to believe in Father God but still don't do it, it might be hard for God to see them as a good person and let them into heaven. But it's not for me to say."

I was impressed with his answer. It was then that I remembered the arrows that Yuway had been fashioning when I had come up to greet him. Now they were lying next to him, elaborately carved and ready for painting with bright-red ochre.

"Those are really nice arrows. Aren't they the kind used to sponsor a young man at an initiation?"

"Yes, I'm sponsoring a young Wapsiayk (a young man from his clan) at Taylmi in probably a month or two."

"Can you still do that and be an SDA?"

"Well, I won't get baptized into SDA myself until after the initiation. It will be the last time for me to eat pork in my life. And if I go just to see the initiation and not because I believe in its spirits, it's okay."

As I mulled over this last response, the sky opened up as if by divine intervention. Suddenly, rain came pelting down. Realizing that it was almost dark—and that the fire for supper was yet to be started at my own house—I smiled and snapped fingers quickly with Yuway and the others before whooping loudly as I raced up the trail. I was thoroughly drenched by the time I reached home.

Reflecting that evening on the day's events, I was struck by Yuway's remarks in relation to what I was finding from the Gebusi who were Catholics or Evangelicals. At Nomad, all three churches featured a fierce God of fire and brimstone—a God who threatened hell and demanded compliance. And all of them held that Judgment Day could come at any time—and that continuing repentance was the only key to salvation. All three churches were "hard," though some were "harder" than others. How was it that different Gebusi belonged to these three different churches—each of which drew members from diverse communities? While I had been visiting with Yuway that afternoon, his two married brothers, Keda and Halowa, had shown up. Keda was a lay leader in the Catholic Church; the previous Sunday, he had been asked to translate parts of the pastor's sermon for the congregation. Halowa, by contrast, was an Evangelical. Each of the three brothers, I realized, belonged to a different church. I found increasingly that Yuway had been right: Gebusi accepted each other's right to choose the religious denomination that suited him best. The "him" is significant here, because most wives attended the church that their husbands had chosen. If Christianity saved the soul of the individual rather than the group, so, too, each individual man, at least, could choose what church to belong to—and whether to believe in God at all. The Gebusi world of moral choices and consequences was no longer governed so strongly by kinship or clanship, but increasingly by a man's choice.

The second thing that struck me involved Yuway's plan to give initiation gifts to a young man while he himself was completing the arduous requirements for SDA baptism. How was this possible? Was Yuway being hypocritical? Or was this a classic case of "syncretism," in which two religions are blended together? Neither of these possibilities seemed likely to me; I suspected that something else was at issue. It turned out that Gebusi distinguish between witnessing a traditional ritual and actually hosting or performing in one. At a remote settlement like Taylmi—the last big Gebusi village that had not yet become Christian—one could attend an initiation the same way that Americans can watch an action movie or a historical epic without being considered a violent person or a creature of the past; they can view it as an entertaining drama or spectacle without adopting its values or lifestyle. Indeed, being exposed to "pagan ways" without succumbing to them can itself indicate commitment to Christianity.

It has often been noted that the process of Christian redemption is punctuated by trials and temptations. Preachers at Nomad repeatedly emphasized the danger of "backsliding" into sin and vice associated with tradition. Although the Gebusi willingly submitted themselves to the harangues of the pastor, it was their deviation from Christian thoughts or interests that spurred their sense of needing atonement—the pang of conscience that begs for moral cleansing. Exposure to and ambivalence about traditional customs was integral to the jawboning process of Gebusi conversion to Christianity. Hopes of salvation seemed directly linked to threats of sin.

Three weeks later, I experienced this dynamic by going with Yuway's family to an SDA service at a nearby hamlet. The pastor's message was bleak. And it became something of a marathon, in that he exhorted the small congregation for a full two hours. Increasingly, they simply hung their heads. That evening, I wrote the following:

> The patience and passivity demanded in church—which I noted immediately among the Catholics—are brought to a firmer and sterner level here among the Seventh Day Adventists. Today, the long sermon by the SDA preacher was a case in point. He placed great emphasis on the trials of Jesus: his forty days in the wilderness in the hot sun without food or water, his agonizing death on the cross, his suffering for us all. "Our own hardships are small; we should bear them easily and ask for nothing. We should think of Christ—be grateful that He suffered and died for us." The preacher's concluding harangue, which repeated itself for a good forty minutes, was similarly somber. Saturday should be a day only for SDA worship. Food and market and other work activities should be finished Friday night. Saturday should be sober and worshipful, both morning and night, with no entertainment or even cooking of food. This was the true way to worship God.

Where is the payoff in this scheme? It is deferred. Set against the austere trials of the present is the glorious image of life after death. Heaven was described as a place full of *bip*, or "cargo," a place where people are endlessly happy, without suffering or sickness. I was reminded of the dramatic cults that some Melanesians developed when they first encountered Western goods. These so-called cargo cults arose as local people attempted to obtain or "produce" European goods by conducting magical rites or by mimicking Western behavior. In their conversion to Christianity, however, the Gebusi had bypassed such attempts, accepting that wealth and salvation would come only in an afterlife and not right away. To attain this bliss, they could not ask for much during life here on earth. But on the day of reckoning, God would give his ultimate reward to those few who had truly followed the path of Jesus. My field entry concluded as follows:

> Now I can see, at least dimly, Yuway's attraction to this church. It is severe; it stresses the need to be hard and disciplined for God. This is the modern path of dignified compliance in and around the Nomad Station as well as a path for everlasting life. It measures the present not against a happy standard of current success but against trials, and rewards, that were infinitely greater for Jesus.

Yuway's choice foregrounds the path that the Gebusi were increasingly taking not only in church but also at school, in the market, and even on the ball field: to wait patiently for future success. Across these contexts spread an ethic of acting with discipline, of listening to outsiders, and of accepting the authority of superiors.

The most dramatic case of religious transformation was undoubtedly that of Doliay. Doliay was the youngest and smallest of the six young men whom we had helped initiate in 1981. In the late 1980s, he married Boyl, Sayu's widowed mother. However, Boyl died shortly thereafter. Following the death inquest, Doliay confronted the person accused of causing Boyl's death through sorcery—a man named Sabowey. Doliay told me that his anger toward Sabowey had come to dominate his thoughts and actions. As he described it, his plan for revenge took on a surgical and almost Zen-like focus. Although Sabowey was almost a foot taller than he was, Doliay sought him out and confronted him alone in the forest. He dodged Sabowey's arrows and split his head with a bush knife. When Sabowey was dead, Doliay cut off his head and left it next to his body in the forest. Then he went to the Catholic compound, told the pastor what he had done, handed him his bush knife, and turned himself in to the Nomad police.

Doliay's killing of Sabowey in 1988 was a watershed. He was sentenced to six years at the national prison in the capital city of Port Moresby. No Gebusi had ever traveled so far. But Doliay hardly saw the city. While in prison, he became exceedingly self-disciplined. He learned to speak *tok pisin*, the national language, converted to Christianity, became a model prisoner, and even became head cook for the warden, who entrusted him with the key to the compound's storehouse of food. In 1998, Doliay proudly kept the letter of reference and commendation that the warden gave him upon his release from prison. He remembered his jailers fondly and with great affection. He still wore the shirt that one of them gave him, and he named his first son Willy after a prison guard who became his good friend.

Now back in Gasumi Corners, Doliay has become something of an ideal Christian. Unlike those who hung around the pastor's compound in hopes of wheedling a favor or gaining a benefit, Doliay did parish work out of a sense of personal commitment. He told me that he waited to be baptized until coming back to Nomad because he wanted to be sure—really sure—that his bad ways were completely gone, that he felt no more hate in his heart. He felt grateful that God could forgive even as great a sin as his killing of Sabowey. And he said that he would wait with a Christian heart until Judgment Day to see if God would accept him into heaven. I asked Doliay if he wouldn't be tempted to kill another person for sorcery, especially if one of his own children were to die of sickness. His answer was immediate: "No. No way."

"Why not?"

"It's not for me to take revenge. That's something for the 'Big Fellow' [God] to decide. Besides, the people of Gasumi Corners don't practice sorcery anymore. Even if they wanted to, they would be too scared of what I did to Sabowey to send sorcery again. If my son died, it wouldn't be from sorcery."

Against traditional beliefs, Doliay's view was revolutionary. Before, the Gebusi had universally attributed fatal illnesses to sorcery. And a man's demand for revenge was greatest when it was a member of his own immediate family who had died from sickness.

While Doliay was in prison, his community had changed. Incited by the pastors, the villagers redoubled their rejection of violence against suspected sorcerers. The penalty Doliay had been forced to pay—six years in prison, away from his kin—reinforced the reluctance of other Gebusi to follow in his footsteps. The killing of Sabowey became renowned as the last execution of a sorcerer, the end of an era. In the wake of this act, conversion to Christianity swelled rather than diminished. Since then, as far as I have been able to determine, no Gebusi has been killed as a sorcerer. This is fairly amazing: a society with one of the highest known rates of homicide has seen it drop to zero. I confirmed this lack of violence by detailing and then cross-checking the cause and circumstances of each of the deaths of the members and descendants of Yibihilu and its hamlets. To me, this underscores the degree to which human violence is not an ingrained or inevitable outcome, but one that is strongly shaped by attitudes and beliefs. And yet, I remained somewhat skeptical of this good-news story. The Gebusi belief in sorcery had been so strong, and their desire to seek vengeance had been so high, that I remained a doubting Thomas—I needed to see in order to believe. Then Uwano died.

A certain depth emerges from the eyes of a man who knows his death throes are starting. Uwano was not old by our standards, probably in his late forties. Perceptive and a convivial joker, he had been my *arga*, my "breadfruit" gift partner, since 1981. We had always greeted each other heartily. But by the fall of 1998, he was a shell of his former self, having only a tiny reserve of strength to fight his death. When I went to visit him at the Nomad Aid Post on his last night, the swelling that would soon consume his body had already taken his right arm and back. He gazed upward with a mixture of knowledge and confusion. Then he turned and seemed to recognize me, and a shadow of a smile flickered across his face.

I knew better than to tell him he would get better. I could only kneel down with a helpless smile, look softly into his eyes, and say *"Koya, koya,"* (friend, friend) as tenderly as I could. I took his hand in mine and stroked it. It was cold, already dead. He looked at me with that slight shake of head that is the Gebusi expression for, "There's no way; it's impossible." Then he was gone from me, eyes drifting into space. His little frame shook with a small spasm, which was all his ravaged body could muster. He did not look back at me as I waited there. After a while, I crept out to the next room to talk with his relatives. The stark glow of the fluorescent bulb in that room with no furnishings cast them all in ghostly stillness.

We always project at death, I think—the Gebusi with their beliefs and me with my thoughts of final human connection. And hopefully Uwano, too, reaching out from his doorway on death's divide. He died a few hours later, on October 9, 1998.

I waited instinctively for the sorcery inquests to start. Back in 1980–82, it would have been unthinkable for a prominent man in the community to die without a full-blown inquest to find the sorcerer responsible. But Uwano's body was carried back to Gasumi Corners for a simple Christian funeral. He was dressed in his best Sunday shirt, his head was wreathed with leaves, and he was buried during a grave-side service led by a Catholic catechist who read from the Bible.

A few of Uwano's closest relatives grumbled that someone must have killed him. Men voiced vague fears that an assault sorcerer could be on the prowl. But there was no spirit séance, no accusation, no attempt to identify a suspect, and no attempt to take revenge. As if to satisfy themselves, the men walked off to one of Uwano's gardens. They pawed around aimlessly in case an obvious sign of a sorcery attack could be found. But their search was half-hearted, and they quickly lost interest. As one man said with a shrug, "If a spirit medium were around, we might have a chance of finding something. But there isn't." In effect, they were simply paying their respects to Uwano by visiting the place where they thought he might have become sick. Not wanting to waste their trip to the forest, the men gathered weathered logs near his garden and shouldered them back to the village for firewood.

In the wake of this experience, the descriptions of Gebusi deaths between 1982 and 1998 finally made real sense to me. Friends had earnestly told me, in case after case, "So-and-so simply died of sickness. We just don't know why. Only God can know. Maybe she was killed by sorcery. Or maybe by some other kind of spirit. Maybe Satan was trying to fool us into thinking that it was sorcery. Not knowing, we just buried the body and had the pastor read from the Bible." Although the dead person's closest relatives might suspect someone of sorcery, there was little they could do. Without firm spiritual evidence, other people in the community would not support their claim. And if they did try to launch an accusation, it could backfire. The person accused of sorcery could now turn the tables and charge the accuser with making a slanderous accusation without evidence, even bringing the case to the Nomad police.

As I thought about all this, my views of Gebusi Christianity had opposing sides. On the one hand, I felt that much of value in Gebusi culture had been lost. The vibrant wonder of their traditional beliefs had faded, and the poetry, symbolism, and musical awe of their spirit world were almost dead. In their place was a demanding new religion, trumpeted from elsewhere. In the history of colonialism and post-colonialism, including in the global spread of Christianity, the pressured or forced conversion of local people has worked hand in hand with powerful forms of social, economic, and political domination. Though the Gebusi had been thankfully spared coercive intimidation in their conversion to Christianity, they nonetheless had become passive recipients of outside spiritual as well as political authority. On the other hand, however, Christian teaching and a new way of life had reduced the Gebusi's extraordinary rate of violence. Indeed, their sorcery killings had stopped altogether. Social life was more peaceful than before. Men, women, and even children could walk to Nomad or in the nearby forest without fear of attack. Although the intense camaraderie of earlier days was gone, so, too, was the threat of lethal violence. Life was tamer in many ways.

What about the experiences of Gebusi women? Previously, they had enjoyed the energy and splendor of the spirit world, but from the sidelines. Although spirit women were key figures in the traditional cosmos, Gebusi women themselves had been excluded from séances and had little influence in sorcery inquests; men controlled the spirit world and the use of violence. Now, however, women were Christian along with the men. The responsibility and the reward of being Christian—of repenting sins and gaining salvation—was individual for both sexes. In the church itself, pews were divided evenly, with women on the left side and men on the right. At the Catholic services, men and women attended in roughly equal numbers, but in SDA and Evangelical services, a decided majority were women. The church pastors and the primary lay leaders in the community were invariably men. And the authority of "Papa God," as he was called, was both stronger and more patriarchal than that of traditional Gebusi spirits. Sporadically but notably, men in Gasumi Corners would echo the tone of the preachers or government officials, adopting a lecturing and authoritative tone in their own community. Finally, the number of Gebusi marriages that were acrimonious as opposed to harmonious was about the same as before.

Adding to my conflicted feelings about Christianity was another uncertainty: To what extent were the Gebusi's previous beliefs really dead? If only vestigially, the Gebusi still worried about sorcery. In many parts of Melanesia—and in parts of Africa, Asia, Latin America, and even Western countries—belief in sorcery or magic has persisted or reasserted itself. Such beliefs have sometimes melded with Christianity or other world religions such as Islam, Buddhism, or Hinduism. In significant areas of Melanesia and Africa, sorcery beliefs play a major role in disputes and rivalries, including between political leaders. If these customs can continue in modern forms, couldn't Gebusi beliefs come back in new ways? Vengeance against suspected sorcerers certainly seemed to be a thing of the past for the Gebusi in 1998.

But just as their religion changed radically since 1982, perhaps it will take another new turn in the future.

No matter what happens, however, and even if Christianity is later rejected or disavowed, its present influence will have a significant legacy. In this sense, the hands of time cannot be turned back. And there is every indication that Christian influence among Gebusi has been growing stronger.

Ultimately, how can we explain Gebusi religion—the complexity of its past, its present, and its indeterminate future? As with many topics that anthropologists study—subsistence, kinship, economics, and politics—the complexities of the present play havoc with the categories of the past. The traditional Gebusi cosmos was full of spirits in the form of humans, birds, fish, lizards, and even trees. Contact with these spirits was made by spirit mediums—spiritual practitioners who had direct, if sporadic, access to the spirit world. Traditional Gebusi religion reflected dimensions of animism and shamanism, which have sometimes been suggested as the oldest forms of human spiritual belief. However, Gebusi religion is now clearly, if not predominantly, influenced by Christianity as one of the major world religions. Historically, world religions such as Islam, Buddhism, Judaism, Hinduism, and Confucianism, like Christianity, have been associated with kingdoms or state empires. The spiritual pantheon of most of these religions is centralized or monotheistic, often focusing on a single God or creative force. In recent years, major world religions have spread yet further and become more influential, including in remote areas such as the New Guinea rainforest. Although it once was thought that religion would decline as cultures became more modern, just the reverse may be increasingly true. And in the process, world religions are themselves shaped by the history and beliefs of many different cultures. Global religions meet local persuasions, conversions, and sometimes resistances. At Nomad, the practice of Catholicism, Protestantism, and Seventh Day Adventism is significantly different from how they are practiced in Western countries. But they remain strongly Christian nonetheless.

At Nomad as well as in many countries and also in the United States, the growth of religion has been strongly connected with politics and political interests. Government officials were among the strongest proponents of Christianity and among its strongest leaders. Christianity was even taught as a subject in the Nomad school—just as the teachers often read scripture or gave sermons on Sunday in church. More generally, there is easily an integral connection between the local force of the State, a national or international church, and the broader process of being or becoming modern.

At the same time, people often find ways to reassert more organic or home-made versions of spiritual and aesthetic expression even as structures or institutions from elsewhere may dominate them. This includes personal experiences that are deeply meaningful and "efferverscent" even though they may not be religious in formal or institutional terms. One day, I found this myself, quite unexpectedly, in Gasumi Corners. This is what I wrote in my field notes:

> Today by my house, I had little idea what hit me. The breeze sent a faint melody, beautiful and haunting, apparently from afar. I had never heard anything like it. I went magnetically toward the music, but I found no houses in its direction. "You want to hear the singing," Kilasui said, and he pointed me to the path. It led from the village to seemingly nowhere, but the sound grew louder. The sound was as stunning as and yet different from the séance songs of old. I wound through the brush to a small fire that had breadfruit warming next to it. No one was there, but the music was now full all around me. I looked up. Smiling down like nymphs on high were seven radiant boys smothering each other in soft harmony.
>
> I drew irresistibly up into their tree, its white branches grown as if they knew where each step would need to be placed. It swayed slightly with my weight and shook with gentle laughs that echoed the boys themselves. They squealed in delight to have a grown gawky companion, white as their tree, take interest in their singing. This soon brought the attention of other children, some of whom also clambered into the tree and distributed themselves carefully, as if to steady a wobbly ship. Even without their hubbub, my juvenile action could not have gone unnoticed. Now I could see a gathered crowd of women, yet more children, and even Sayu, who grinned at me through the foliage below. Their happiness, mine, and that of the boys made its own harmony, suspended in air with their song.

I had several of those indescribable minutes in that tree—the kind that convince you to the bone that you've done the right thing to go so far, that you have reached an enjoyment and bonding that transcends culture and that words cannot express. The sky was bluest blue, a cool breeze laced their melody, and I looked out thinking I had captured the innocence and joy of forest peoples that others have written about so nostalgically in decades past. I cannot fully share or reproduce that nostalgia; there are too many complexities, uncertainties, and problems for that. But those stolen moments of innocence, full and beautiful, when one finds oneself inexplicably a young boy again drawn up in a tree, caressed in a sea of angelic smiles, tender harmony, and rainforest awe, can be neither denied nor suppressed. These are the moments that make life not just worth living, but a thousand times over. If music marks the sound of the soul and the wheels of time, the songs of the Gebusi present may be as rich as their spiritual past.

CHAPTER 9

Women waiting to sell their produce at the Nomad market. (PHOTO: Bruce Knauft)

Pennies and Peanuts, Rugby and Radios

BOSAP WAS NOT HAPPY. The market was winding down, and her piles of bananas and sweet potatoes lay primped for sale like wallflowers that everyone saw but nobody wanted. The other women were similarly forlorn; their produce was still competing with Bosap's on the sellers' tables. Thinking to make light of the situation, as well as to collect more information, I tried to view her glass as half full: "You sold at least a little, right? Maybe two or three sales at 10 cents each?" Bad questions, bad timing. Bosap's normally congenial features, already sober, flashed to a scowl. "Not interested," she said, and turned away. She had sold nothing.

So, too, in her life, Bosap had been passed over, though she usually took everything in stride. As she had laughingly said when I talked to her before, "No man wanted to marry me. But then, I didn't want to marry any of them, either!" Among the Gebusi, Bosap had the rare distinction of becoming an older woman, now in her mid-fifties, without ever having married. When she had been in her thirties, this hadn't stopped her from having a sexual affair with a young man in his late teens. It had created a scandal when Bosap became pregnant, but she had carried on with determination. She did not marry her young lover, who had not yet been initiated, nor any of his older clan-mates, who might have been willing to claim the infant boy and take Bosap as a second wife and domestic helper. Despite the anomaly, Bosap had raised Kuma by herself, with the help of her own kin. It was now the pride of her life that Kuma had become a strong and decent young man who was now almost ready himself to be married. As long as I had known her, Bosap had maintained both her pleasant disposition and her ultimate determination to go her own way. Her good-spiritedness was attested by the fact that, even as an "old woman," she had never been suspected of sorcery in previous years, in contrast to many other older women in Gasumi Corners.

Because Bosap was usually friendly, I was caught off guard by her reply to my query at the market. Bad sales were a touchy personal issue, and there were few buyers—mostly government officials and their wives from the Nomad Station. Nevertheless, women from Gasumi Corners and other communities continued to invest effort in taking their best produce to market in hopes of selling it. At dawn on Tuesdays and Fridays, they packed their foodstuffs in cavernous net bags and hauled them across the Hamam River and down the muddy path to the Nomad market. Even on a "good day," many women came back loaded down with the same food they had brought. And prices were low. For the equivalent of 60 cents, a buyer could purchase a large bunch of ripe bananas, a pile of shelled Tahitian chestnuts, and a bundle of cooked bamboo shoots. Even at that, few people aside from government workers and pastors had money to spend on food, and their own wages were small, erratic, and undependably paid. But local women kept bringing food to sell, twice every week. The market was their way to have at least some small place in a cash economy.

Wanting some insight into this dynamic, I determined to find out exactly how much food the women brought to market, how much they took back or gave away, how much they sold, and how much money they earned. As I realized from my encounter with Bosap, however, this was going to be tricky. Women were eager to hide their many failures and even their few successes—for fear of jealousy. Only a very few of them could actually add up the value of the coins they received in any event, and they quickly shoved their proceeds into tightly wadded bundles. When they did occur, transactions were downplayed or shielded from public view. A purchaser would have the exact change ready and pay it in a lump sum rather than publicly counting coins. Sometimes, he or she would saunter behind the table, privately make the purchase, and furtively sweep the food into a net bag before walking away. Because prices for each pile of food were standardized, there was no need for bargaining or even, in most cases, conversation at all.

In typical fieldwork fashion, I discovered this etiquette by seriously violating it. I had been pleased to see so many new foods for sale at the first market I attended. Wanting to stimulate the local economy and to obtain some different foods for my own supper, I approached a woman who had bamboo shoots for sale. Lacking pocket change, I pawed clumsily through my various pockets, only to find that the smallest currency I had was a 2-kina bill. As I extended this to her across the table, I could see the color drain from her face. Though worth only one U.S. dollar, the bill was ten times the price of the shoots I was buying. The poor woman had neither the arithmetic nor the coins to make change, so she was forced to initiate a confusing chain of inquiries that rippled in domino effect through all the people around her. Ten-cent loans and other transfers of coins ricocheted through the crowd. After several long and awkward minutes, my requisite 90 cents in change was amassed and dutifully counted for me—as everyone looked on. By this time, I had half a mind to let the unfortunate women simply keep the change. Except for two things. First, I would be wildly undermining the standards of the market, which were predicated on fixed and standardized prices for each pile of food. Second, my transaction had attracted the attention of perhaps half of the two hundred or so people at the market. Setting a precedent of overpayment could have jacked up the cost of my future purchases by as much as 900 percent! So I smiled gamely and apologized pleasantly, trying not to call yet more attention to my gaffe.

How much is a dime worth in Gasumi Corners? The episode reminded me of how cultural meanings, rules, and assumptions—whole worlds of understanding— underlie the smallest of material exchanges. Back in the United States, I walk into a store and don't give it a second thought. The impersonality of buying an item from someone I don't know, of handing over money in public, of receiving change, and of having other people witness it—all this presumes a series of market assumptions that the Gebusi and their neighbors are just beginning to engage. But—and this is the more important point—Gebusi seem more rather than less motivated to engage this market world at the same time and in some ways for the very reason that they are marginal and awkward with respect to it. Notwithstanding the embarrassment of my conduct at the market, the woman I bought produce from had earned not just my 10 cents but the prestige of selling to an outsider who had money. Of all the sellers with bundles of bamboo shoots, I happened to have chosen hers. She and her kin now had the ownership, presumably collective, of not just some coins but a 2-kina bill that was received very publicly. Notwithstanding its awkwardness, the transaction also conveyed value, which I judged from the grinning palaver of the woman's kin as I walked away. If I had unwittingly trampled on local etiquette, I had also unwittingly reinforced larger assumptions of a market economy: that monetary exchange is at once public, impersonal, and prestigious.

Being either a good or a bad ethnographer (sometimes, it is hard to know which is which), I became more interested than ever in finding what market women at Nomad actually accomplished. Like the churches, the Nomad school, and the local sports league, the market is an interethnic affair—people come to it from various sides or "corners" of Nomad. These corners are inhabited by persons with different ethnic or tribal affiliations. As such, women from Gasumi Corners form only a small fraction of those at the market. But because they were from my own core community, I decided to keep them as my focus.

The first and easiest thing to discern was that most of the sellers were, in fact, women. By counting the sellers from Gasumi Corners on twenty-five different market days, I found that over 91 percent of them (285 of 313) were female. This paralleled my rough sense of the percentage of female sellers attending from other communities and ethnic groups. Although men and boys also came to the market, they seldom sold anything; they tended to converse with one another around the periphery of the selling area. Occasionally, they would saunter down the aisle of selling tables under the market's large thatched roof. And once in a while, they would buy a pile of peanuts for a dime. But the center of action—or lack thereof—was the women and their sales. All the women from Gasumi Corners participated; each would gather her best foodstuffs and bring them to market an average of once every ten days. All in all, the market was the prime place for village women to aspire to a new time of material prestige—a place to be modern. Gebusi women also went to church, of course. And in recent years, girls had increasingly become students along with boys at the Nomad Community School. Only at the market, however, were women not merely present but the dominant and central focus of attention. Although they tended to be quiet and retiring rather than talkative or aggressive, they did visit casually with their female kin and relatives, including women from other villages or communities.

How much money did women actually make at the Nomad market? I couldn't easily ask them, but I found that I could count the piles of food they initially placed on the selling tables. As the market progressed, I could stroll casually up and down the aisles, chat with the women and note which piles of food had been reduced by sales and in what amounts. Because prices were standardized, it wasn't hard to figure how much the women had sold by the end of the market. Women who were lucky enough to have sold several items were willing to clarify, if I was unsure, how many units they had sold.

Over the course of twenty-five market days, I calculated that the women sold less than half the food that they had brought to the market for sale. The rest was carried back home or given away. A woman's average total earnings per market day were 20 cents—for selling food weighing several pounds or more. More than 20 percent of the women who brought food to market on a given day sold nothing at all.

The inflated price of the few things that could be bought with money at Nomad's tiny home-front stores underscored the difficulty of the women's enterprise. The benchmark goods bought at these stores were one-kilo bags of rice and twelve-ounce tins of low-grade mackerel. Each of these items cost the equivalent of $1.50. This meant that the average woman's sales from almost an entire month of marketing were wiped out when she purchased a single bag of rice or a single tin of fish. In assessing the nutritional value of the rice or fish against the many hours and calories involved in raising surplus food and hauling it back and forth to market, it became obvious that the energy cost of women's marketing far outweighed the benefits they gained from it. In these terms, the market activities of Gebusi women seemed irrational.

Why would someone put more time and effort into an enterprise than they get out of it? This question grew increasingly poignant as I saw women from Gasumi Corners processing and carrying food and then waiting aimlessly at the market, week after week.

The onus seemed greatest for two young adolescent girls, Danksop and Waygo, who would sit wooden or sighing behind their piles of food for hour after hour. But the answer to my question was one that I should have realized all along. In a word: culture. As we know from the things we ourselves buy, there is much more to a purchase—and more to the work that pays for it—than the trade-off between the dollars we spend and the functional use of the things we buy. Why do we prefer a Ferrari to a Ford, Godiva chocolate to Hershey's, or a gold ring to one made of tin? Similarly, why do the Gebusi prefer a single kilo of rice to a dozen pounds of potatoes? The answer is the same in both cases: items of value afford prestige and cultural status. If Gebusi marketing seems "irrational," it carries the value and prestige of earning money, of being modern. And it does this for those who are otherwise most shut out of the local cash economy: village women. If men obtain occasional paid work—cutting the grass on the airstrip, doing odd jobs for government officials, or acting as carriers for visitors on a trek—women earn coins at the market.

❧   ❧   ❧

I realized the cumulative significance of women's marketing when I found my "banker" in Gasumi Corners. Nolop was the cleverest old woman in the settlement. On the way back from the market one day, I joked that though I had money, it was difficult to buy things—I had bills but not enough coins. At the next turn in the path, Nolop quietly motioned me away from the others. "I've got coins," she said. "Come to my house." We then continued to our respective homes. After stowing my things, I walked back to her little dwelling. As I did so, I remembered her personal history. This was as colorful as it was fascinating—and it helped explain her initiative in exchanging coins for my bills. I knew Nolop well from 1980–82; she had lived in the house that was second closest to our own at Yibihilu. At that time, she had been married to the easygoing Wosip and raising two boys. She had also been a bold character. Not only had Nolop been caught having a sexual affair with the uninitiated Doliay, but she was also the only Gebusi woman we ever knew or heard about who had dabbled in the otherwise all-male art of spirit mediumship. On one occasion in 1981, Eileen had tried to arrange for Nolop to sing a full séance at our own house—with other village women serving as her chorus. However, the men of the village came by so frequently and intruded so petulantly that the women's singing was quickly terminated and not repeated.

Since we had left in 1982, Nolop had endured much. The cyst on her right wrist had grown larger, and it became hard for her to use her hand. About 1990, her oldest, cherished son had been gored to death by a wild pig. Almost immediately afterward, her gentle husband had also died; villagers said that after his son's demise he had lost all appetite and grieved himself to death. Nolop had been left with her remaining son plus a younger daughter, Kwelam. Shortly thereafter Kwelam became seriously ill from a bone deformity in her hip. But Nolop was as tough as she was smart—always ready with both a witty smirk and an astute way to solve a problem. She had somehow finagled the medical officer at the Nomad Aid Post to have Kwelam flown out for an operation to the Kiunga Hospital— along with Nolop herself. While in Kiunga, without money or kin, Nolop had had to rummage in garbage heaps for daily scraps of food. Lacking a blouse or bra, she had felt the powerful stigma of going bare-breasted in town and had scrounged for rags to cover herself. Despite these abasements, Nolop had cared for Kwelam until she recovered and they could both be flown back to Nomad, at government expense. Today, Kwelam walks with a limp but is otherwise healthy, and she seems to be one of the happiest girls in the village. Nolop's surviving son, Damya, is now married and has an infant daughter of his own. He is one of the most decent lay leaders in the Nomad Catholic Church and also the lead singer in the community's string band chorus.

As Nolop saw her children grow up successfully, she felt pressure to marry the widower Gono—the silent, wiry man who had been one of our carriers during our first foray into Gebusi territory. Perhaps she had found him a useful partner at the time. As he aged, however, Gono became crotchety, and he resented his wife's feisty wit and lack of deference. On more than one occasion in 1998, he beat Nolop. As an unusual stigma, Gono was criticized for his actions by both the men and the women of Gasumi Corners.

Quite her own person, Nolop went her own way; though she still lived in Gono's small house, she kept her affairs to herself. These included her earnings from the market, which she squirreled away without telling him. Although most wives try to keep their market money at least nominally to themselves, it tends to become part of the household economy and subject to the decisions of their husbands, especially if the proceeds accrue over time. Women earn money with painful slowness, but men typically decide how any larger sum will be spent. That said, women took pride in the knowledge that their hard-earned funds pay for prestigious tins of fish and bags of rice at community feasts—though their husbands presented these gifts and took credit for them. Even if they keep their own money, many Gebusi women were uncomfortable or embarrassed to make significant purchases by themselves at one of the Nomad stores.

By dint of personal will, however, Nolop had kept her small earnings to herself and for her own children. And she had wisely focused on raising and marketing peanuts, which were the one item that sold most widely and regularly at the market, even though it was not the splashiest or most prestigious thing to sell. Week after week, Nolop sold little piles of peanuts from her big bag. And over time, her 10-cent sales added up. After we were safely in her house, Nolop smiled wryly and carefully unwrapped several unobtrusive bundles. To my amazement, pile upon pile of coins poured out. She didn't know how much she had earned. When I counted up her earnings, they totaled more than 40 kina, or 20 dollars. This was equivalent to two hundred sales of 10 cents apiece at the market—approximately two years of market sales for the average woman of Gasumi Corners.

With easy trust, Nolop was delighted to give me the bulk of her coins in exchange for two of my crisp 20-kina bills. Everyone knew that the bright red pigs head money, as it was called, was the biggest and most important currency that circulated at Nomad. That Nolop now had two of these bills seemed to give her a profound sense of satisfaction. As she carefully tucked them away, we both knew that she could use them however she wished. And they would be easier to conceal from others' prying eyes than her piles of coins had been. Perhaps Nolop would contribute unexpectedly to a major feast. Or give a gift to her children. Or buy something extraordinary at a special time. As for me, I now had all the coins I needed. As I walked home, I tried to carry my stash in my own net bag as unobtrusively as possible. I smiled at the thought that an economy of new money could, at least on rare occasions, benefit both a Gebusi woman and an outsider—without compromising the integrity of either. The economy of money in Gasumi Corners was paltry and in many ways unproductive, but its economy of culture was strong and important.

🌿   🌿   🌿

My experience with Nolop got me thinking about how women's relations with men were changing. If the Gebusi market foregrounded the hopeful and compromised role of women in a fledgling cash economy, it was complemented by their new role in other spheres. The Christian churches had given women a new sense of spiritual participation, even though men were ultimately in charge. Other institutions and activities at Nomad also reflected gendered change while simultaneously providing new forms of male dominance. These trends were particularly notable in education, in sports, and, perhaps surprisingly, in theft. But it was difficult for me to talk with women about these developments. For an unrelated man to talk with a Gebusi woman invariably implies sexual interest. Older women like Nolop and Bosap were easier for me to approach because they were no longer considered desirable as sexual partners or wives. But younger women were a different story. Even for married women in their thirties and forties, a personal interview was difficult to arrange and even more difficult to carry out. I could talk to a woman if her husband or brother was present. But then the man would reinterpret my questions and answer many of them himself.

The same was true of my attempt to talk to schoolgirls at the Nomad Community School; the boys took charge in responding. To be fair, part of the problem involved all the students. Repetitive drills and copying from the board took a toll on a class of forty, sixty, or even eighty pupils who sat cross-legged on the floor or on hardwood benches for hour upon hour. Students were not just Gebusi but came from several different language groups. Their language of instruction was that peculiar dialect of my own native tongue that is "Papua New Guinea English." After a year or two in school, students could understand this form of English fairly well. But the rote process of learning it left them collectively passive and reluctant to speak individually in class. As in church, powerful outsiders controlled the expression of important knowledge. Villagers were generally too shy or embarrassed to voice an understanding or express a point of view in a language that was not their native tongue. So, like members of the congregation, students from Gasumi Corners and the surrounding communities rarely spoke up. This problem was by far the worst for the girls. To the teachers, however, the students were like the school's leaky water tank: when something new and good was imparted to them, they couldn't retain it but let it seep away.

I got my chance to break this mold when the teachers welcomed me to give guest presentations in each of their classes. My idea was to explore a more interactive form of teaching. Being demonstrative and something of a ham, I showed the students glossy photo essays that my parents had sent me from *National Geographic*. Using the pictures as props, I talked about what it might be like to be a Tibetan pastoralist, sell crafts in Oaxaca, be a Navajo dancer, or raise ponies in the Shetland Islands. I showed them pictures of Atlanta and explained features of living in the United States. Closer to their own homes, I described my early experiences among the Gebusi, showed them photos from my first Gebusi ethnography, and tried to get their views about what had changed at Nomad in recent years. The kids seemed to love my presentations. But when it came to saying much about themselves—indeed, when it came to saying much of anything that wasn't a collective repetition—they were tongue-tied.

At first, I thought they might be reluctant because of my status as a tall white American. Or maybe my words and intonation didn't make full sense to them. So, I took pains to re-express myself in *tok pisin* and in the Gebusi vernacular, as well as in Papua New Guinea English. Given the amazement many of them had shown when I spoke in Gebusi, I knew they understood. It was only after conducting repeated sessions with all the grades and listening to the teachers lead their own classes that I realized how completely the students had internalized a sense of "active passivity," of listening or parroting without individually speaking. I remember asking a fifth-grade class to name pictures of things without my saying the names first. Although they knew all the words, this simple task was painfully difficult, especially for the girls. I gave one group of girls three photos of pretty flowers. I knew that they knew what they were. I coaxed them with antics and pleasantries to say the word "flowers." They wanted to say the name in the worst way; they beamed as they squirmed. But none of them could get it out. Finally, I gently leaned close so one of them could whisper very faintly in my ear, "Flowers."

Although girls from Gasumi Corners and other communities increasingly go to school, the gender gap between them and the boys is as strong as the heat of the midday sun. Girls drop out of school much more frequently than boys. In Gasumi Corners, only 12 percent of the women know *tok pisin*, the national language, as opposed to 60 percent of the men. And unlike a significant number of boys and young men, no girls from Gasumi Corners have completed elementary school.

Outside school, boys dominate in physical activity through sports. Although sports were hardly important to Gebusi in 1980–82—as opposed to ritual fighting and even warfare—competition on the ball field has since become a more modern, more organized, more disciplined, and less violent arena of collective male rivalry. Schoolboys from Gasumi Corners avidly play rugby and soccer. As they get older, they join community teams that play on the Nomad ball field for much of each weekend afternoon. The games are interethnic occasions at which several hundred spectators ring the field. But (as was also the case in ritual fighting and warfare display) women can rarely be found on the field. Indeed, they can seldom be found even on the sidelines. In contrast to the dozen or so men's matches each weekend, there is a single game of women's soccer, and this is played almost entirely by the wives and elder daughters of government officials. Women from Gasumi Corners told me quite earnestly that they would be glad for their daughters to learn how to play soccer. And they added that they would themselves be glad to go as spectators to see their daughters play. But athletic field sports have become a de facto male province, beginning at school during recess. Few girls feel comfortable learning how to play or joining a team.

Ironically, men's dedication to sports was the ultimate solution to my difficulties in trying to talk more earnestly with Gebusi women. After several sun-bleached weekends of watching one game after another of rugby and soccer, I got bored. It wasn't that I disliked sports. When I was younger, I enjoyed playing and watching a wide range of sports, and I had even been a starter for my high school soccer team in the Connecticut state finals. But I never enjoyed life as a couch potato. And this certainly didn't fit my expectation of fieldwork with Gebusi. To some extent, I had to look beyond my own resistance. Since watching and playing sports were important to Gebusi men and boys, my hours of watching yielded insights. These concerned not just their style of gentlemanly competition on the field and the caliber of their play (which was surprisingly good, even in bare feet) but the dynamics of their spectatorship. Men in the crowd could interact across community and ethnic lines without the demands of hospitality, etiquette, or reciprocity that accompanied formal visits between settlements or communities. Having uncovered these dynamics, however, I still felt apathetic. So one fine Sunday afternoon, I simply stayed home.

Predictably, the men and boys were all at the Nomad ballgames. But as I quickly realized, this left the village an entirely female place for a few precious hours. Away from their husbands, brothers, and older male children, women's talk became freer and more relaxed. I found that I could interview women fairly easily as long as some of their female relatives were also present. It turned out that most of the women were eager to participate in my "talk-work" sessions. It helped that I had brought special trade goods for women that were otherwise hard to get— including dresses, bras, and costume jewelry. I had known that the bras and jewelry would be hard to find in bulk in Papua New Guinea, so I brought stocks of these with me from the United States. I can still remember the look on the saleswoman's face in the Dollar Store in Atlanta when I heaped fifteen inexpensive bras into my shopping basket along with mounds of cheap costume jewelry. Sensing that I should somehow "explain myself," I had said to her, without thinking carefully, that I was buying gifts for my many female friends in the rainforest. Aghast at the implications of my statement, I gulped as I guessed what she must be thinking. But it all turned out fine. The sales clerk was Malaysian, and she knew a good bit about rainforest peoples, the difficulty of obtaining trade goods in remote areas, and the politics of gift giving. In fact, she ended up advising me which bras were most likely to fit the short but sometimes well-endowed women of Gasumi Corners. I came away with a fresh understanding about crossing cultural boundaries with women—in Atlanta as well as in New Guinea.

Back in Gasumi Corners, the women greatly appreciated the goods I had brought. I talked with each of them individually as primary interviewees—listening to the woman's life history and getting her opinions and reflections on various subjects. Particularly with less articulate women, their female kin and friends chimed in with helpful promptings, clarifications, and elaborations. Young women and adolescent girls remained the most difficult to talk with. Even when asked by a not-so-young and weirdly acceptable male such as myself, and even with other women supporting them, their responses were often only shuffling feet, embarrassment, and blank looks. I tried to ask what kind of man would make a good husband. Or if they would like to see their own future daughters-to-be go to school. But their charged status as eligible young women overwhelmed their responses. Discussing positive husbandly characteristics implied a young woman's embarrassing preference for one or another young man in the village. Talking about unborn children awkwardly implied that she herself was almost mature enough to be a mother. Nonetheless, all the women, even the younger ones, maintained their desire to work with me. This was partly because the other women were also doing it, and perhaps partly because my interest and history in their community provoked a sense of obligation on their part. But mostly, I think, they wanted the trade goods that I gave them at the end of the sessions.

The final link in my investigation of gendered change—across developments in church, the market, school, sports, and domestic relations—concerned the heightened yearnings of women and men for modern goods and a modern way of life.

During the latter part of my fieldwork, I sponsored a contest in which Nomad schoolchildren drew pictures of how they envisaged themselves in the future. I was amazed how eagerly and effectively they took up this task, not to mention the high quality of their results. Burgeoning on the pages were full-color drawings of the children in modern walks and ways of life. Boys drew themselves as heavy machine operators, pilots, doctors, and even as an actor or newsman. Girls drew themselves especially as nurses, teachers, or housewives in nice Western dresses. It was significant to me that girls as well as boys drew themselves in highly modern futures. A few actually drew themselves as living in a Christian heaven. By contrast, very few of the students—just 6 percent of the boys and 5 percent of the girls—drew their future selves as pursuing traditional livelihoods such as gardening, hunting, or fishing.

The optimism of the school children notwithstanding, it seemed to me that many of their desires were unrealistic. It was very unlikely that many or perhaps any of them would be able to actualize the lives they envisaged for themselves. The economy of Nomad is too paltry and the ability of local people to change this is minimal. So what will happen to the expectations of young people as their aspirations for the future are frustrated if not dashed?

If gender does not divide the modern aspirations of young people at Nomad, one important contrast did emerge. Virtually half of the boys envisaged their future as a forceful, gun-wielding member of the Papua New Guinea Defense Force or the National Police. The gravitation of boys to images and roles of forceful power is of course not surprising. But this predilection does carry distinctive modern implications in the context of the Papua New Guinea. In a local world where manufactured goods and commodities are increasingly desired—and expected—the temptation to forcefully take or possess them can also increase, especially for young men. This has been an increasing problem across much of Papua New Guinea. Back at Yibihilu in 1980–82, people had craved our Western commodities, but we had never feared theft. Living so communally, Gebusi had made a virtue of necessity by respecting each other's property and sharing it with others at will. By 1998, however, things had changed. Villagers were more possessive and private with their manufactured goods. Money was an increasingly important and anonymous commodity. And activities at the Nomad Station entailed interaction with many people who were strangers—and potential thieves. Families living in separate houses were concerned about theft, and desire mounted for metal boxes, chains, and locks. In the Nomad police register, theft was the most frequently reported offense—almost twice as common as any other crime. The vast majority of these accusations were both made by and targeted against men. Although theft in Nomad was only a small problem when compared with the robbery, theft, and violent crime in Papua New Guinea's larger towns and cities, it was still a focus of moral concern.

During the months I was there, the biggest case involved the theft of two boom box radios from the Nomad Community School. Boom boxes had become a major icon of modern identity at Nomad, especially for young men. They referenced a prestigious world of commodities and accomplishment, of fluent speech in *tok pisin* or English, of rock music, and of sexual allure. The radios in question were also important signs of modernity for the school. In addition to playing music and tapes, the players broadcast national education programs in classrooms each morning. Students throughout the country were presumed to listen to the same program for their grade level at a specific time.

Given their significance, the theft of the school boom boxes was a blow to the modern dignity and prestige of the Nomad community—and it highlighted the increasing possessiveness and frustration of young men in and around the station. At a large public meeting, officials harangued villagers and criticized them for letting local boys carry out and get away with such an awful crime. If this trend continued, they suggested, the schoolteachers would not want to live and work at Nomad. They opined that maybe the school itself would have to be shut down. Given a general shortage of teachers and funds, this was a very real threat—many village schools in the Nomad Sub-District are shut down due to a lack of instructors or money to pay them. If the central station at Nomad itself was going to be a "bad" place, a place of theft and "backsliding," officials continued, airplanes bringing supplies might stop landing at Nomad Station altogether. As the cause of this potential development, villagers and young men in particular were disparaged as sinful and un-Christian, untrustworthy and deceitful. They would face the onus of living in a remote rural area in a state of moral, religious, and economic backwardness. As in church, some villagers hung their heads.

For many people, the loss of the radios reflected the difficulty of becoming modern in a place like Nomad. Institutions such as the churches, market, and school have brought people together in new ways and in the service of new endeavors. But they have also created an increasingly impersonal world. This world is marked by new inequalities and resentments, for instance, between government workers who can afford boom boxes and villagers who cannot. Particularly for young men who are unable to earn a modern living and achieve its way of life, pressure mounts to simply take what they can—to resort to force and to reject the slow, frustrating process of becoming modern through tedious and often fruitless effort. The problem of crime has become a major blight in the larger towns and cities of Papua New Guinea, as it has in urban areas of many other countries. In 1998, the problem was as yet small but increasing at Nomad.

These issues link us back to the role and significance of gender under changing circumstances. If local men used to control the means of traditional violence, the access to the spirit world, and the prestige of public festivity, their modern authority and sometimes their dignity can be undercut by status inequalities and relative impoverishment vis-à-vis powerful outsiders and the perceived largesse of a wider world. In some case, these tensions can be redirected by men back on local women—as was the case of Gono beating Nolop, his economically successful wife.

If local modern institutions afford women the potential for greater and more active participation than they had in the past, they can also threaten masculinity and increase the tensions that young men face as they pursue modern forms of prestige and success. At Nomad, men's preeminence and growing impatience—in school, athletics, church, and government activities—seem to contrast with the activities of most Gebusi women. In this regard, patient market women such as Nolop and Bosap form a counterpoint to younger and more restless desires, particularly among men, for quicker and more forceful routes to modern success.

CHAPTER 10

Two women from Gasumi Corners at a village dance, 1998. (PHOTO: Bruce Knauft)

Mysterious Romance, Marital Choice

HE ALWAYS SEEMED TO me as spare with his words as he was decent and direct in his actions. He was clearly troubled, so I asked him in. He came inside and hesitated, strong young man that he was, until the urgency of his question overcame his embarrassment. "Do you have any *adameni?* I would really like some." I had no idea what he was talking about, so I asked him what *adameni* was. He stammered and continued on: "*Adameni* is something special. It has to do with an unmarried woman and an unmarried man. When they really like each other and think of coming together." I still had no idea. Whatever adameni was, it related to sexual desire between young people. Wayabay was the oldest of the bachelors, and he was actively trying to find a wife. But what was *adameni?* I wracked my brain. Whatever *adameni* was, it was important to Wayabay. I was as concerned as I was curious.

Could Wayabay be asking me for a condom? I knew that he had worked for a trail-clearing crew a few years back and that he had been out to the town of Kiunga. He had a wider scope of knowledge and experience than many of the young men. Perhaps he was now in a romantic liaison and wanted to protect either himself or the girl. This would explain his embarrassment. Although Wayabay seemed too proper a young man to be involved in a casual sexual affair, I had certainly been surprised in the past by the public revelation of Gebusi sexual trysts. So I tried, gently, to describe a condom in the Gebusi vernacular: "There is this thing that men wear when they have sex. Is this like *adameni?*" Wayabay replied, "Well, maybe. I'm not sure." My unease was mounting, but I forged ahead: "This is something that a man puts over his 'thing,' his phallus. It stretches like rubber. He puts this rubber thing over his phallus before he has sex. He has sex with the woman but his 'thing' doesn't touch the woman's 'thing.'"

Now it was Wayabay's turn to be uncomprehending—and mine to be embarrassed. I tried to explain that men can use these rubber coverings when they don't want the woman to get pregnant or when they worry about getting sick from having sex. All of which sounded no better and, indeed, much worse when spoken in Gebusi. Wayabay shook his head vehemently; this was definitely NOT *adameni.*

In despair, we invited Sayu and Didiga into our conversation. Both of them spoke a smattering of English, and both had had more schooling than Wayabay. I mentally cursed myself for not knowing what *adameni* was—this term that was obviously so important in Gebusi sexual culture and that I hadn't uncovered during all my time with them. But Sayu and Didiga had no better luck finding a translation or an explanation. Yes, they said, *adameni* was something for a man. And, yes, it had to do with sex. It also had something do to with *oop*, the generic Gebusi word for "slippery, milky substance" that was especially associated with semen.

Sex. Men. Semen. I was stymied. Could they be referring to some custom or substance having to do with traditional practices of sex between men? This would certainly explain Wayabay's embarrassment. Perhaps he was having sexual relations with one or another young man before finding a wife. I took another deep breath. "Does this *adameni* have to do with Gebusi sex customs between men?" They looked puzzled, so I persisted: "Does it have to do with traditional Gebusi customs? You know, the sex custom in your initiations in which the adolescent boy sucks the phallus and swallows the semen of the man—so he can grow big and achieve more manhood."

Culturally speaking, I had dropped a bomb. Their mouths hung open in disbelief, and their faces grew ashen. Sayu finally broke their silence: "Did our fathers and boys really do that? In the olden times? Did they? Really?!"

Double ouch. I had been terribly rash. Although the three of them had all grown up in a world of male banter and horseplay, none of them, I now realized, had been initiated; the final initiation ceremony had been held before they would have been old enough. They had never been indoctrinated into sexual relations with other men. And given the community's conversion to Christianity, it was quite possible that they had never been told about the practice. Perhaps my three companions had suspected or wondered about men's sexual customs. But perhaps not. Against their willful ignorance, I had asserted the reality of a strange sexual practice, a custom that was hard to believe and that was highly distasteful to them. I had divulged a secret of my own generation and had shocked them. I felt awful. But I also felt that I had to answer them truthfully: "Yes, that is the custom that the men and initiated teenagers followed at Yibihilu when I was here before."

After shaking their heads in disbelief, they stressed, as if it needed emphasis, that *adameni* had nothing whatsoever to do with sex between one man and another. *Adameni* was for use between men and women. This was the only sex that the three of them knew or cared about. What about *oop*? This wasn't semen. The *adameni* liquid was thick and viscous, but it smelled sweet and tasted good. It was something that a man would dab about his eyes, and when a woman looked at him, she would find him irresistible. *Adameni* was evidently some kind of love potion. White people knew all about *adameni*, they continued. In fact, they said, it came from whites and not from Papua New Guineans. Wayabay had heard about *adameni* from men who had been with white people at a logging camp in the southern part of the province. The potion came in a bottle and was quite expensive. But the whites reportedly said that it really worked to attract women. The bottles of *adameni* had a picture of a naked man and woman on the label—just as described in the Bible.

White people. Nakedness. Bible. Irresistible sexual attraction. Eureka! *Adameni* wasn't a Gebusi word after all; no wonder I hadn't known it. Their accent and intonation had completely thrown me off. It was a Western sexual idea. *Adameni* was "Adam and Eve." It was a love potion that unscrupulous traders to the south had peddled at inflated prices in bottles featuring pictures of biblical sex and lovely sin. Wayabay wanted *adameni* to attract a woman. As a quiet and hard-working but traditional young man, he felt that he needed a modern potion to gain a wife.

My companions persisted. Did I have any *adameni?* And if not, could I get any for them? Though I now understood their question, it still wasn't easy to answer. The three of them believed in this love magic, almost desperately in Wayabay's case. I had already deeply embarrassed both them and myself. I recalled the anthropological theory that holds magic to be an exercise in spiritual confidence boosting. The idea is that magic reduces uncertainty and instills faith in one's actions, like in baseball when a batter fingers a lucky charm as he steps up to the plate. For a moment, I debated enhancing Wayabay's confidence with women by giving him some of the scented cream I had brought for my skin rashes and telling him to dab some on his cheekbones. But I quickly dismissed this as a bad idea. I had already caused enough cultural confusion for one day. After all these years of knowing about the Gebusi, I thought, I was still challenged, surprised, and sometimes at sea. Learning culture is certainly a lifelong experience.

I showed them my skin cream, which they smelled carefully. I said that it wasn't really *adameni* but that they were still welcome to try some if they wanted to. As for real *adameni*, I said, I didn't know how to get it and thought it might be a waste of good money in any event. They declined my skin cream. Disappointed but at least in mutual comprehension, we finished our conversation, and the three of them departed.

I was left with much to think about. If Gebusi culture had been hard for me to learn in 1980, its changes were now chewing up all my seasoned understandings—with plenty of spit left over. Over the course of sixteen years, cohorts of young Gebusi men had gone from actively and proudly having sex with one another to apparently not even knowing about the practice. Could this really be? Maybe my young friends had suspected or been vaguely aware of the custom from their boyhood years. But if they hadn't been directly exposed to or told about it, their knowledge would have been hazy. Compare it with our own knowledge of sexual practices among those who preceded us—for instance, our often vague knowledge of the different types of private intimacy that our own parents may have had with each other, much less with other partners at earlier times in their lives. Like many peoples, the Gebusi distinguish carefully between things that are possible but unsubstantiated and those that they have either seen with their own eyes or heard with their own ears from a reliable witness. In this sense of knowing, Wayabay, Sayu, and Didiga had probably not known about sex between Gebusi men. Until I had told them.

Although some cultures have a strong and deep sense of their past, the historical concern of other peoples can be shallow and weak—and Gebusi are decidedly in the latter camp. Gebusi life cycles are short. As a forty-four-year-old, I was one of the oldest men in the community. The Gebusi have not revered, maintained, or recounted historical knowledge in a systematic way. In fact, many of them do not know the names of their own grandparents. It was not uncommon for me to know more about Gebusi family ancestries, based on the genealogies and life histories that I collected in 1980–82, than it was for younger and middle-aged Gebusi. In retrospect, the gap between my young companions' knowledge of traditional Gebusi sex practices and my own was not so surprising. In my conversation with Wayabay, Sayu, and Didiga, however, I had unwittingly bleached out the rich meanings and personal variations of Gebusi's same-sex practices. These came across to my young friends as a stark custom that was as out of context as it was distasteful.

Beyond the shock, the apparent unawareness, and the possible collusion of ignorance among my three companions, the fact remained that their desire to attract women was much more important than their concern with sexual behavior between men. That their fathers had inseminated teenage boys may have been offensive, but it didn't change Wayabay's need or desire to find a wife. In the past, insemination had itself been an asset for marriage; a young man who "became big" in his beautiful initiation costume attracted women by his very presence. Initiation had been a natural conduit to marriage; within a few months, all the initiates had been married. Ideally, a woman came to a new initiate of her own accord—or at least allowed herself to be claimed for him by his initiate sponsors. The months leading up to the initiation had provided both a special opportunity and a special mandate for sexual trysts among young men themselves. But now, with the demise of initiations, this custom was gone, along with much of men's collective camaraderie.

As I was finding out, the same was also true of women's obligations to marry through sister-exchange. Whereas more than half of women's first marriages had previously satisfied the demands of marital reciprocity, not one of the sixteen marriages in the community between 1982 and 1998 had been a sister-exchange. Although men still insisted rhetorically that their daughters and younger sisters would marry only if the groom supplied a "sister" in return, the practice was moribund in fact. Correspondingly, men could no longer count on obligations of kinship and reciprocity to obtain a wife—any more than they could count on the splendor of ritual attraction. Increasingly, young men were on their own and had to attract a wife through new and more modern forms of courtship.

Wayabay had not been successful in these pursuits. He was several years past the age of normal marriage and was increasingly concerned to find a wife. He was also among the small minority of young men who had not developed a keen interest in activities associated with life at the Nomad Station. He had not been baptized and did not go to church. He played soccer and rugby only intermittently and awkwardly, he would not dance to Papua New Guinea "disco music," and he did not sing in the community's contemporary string band. Instead, Wayabay honed his traditional skills and spent many days hunting in the forest and many hours building his house in the village. He was unusually devoted to indigenous dancing and was proud of his ability to travel to feasts and initiations in remote Gebusi villages and dance in traditional costume. In a sense, Wayabay was a good traditionalist born a generation too late. In this context, *adameni* had become a hopeful substitute for the allure of the male initiation costume that Wayabay would never wear.

By contrast, the young Gebusi men who were most successful in attracting girl-friends and brides were those who were, for lack of a better word, more modern. They could joke with some facility in English or *tok pisin*, had been to school for at least a few years, and were more comfortable with the lifestyle associated with the Nomad Station. They managed to finagle a little money, which they used to obtain a jaunty baseball cap, sunglasses, or a colorful shirt. Perhaps they even had a boom box on which they could play cassettes of rock music. They enjoyed play-ing rugby and soccer if not also dancing to disco music, and they appeared more at ease outside their own settlement. For Wayabay, however, being locally modern was difficult if not impossible. He could kill a wild boar in the forest but he could not shoot the modern breeze.

Even for bachelors who were relatively self-assured, modern courtship could be a stressful experience. On one occasion, Wayabay's two comrades worked up the courage to go to a disco dance on the far edge of the Nomad Station. (Wayabay himself was too reserved to go.) I decided to go with them to see what it was about. For them, it was an alluring adventure that held out the prospect of not just seeing marriageable women from another community but possibly dancing with them to disco music. This hoped-for attraction paralleled the modern romance that was sung about in cassettes and in the Gebusi's guitar-and-ukulele bands. The goal was to captivate a woman not by a display of traditional ritual but with modern confidence and aplomb—to talk to her directly and gyrate with her publicly in contemporary dance.

The risks of this endeavor fueled avoidance as well as desire. In fact, we never got to the disco. We approached it at night, stealthfully, as if stalking a wild animal. We crept slowly and noiselessly down the path, the boldest in the lead. Whispered discussion ensued every few yards as to whether we should go through with this chance for public display and humiliation. Flashlights were turned off so no one would know we were there. We strained to hear if there was any music in the distance. Eventually, however, we turned back, too nervous to proceed. During six months and despite several concerted attempts, I never did manage to attend a disco in a community on the far side of the Nomad Station.

The awkwardness of contemporary romance for young Gebusi men reflects not just new standards of courtship but also new material demands—for colorful clothes, sunglasses, shoes, and boom boxes with cassettes. Failing to obtain these, young men may crave a manufactured elixir with a naked man and woman on the bottle, a potion that, with just a magical splash about the eyes, can attract women. In many rural parts of the world, there is great demand for goods that convey a locally modern sense of sexual attraction. New commodities, clothes, cosmetics, and styles of using them frequently combine the allure of a modern way of life with emerging types of romantic desire. I remembered a story on National Public Radio about a Brazilian woman who canoed into the upper reaches of the Amazon and made quite a profit by selling Avon products like deodorant and makeup to Indians in the rainforest.

For young Gebusi men, the desire for modern commodities is further complicated by economic pressures to pay bride-price or bride-wealth. In the absence of
sister-exchange, the brothers or fathers of young women often say that they will be
satisfied only with a large cash payment from the would-be groom. In some parts
of the world—including regions of Africa and South Asia as well as the South
Pacific—inflated demands for bride-wealth or dowry cause major problems for
young people who want to get married. Fortunately for young Gebusi men, the
amount of money they actually pay in bride-wealth is quite low in comparative terms.
Of the first marriages in Gasumi Corners between 1982 and 1998, the average bride
payment was only 56 kina, or 28 dollars. Even this small amount, however, can be
difficult for many young men to amass. And the demands of a prospective father-
in-law or brother-in-law can easily fuel the groom's sense of inadequacy.

In all, Gebusi courtship is now sandwiched between a rhetorical mandate for
sister-exchange, inflated claims for bride-wealth, the desire for commodities, and
the demands of modern styles of social interaction. Bachelors in Gasumi Corners
often told me that they would never get married. So how do young men find wives?
In large part through the idiosyncrasies of romantic attraction. In the present as in
the past, a young woman and a man who are strongly attracted to each other may
get married despite the objections of her father or her brothers. If romantic marriage had previously been a "minority option," it had now become the principal,
if ever more stressful, way of getting married. Especially for a man, being locally
modern had become an important part of this mix.

To review then, courtship and marital practices in Gasumi Corners had, by
1998, been impacted by the decline of previous customs such as initiations, sister-
exchange, regular male dances, and other traditional displays of male splendor
that were considered to attract women. If young men now had a wider range of
potential female partners, including at school and the Nomad station as well as
other settlements and Gasumi Corners itself, this circumstance could also be
stressful, especially for men such as Wayabay. But what about women? How did
they perceive the new potentials and challenges of romance and of finding a mate?
In Gasumi Corners, these dynamics became poignant in the one attempt that was
made to resuscitate older marriage patterns and forge a sister-exchange—a paired
set of reciprocal marriages in which the "sister" of each prospective groom was
supposed to marry the "brother" of the groom's anticipated bride.

Guyul was a cheerful, strapping bachelor about twenty-one years old; his true
sister was the comely and straightforward Kubwam, a mature fifteen- or sixteen-
year-old ready for marriage. On the other side was Mako, a slight young man
about nineteen and his adopted "sister," the vivacious Gami, who was only sixteen
but full-bodied and, if anything, readier for marriage than her elder "brother."
Gami was to marry Guyul while her "brother," Mako, was to marry Guyul's true
sister, Kubwam.

After spicy rumors that spread throughout the village, the courtship of the
two young couples started off well enough. Following Gebusi custom, on the way

back from one of the markets, each young woman was "seized" by the wrist and led away by a male kinsman of her husband-to-be. Although the show of force conformed to the dictates of public display, neither woman resisted or tried to get away—which they could easily have done. Kubwam appeared forlorn, which is the proper etiquette for a woman taken in marriage. But Gami could hardly keep from smiling despite her presumed sobriety. The four new spouses were told to sit down together and exhorted to attend to their duties as husbands and wives. Much was made of the fact that the brother of Guyul's new wife was also the husband of Guyul's sister, and vice versa. It was not simply a double marriage but a linkage among the four of them. Everything was going according to plan.

The two women, Gami and Kubwam, proceeded to swap residences across the four-minute walk that separated their husbands' respective households in Gasumi Corners. Each extended family simultaneously gained a daughter-in-law while losing a daughter. The two mothers-in-law made special efforts to ensure that the incoming brides felt welcome and at home. I paid visits to both households and gave small gifts. With her typical pleasant reserve, Kubwam seemed comfortably ensconced in Mako's household. For her part, Gami was practically ebullient in Guyul's family house; she smiled broadly and engaged eagerly with Guyul's female kin.

The first crack in the arrangement appeared after only a day and a half. Mako started spending time away from his household and away from his new wife, going off with the remaining bachelors. Not yet twenty years old, Mako was still "young" to be a Gebusi husband. In sister-exchange marriages, the younger husbands sometimes took a while to settle fully into the new arrangement. In the present case, Mako's marriage was not yet consummated. But his new wife, Kubwam, continued in the interim to live with Mako's female kin. By themselves Mako's actions represented only a small wrinkle and not a major cause for concern. On the other side of Gasumi Corners, Gami's relationship with Guyul got off to a good start. She had been the village belle—friendly, easygoing, buxom, and with a bright, quick smile. In the preceding months, I had been surprised that the community had allowed her and some of the other young women to joke directly with eligible young men. Outside of ritual occasions, public joking between men and women had been strongly discouraged in 1980–82.

Within a few days, Gami and her new husband "went off together" to the gardens. When they came back with moony dispositions and euphoric smiles, village gossip was as ribald as it was irrepressible. Guyul and Gami had consummated their marriage, and everyone knew it. But this happiness did not last. Exactly what went wrong I never learned, least of all from Guyul or Gami themselves. But all signals pointed to an abrupt U-turn in their sexual compatibility. Gami's disposition turned suddenly from sweetness to sourness. She wouldn't look at her husband, wouldn't work in his household, and wouldn't eat. She tried to go back to her adopted mother's home but was forced back to her husband's house. She tried again and was again forced back. She refused to cooperate and returned yet again to her own family home. No entreaty made headway; no inquiry bore fruit. "Who knows what goes on in a young woman's heart or mind?!" "Gami is just stubborn and big-headed." "She just won't be married." "But why?" I would ask. "Just because," I was told repeatedly. "That's just the way she is."

As the hours passed, Gami's recalcitrance fueled increasing anger against her in the village. It is a very serious matter for a Gebusi woman to consummate her marriage and then to repudiate it. That a woman could have sex with a husband she had publicly accepted and then reject him after several days of romance struck at the heart of Gebusi morality. Not only was Gami's virtue on the line but also the manhood and self-esteem of her husband, Guyul. The stakes were also higher because the marriage was a sister-exchange. Gami's rejection of Guyul also compromised the union between her "brother," Mako, and Guyul's sister, Kubwam; if her marriage dissolved, her brother's would also be forfeited.

In short order, everyone in Gasumi Corners turned against Gami. Her new husband disdained her, and her mother-in-law was incensed. Her adopted mother was even more furious, as was Mako. Her "mother" slapped her, her "brother" beat her, and she endured a barrage of verbal abuse. "What is WRONG with you?!" "You good for nothing!" "Guyul is a fine man!" "You think you can 'open your skirt' to your husband and then just turn around and say you won't be married?! Huh? HUH?" "Don't you care about your 'brother'?" Don't you care about your 'mother'? No one in this village is going to protect you." "Where are you going to find a new husband? Do you think any man would want you now? Huh? HUH?" "You are alone, no one cares about you." "You can't stay here. You have no home here. Your life here is finished."

Gami never once explained and never argued back. But she wouldn't budge, wouldn't go back to Guyul's household. As the hours mounted into a second day, the tension worsened. Women from other households took up the banner of village honor. Senior women tore into Gami, badgering her in every way they could think of. Finally, Mako had had enough. He grabbed Gami and dragged her bodily out the door of his house. She shrieked and screamed, refusing to leave. Heavier and at least as strong as he, she held her ground. But as Mako grabbed one of her arms, his mother and another man took hold of the other. Gami was dragged screaming and crying, feet trailing and flailing. By the time they had hauled her fifteen feet from her house, she was covered in mud and bloody scrapes. Still she refused to cooperate. They pulled her by the hair, but she would not give in. Panting and screaming, they told her she could lie there and rot.

Then one of the senior women came over. She was a woman, here nameless, whom I otherwise liked and admired, but whom it has been hard to forgive. She silently walked up to Gami, leaned down, and talked to her in low tones. Watching from my doorstep, some forty feet away, I had a sinking feeling that I knew what she was saying, and my suspicion was soon verified. It was terrible to have seen Gami being hit and dragged. But it is almost unimaginable for a young woman to be threatened with a public stripping. For Gebusi, this idea is so deeply shameful as to be a kind of social death—never forgotten, never expunged. And it is triply so for a nubile young woman. It was true that Gami had badly misjudged the game and the stakes of her marriage. Her girlish, fancy, flirtatious behavior and mature body had led her to the four-sided vise of a sister-exchange. At first, she had complied willingly, even enthusiastically. But then she had come to realize that her actions were an appalling mistake that she would risk her reputation and even her life to repudiate. This new threat, however, made it too costly for her to resist any longer. A minute or two later, Gami calmly got up and walked life-lessly back to Guyul's household.

I assumed that would be the end of the story, that both unhappy marriages would remain intact. I was wrong. Over the next few days, Gami stayed in Guyul's household, but she would not respond or cooperate in any meaningful way. She remained defiant, a living dead person. In exasperation, her relatives took the mat-ter to a higher authority, the Nomad police. As chance would have it, I was in the police station studying the police register when they trooped in. The village men and a Nomad police officer sat Gami down in a chair, surrounded her, and began their inquisition. A uniformed constable took the lead: "Why won't you marry this man?" "Why did you have sex with him and then refuse him?" "Do you really want to reject your own family?" "What are you going to do if you don't stay married to Guyul?" "We can start charges to put you in jail for immoral conduct." I thought for sure that Gami would crack. Alone, she faced the most powerful men not just in the village but at the Nomad Station. But she refused, not just to comply but to speak. Her only words were "I don't know" and "I don't want to," as she hung her head and sobbed. Fortunately, the men did not touch or strike her. I don't know if my presence deterred them. But I was knotted up inside, frustrated at not being able to intervene. Ultimately, they gave up in des-peration and returned Gami to our settlement. A public meeting was then held in Gasumi Corners. Again the invective started as people debated what steps to take next. They also aired their opinions of women's morality in the village more generally—how shameless and loose young women had become.

I had never made a formal speech at a public Gebusi meeting; I had never felt that it was my place to do so. And my mastery of the Gebusi language was never good enough for me to wrap myself in their oratory. But this time I felt I had no choice. I knew I couldn't change Gebusi customs, alter Gami's predica-ment, or impose my will on theirs. Still, these were people I had lived with, and they were my friends. I thought what they were doing to Gami was very wrong. As I got up to speak, I started to tremble. It was like that first speech you make to your junior high school class, when you can't remember the words and you know your voice and your bearing betray that everything about you is awkward. But I had to continue. What I said, or at least what I tried to say, was that my Gebusi friends had to respect their own custom—the custom that no one can ulti-mately force a woman to be married. Even in the old days, I said, some women had refused to be married. No matter what anyone had done, and no matter even what the women themselves had done, they had simply refused. I alluded to some of the failed first marriages of the people sitting around me, including some of the older women who had berated Gami. They, too, I reminded them, ultimately had refused the men they had been pressured to stay with in marriage. The police, I said, respected the same custom, following the laws of Papua New Guinea. People could try to persuade a woman to marry, but they simply could not force her to do so. That was all.

I don't know if my words had any effect. I was too nervous to judge people's reactions or to recall things clearly afterwards. I wasn't saying anything revolution-ary but merely putting into words the reality that I hoped they would accept—and that they were grudgingly beginning to accept anyway. Then I did something else that I had never done before. After the meeting was over, I asked to talk with Gami. Alone. Of all the things I have intentionally done with the Gebusi before or since, this was the most awkward. An unrelated man simply does not talk with an unmarried woman alone—especially one like Gami, who bore the stigma of sexual immorality. In addition, Gami had been a flirtatious and endearing young woman. And anthropology is littered with tales of well-meaning white men who scheme to help attractive women of color, only to unwittingly leave them worse off in their own culture than they had been before. I had to be very clear about my motives.

My request, in fact, related to Gami's family situation. Gami's father had died, and her biological mother had remarried. She was now living outside of the town of Kiunga with her new husband; she was the only woman in the community to have left the Nomad area. Without money for another airfare, Gami had been left behind with her aunt. Now, however, Gami's true mother was the one person who might have cared enough to help her out. I knew Gami's mother from 1982 and thought she was a good person. Because Gami could not read or write, I thought she might like me to write a letter to her mother in Kiunga—to communicate with her and solicit help. This practice is not unusual in many parts of Papua New Guinea. For example, when I had previously visited male inmates at the national prison in Port Moresby, many of them had immediately accepted my offer to write letters on their behalf and to send them to their families back home. In some ways, I thought, Gami was now a prisoner in Gasumi Corners.

Apart from this, there was something else that I wanted to communicate. I wanted to tell Gami that I didn't think she was a bad or wicked person. Many young women struggle to find a man they can live with. I wanted to tell her that I thought she had courage to stand up for herself. I knew I was on cultural thin ice. I had no idea if these words would make sense or if they would backfire. But I had to try. And there was no way I could talk to her with other villagers intervening.

In the village clearing, I told Gami's adopted mother and the others gathered there that I needed to talk to Gami, alone. They looked at me, and I looked at them back. I told them not to worry, that I was only an "old man" and that we wouldn't be long. My excuse was that Gami had never shown me the abandoned spur settlement, just two hundred yards away, where her true mother had previously lived with her. (I also thought that this might be a good place for her to think of her mother and to tell me anything she wanted me to write in a letter.) I was touched that the villagers trusted me enough to let Gami go off with me. Gami herself had been through the wringer already, and who knows what she thought now. She had every reason to be scared of any new development, and she was, in culturally appropriate fashion, reluctant to go with me. To my distress, her relatives now ordered her to accompany me to her mother's old settlement. As I walked slowly out of our hamlet, Gami trailed a good fifteen feet behind. My first thought was to wait for her and say something innocuous. But when I slowed, so did she. It got worse when a twelve-year-old boy crossed paths with us. Gami and I were the spitting image of a married couple—adult man up front and younger wife coming behind. The boy was incredulous. I mumbled that Gami was going to show me her mother's house and that her "mother" had said it was okay. As we neared the site, a second boy, fourteen, appeared. I repeated the story. But he was too captivated by the remarkable sight of Gami with me to be easily deterred. Even as I told him to move along, I could see him scurry away only to hide and watch from the bushes.

My conversation with Gami took place close to the main path and was very short. We stood about a dozen feet apart—as close as we ever got. Both of us looked at the ground or anywhere except at each other. I said that I was sorry for her. I said that I thought she was not a bad person, but a person who had much inside that was good. I said, without repeating the obvious, that I knew she had "worries." Then I said that I had known her mother and that I had been told that she was now living near Kiunga. And I asked her if she wanted me to write a letter to her mother to see if there was any way she or other members of her family could help. Nervously, Gami said simply, "No." I continued, "Is there anything else you would like to say? Is there anything that you would like to talk about or that I might do?" She replied again, "No." I responded, "That's fine. I just wanted to ask. We'll leave it go." Then we walked directly back to the village. Gami took the lead, walking much faster than she had before.

🌿   🌿   🌿

I will never know if my awkward attempt to help Gami was an abject failure or merely a nominal one. Perhaps the thought of her mother finding out about Gami's predicament only added salt to her wounds. Perhaps the idea of telling one's long-lost mother about one's indiscretions wasn't that appealing. Perhaps I was guilty of cultural insensitivity or of taking license with Gebusi rules of gendered interaction. I could not know and could hope only that some part of Gami sensed, amid my ineptitude, that I was trying to help rather than hurt her. I know that the best intentions can sometimes have the worst results. But I felt I should try.

What conclusions can we draw? On a personal level, my experiences, both with Wayabay and Gami, led me into the uncertain territory of trying to connect my own cultural understanding of the Gebusi with an active desire to help some of them with their problems. In addition to being researchers, anthropologists in the field are also people, and we sometimes feel compelled to act on behalf of those in our community. But we can't know the consequences of our actions or even if our good intentions will be recognized. It seems as important as it is difficult to balance our positive intent against our awareness of its unpredictable result. The interventions of Westerners among foreign peoples often have led to unfortunate consequences even when the intent was noble. This pattern continues to the present; some of the largest and most expensive international aid projects in Africa, Asia, Latin America, and the Pacific create little long-term benefit and sometimes do greater harm than good to local people. To correct for this possibility, a sense of humility and an awareness of our own limitations—as searchers, as advocates, and as human beings—is called for.

In topical terms, Gami's case and that of Wayabay illustrate the challenges of finding a marriage partner in a world of greater choices and also greater risks. In many parts of the world, increasing personal options, including for women, are noted as a modern phenomenon. Correspondingly, in a number of world areas, the idea of "marriage by choice" is gaining emphasis vis-à-vis or alongside marriage by arrangement or kinship. Gami's plight and Wayabay's illustrate a similar pattern in Gasumi Corners. By engaging these challenging conditions, marriages build on the spine of determination, physical attraction, and romance that women and men have long if not always had—and also ratchet up the stakes of choosing from among greater numbers of potential partners. Who can say if women or men lead happier lives as a result? But in a modern world of increasing alternatives, the lives of many young men and women are increasingly shaped by the intended or unintended consequences of their own actions rather than those of the elder members of their families and communities.

Amid the clash of choice and constraint, some predicaments work out better than one might have guessed. This was ultimately the case for Gami and also for Wayabay. Despite their respective trials, each of them ended up finding an acceptable spouse after I left the field. In each case, their partner carried a history of difficult choices that complemented their own. And in each case, their partner had been living in the house next door. In December 2001, I received the following in a letter written on behalf of Sayu from Gasumi Corners: "Wayabay got married already to Gami. And ready to deliver baby."

Long live their lives together. Long live their resilience.

A man and woman in semi-traditional costumes introducing their village dances on Independence Day. (Note: The T-shirt of the man standing in the middle reads, "Compulsive, Antisocial, Manic Depressive, Paranoid, but Basically Happy.") (PHOTO: Bruce Knauft)

Sayu's Dance and After

SAYU SIDLED AHEAD OF me, down the trail and into the dawn. Daybreak bathed us in its softest light as we returned from our all-night ceremony. The previous evening, in a rare expression of a fading custom, Sayu had been the visiting dancer at the village of Kotiey-masam. In the traditional costume, painted and plumed, he had enacted the spirits of old in their full splendor to the beat of his crocodile-skin drum. His jaw had been as firm as the pearl shell just beneath it, his eyes as bright as the red bird of paradise he had become. With a magnetic aura, he had been wonderfully transformed.

As we walked back to Gasumi Corners, I remembered Sayu from sixteen years before, when he had been five years old. His impish smile had lit his face like sunlight streaming through a break in the forest canopy. His play had been as full of Gebusi tradition as it could be. He would wrap his small body in leaves, smear soot on his face, and put a feather in his hair. With supreme whimsy, he would take a length of bamboo as a make-believe drum and dance resplendently at an imaginary feast. He would lisp a fetching echo to the men's songs at night. Or pretend to marry a little girl in sister-exchange. Or cook some sago to divine and accuse a make-believe sorcerer. More than any other child, Sayu had been in our house and in our lives at Yibihilu. Women had said that Eileen was his *wi-helof*, his "side-mother." Now, this dancer of childhood returned home with me at a new dawn in this rainforest of memories.

Since we had left in 1982, Sayu's life had not been at all as I had thought it would have been. In 1985, his young father, Silap, had died. Sayu's mother, the fun-loving Boyl, had perished suddenly just two years after that. Recently remarried, she had been foraging for sago grubs deep in the forest with Sayu and his younger brother, Huwa. Far from the settlement, and before they could return, she had fallen suddenly and fatally ill. The two boys had cried and clutched at their mother as she writhed in agony in the forest at night. A search party later found them and carried Boyl's body back to the village. Sayu was eleven or twelve years old, Huwa was about five. Sayu's new father-in-law, Doliay, was enraged by the death and pursued the sorcery inquest for Boyl with great intensity. Shortly afterward, as previously described, Doliay avenged her death by killing Sabowey and beheading him.

When Doliay departed to serve his six-year term in prison, Sayu and Huwa were left behind at Gasumi Corners. Five years later, following a dispute in the village, Sayu decided to leave the community and embark on a young man's adventure. At age seventeen, he and a friend walked eighty miles to the town of Kiunga—through lands he had never seen and groups he had never encountered before. Kiunga was the district capital of three thousand people, a muddy gateway to the modern world and emerald city to those in the forest for hundreds of miles around. Quick and smart, Sayu finagled work in Kiunga as a domestic helper and "houseboy." He lived the life of a successful teenager in town: washing dishes, doing laundry, running errands—and learning to live in his employer's house, ride a bike, watch satellite TV, and dance disco. Two years later, he returned home to the outskirts of Nomad, where his treasured boom box broadcast music to everyone's delight. He had become a dandy, but he remained thoughtful and worked hard.

When I came back to the Gebusi, two years after his own return, Sayu quickly became my companion, helper, and confidant, along with Didiga, who was a good friend to both of us. I helped support them, and we shared many good times. On one occasion, Sayu delicately withdrew from a budding relationship with a flirtatious young woman in a neighboring hamlet. Although things had not turned serious or physical, the woman's father and brother suspected otherwise. The next day, while Sayu and I were doing chores, her male relatives charged out of nowhere, brandishing their bows and arrows. Sayu and I stood side by side as we turned to face them. I told myself to remain appropriately passive but defiant. Livid, the young woman's brother came at us in a dead run. As he closed to about twenty feet, he cocked his bow, drew back his arrow, and snapped his bowstring at us. Then he veered away. I knew well enough from my days at Yibihilu that this was merely a display of aggression, and I bore him no anger. We all laughed about it days later. But my spine had stiffened at the time. At a public meeting, the village councilor concluded that the woman's brother and father had been wrong to intimidate us; they had to pay a fine to Sayu for falsely accusing him of impropriety.

My many memories of Sayu linked back to the present as I walked back with him from his all-night dance at Kotiey-masam. He had danced until dawn for the first time, not to disco, as he had before, but in stately traditional costume. He had become an impressive and handsome young man, both in an indigenous and a modern sense. As his friend and part-parent, I felt a surge of pride in and affection for him. I thought how deeply pleased Sayu's true parents and his side-mother, Eileen, would have been to see him now. I told him what I felt: my eyes had seen his traditional dancing with the happy heart-spirit of his dead father, his dead mother, and his side-mother back in the United States. Suddenly, my eyes got misty. His lip quivered. I turned away so as not to cry.

The drama of the night receded slowly with the dark. Dawn approached as the trail took us back to Gasumi Corners, where traditional dancing is all but dead. We finally walked by the Nomad Station, winding our way past its airstrip. The light was growing brighter. I could now see that Sayu's pearl shell was crooked, his feathers skewed, and his red-ocher paint smudged on his taut skin.

Even on Saturday morning, he was concerned that someone from Nomad might see him in the grass skirts of a traditional dancer. Although he had been the center of ceremonial attention all night long, this had occurred in an old forest village. Slipping behind a shrub, Sayu exchanged his skirts for a pair of shorts. Now hybrid, he left the signs of his dancing above his waist but kept the security of Western clothes below. Around his neck, he now hung the blue beads and cross from his Catholic baptism.

As Sayu had anticipated, we met others along the way. We snapped fingers firmly with them before continuing on and finally reaching Gasumi Corners. There we were greeted by those who had not made the trek—which was most of the village. They asked whether they could hear the tape recordings I had made the previous night. As the cassette played, we listened to the men's joking, Sayu's drumming and dance rattles, and the women's traditional singing. But there were other sounds that I had barely heard amid my focus on Sayu: the guitar and ukulele of the evening's string band, and the rock 'n' roll of a Papua New Guinean band that one of the visitors played on a boom box. The clash of musical styles had mirrored the mix of celebrants in that old longhouse. Some had adorned themselves in leaves, body paint, and beautiful bird feathers. Others had sported a colorful shirt or hat, or even worn sunglasses in the night. Still others had mixed and matched cheerfully—a collage of body paint here, Western clothing there, a headdress on a hat. They had drifted through shadows thrown alternately by traditional resin torches and modern wick lanterns. All of them had paused appreciatively and even gratefully to pose for my flashing camera—as if the prize of my modern photography would validate their hybrid tradition.

In Gasumi Corners, the men listened to my tape recording and talked of getting dressed up themselves in traditional costumes—but not for a traditional ritual. Instead, they wondered if they could scrape together enough decorations to perform in traditional costume for the government-sponsored contest that was going to be held at the Nomad Station on Independence Day. Competing communities would stage reenactments of their indigenous dances. Officials would judge the performances and award a pittance of prize money to those whom they thought were best. The men of Gasumi Corners wanted to have at least some chance to be among the winners. They mused that maybe they would dress up Wayabay or one of their other bachelors in the full regalia of initiation—even though none of these men had been initiated nor ever would be.

Listening to the tape recording and then to the men, I felt I was in a time warp between the past and the present. This was partly from a lack of sleep. All-night feasts invariably give me vertigo the day after—as they seem to do for most Gebusi. By traditional design, staying up all night mixes things up and turns them back to front; the spirits of the dark meld with the humans of the day; the performance of the present enacts the cosmos of the past. But now the spirits had not just vanished with the morning mist; they seemed to be gone forever from Gasumi Corners. It was now midday on Saturday. Only a few men from our village had gone to the feast; most of the men and boys were now preparing to leave for the ballgames at Nomad. Tomorrow, we would sing praises to God in the hot Sunday sun. Then there would be more rugby and soccer. When the men returned from the ball field on Sunday evening, their children would be going to bed—so they could get up and be off first thing Monday morning for a full day of school. As I drifted to sleep, I wondered if my memory of Sayu's dance was already fading. I realized that I was now immersed in the changing of Gebusi culture itself, beyond specific new activities or values or forces derived from afar. I was confronting new meanings and subjective emphases created by Gebusi themselves in both their daily self-expressions and shared ceremonial life.

The following day, my schedule got back to normal. But I didn't know what to expect over the next few weeks. Independence Day was coming up, and ceremonial life would be taking another turn. Would the festivities be traditional, modern, or somewhere in between? Everything now seemed geared to this next celebration. This was true even at Yulabi, a remote Gebusi settlement where a large initiation was being held. The arrangements were timed so that their ceremonies would take place just one week before the national holiday. This would allow the new initiates at distant villages to get dressed up again and parade in full regalia before officials at the Nomad Station.

In Gasumi Corners, preparations for Independence Day also intensified. Young men talked excitedly about their local genre of so-called string band singing. I became curious. A quartet of young men from Gasumi Corners had formed a singing group that featured two guitars and a medley of original songs. The leader was Damya, Nolop's son, and one of the singers was Huwa, Sayu's brother. I went one night to hear them perform. And I was blown away. The songs were as stunning and soulful as those of the young boys I had heard earlier singing up in the tree. And their tone was even crisper. The music soared with rich melodies, undulating rhythms, and resonating harmonies. Hard as it was for me to admit it, their new genre was more beautiful than the séance singing of old. How to describe it? The songs were both indigenous and original. They drew important threads from séance singing, including haunting nasal tones, falsetto harmonies, and surging refrains. But their quickened tempo, lighter lilt, and instrumental accompaniment rang clearly modern. The lyrics of the songs borrowed variously from Gebusi, English, *tok pisin*, the vernaculars of neighboring ethnic groups, and even phrases that had somehow been transmitted from distant New Guinean languages that very few Gebusi could translate. As in séance singing, the songs compressed poetic images that were evocative, longing, and nostalgic; they were short on content but lovingly repeated. Most of them involved contemporary contexts such as school, work, and romance. The following song was especially popular:

I go to school.
I look at my friend from before.
She looks at me and I look at her.
Her eyes fill with tears.
Why did you come to tease me?

Unlike séance singing, which had been spontaneous, string band songs were carefully rehearsed. When the people of Gasumi Corners gathered late in the evening to hear their singers, they were not communing with the spirits but listening to a musical performance. Men in the audience did not chime in with their own singing. There was no spirit medium, no dialogue with spirit women, and no divination for sickness or sorcery. Although some senior men might call out in emotional response, this was the exception rather than the rule. The audience was attentive and respectful, not ribald or raucous.

In a way, string band music had the same relation to séance songs that black American jazz had to the Negro spirituals and folk songs that preceded them. In both cases, a deep cultural tradition of singing gave rise to a modern form of music that was strongly instrumental, had a quicker pace and livelier tone, and carried a more nuanced and playful sense of rhythm. In both cases, the new music spoke to current social conditions in ways that were powerfully evocative and soulful but without being directly religious or spiritual. In the United States, my favorite music has long been jazz. In Gasumi Corners, it was clearly string band singing. To be able to hear how Gebusi music had evolved was a wonderful and unexpected pleasure.

But what about the costuming the men of Gasumi Corners had talked about? As Independence Day loomed closer, they scurried to locate or trade for items of traditional costuming. How would they use them? Judging from their winks, nods, and smiles, it almost seemed as if each man had his own plan. As I slowly came to realize, there was going to be more to Independence Day planning than either the rehearsal of songs or the presentation of dances. Sports practices also increased based on talk of fierce competition on the ball field. So, too, there was talk of other contests and displays, including disco dancing, "dramas," and a host of humorous as well as serious games.

If initiations had previously been the biggest and grandest spectacles of Gebusi culture, the celebrations of National Independence Day had since been geared to supplant them. But the festivities at the Nomad Station would include more people than the Gebusi. Certainly, Gebusi dancing, athleticism, music, and who knew what else would be on display. But so would those of other ethnic groups that ringed the Nomad Station: Bedamini, Kubor, Samo, Oybae, Honibo, and even distant peoples such as the Pa and the Kabasi. Nomad is the administrative center for a subdistrict that includes some nine thousand people scattered across 3,500 square miles of rainforest. During the week prior to Independence Day, visitors and families from many settlements within several days' walk arrived and stayed in the "corner" of Nomad to which they were most closely affiliated. Gebusi culture was going to be presented as part of an interethnic and even regional festival that was linked, in turn, to celebrations of the independence of the nation as a whole held each year on September 16.

State employees at Nomad took a special role in organizing and planning the events—and finding government funds to pay for materials, organization, and prize money. Given the disgruntled perception that many in the Nomad area have of government programs, which often underpay or fail to pay local workers, the thousands of kina obtained by the Nomad officials to host the Independence Day festivities were important both as a message of local governmental support and as a kind of insurance against rebellion against the government, especially by those from larger ethnic groups in the area, such as the Bedamini and Samo.

As part of this mix, Gebusi culture has become enmeshed with the activities and institutions of the Nomad Sub-District, its various ethnic groups, and the national and provincial governments, which control the schools, police, and local administration. In the realm of religion, the Gebusi were now identified with Christian denominations that spanned their area, their country, and, indeed, the globe. On Independence Day, Gebusi culture would be laced with symbols that connected them with other ethnic groups, the Nomad Station, the country of Papua New Guinea, and various forms of Christianity. I realized that my conception of Gebusi culture was expanding to include a much broader range of identifications, meanings, and institutions. Anthropologists often look to rituals of display and tradition as key expressions of a culture's values and history. But as cultures interconnect, their associations increase, and the lines that distinguish them blur. Meanings, identities, and values cut across local boundaries and become regional, national, and even international in scale.

Independence Day at Nomad ended up featuring almost a week of festivities and celebrations. More than a thousand people attended. The ceremonies began with two days of team sports on the Nomad ball field. These competitions escalated through several rounds and climaxed with all-star games that pitted the best players from different ethnic groups against each other. For the Gebusi, their key matches were against the Bedamini. Of course, the Bedamini had raided and sometimes decimated Gebusi villages in the past. Numerically, the Bedamini population remained seven or eight times larger than that of the Gebusi, and they retained a reputation for aggressiveness. But the Gebusi had important advantages. Whereas most Bedamini settlements were distant from Nomad, the people of Gasumi Corners and neighboring communities lived in close proximity to the government ballfield. It was difficult for the Bedamini to hone their athletic skills without regular practice and league competition. And Bedamini fighting tactics didn't work as well on the playing field. The matches were closely and vigorously officiated by government referees. And the Gebusi—especially those from Gasumi Corners itself—also had a home field advantage; the matches were played on the same pitch, with the same referees, and with much of the same crowd that they encountered every weekend.

At the end of the competition, the headline could have read, "David beats Goliath!" In an amazing coup, the Gebusi won all except one of their matches against the Bedamini. Their defeated rivals were so frustrated and angry that they accused the Gebusi of using magic to sabotage them. But government officials upheld the Gebusi victories. What was the Gebusi response? From an American perspective, I expected a big celebration and at least a little gloating. But Gebusi were subdued and circumspect. They worried that their Bedamini adversaries might take revenge by breaking into the little store that we had started in Gasumi

Corners or even that they would break into and loot my house while I was attending festivities at Nomad. This lack of boastful or gleeful behavior fit with Gebusi reactions after their victories during the regular season; they remained even-keeled and sportsmanlike.

On the eve of Independence Day, the festivities switched gears, and I struggled to keep up. There was excited talk of "dramas." But I had little idea what this meant. As dusk turned into night, a large performance area was roped off next to the government station. Gradually, hundreds of people amassed to watch the performances. When they started, what a shock! The bulk of the dramas were spoofs, farces, and parodies of local traditions. These were acted out by villagers themselves dressed in elaborate indigenous costumes. In one skit, for instance, a man in black paint, wearing a cassowary headdress and an old loincloth, groaned buffoonishly as he tried with clumsy and exaggerated effort to hack down a tiny tree using a traditional stone ax. After every few swings, the stone would fall from the ax handle and the man would stumble and grunt stupidly while looking for it in the grass. Then he would try to sharpen his ax with a traditional grinding stone, while cursing in the coarsest traditional manner. His slapstick antics and rudeness were really quite funny, and the audience laughed loudly. Meanwhile, the man's sardonic companion smoked a traditional pipe and refused to help cut the tree until they almost got into a fight. Again, the audience erupted in laughter. At the end of the skit, the performers explained its "meaning" to the audience in *tok pisin* over a battery-operated bullhorn: "In the old days, we were ignorant. We didn't know about steel axes, and we tried to chop down trees using stone axes. This didn't work, and we got angry and fought with each other."

In skit after skit, one or another traditional practice or belief was skewered to the audience's delight. Many of the customs were ones that I had seen practiced quite genuinely back in 1980–82. Rites that had once been performed with dignity and grace—including magic spells, origin myths, fish poisoning rituals, spirit séances, divinations, and dances—were turned into farce. What bittersweet comedy! As an anthropologist, it was sad to see such a mockery of rich local traditions—and by the very people who used to practice them. And yet, the skits *were* very funny, sometimes uproariously so. I fought back tears of laughter even as I felt pangs of nostalgia for customs that I had seen very much "for real" sixteen years before.

For me, the most dramatic skit was performed by some of my friends from Gasumi Corners. It was a spoof of sickness, death, and sorcery divination. The opening performer was Mora—the teenager who had sought to be my romantic partner in 1981 and who was now a senior man with several children. He was caked with mud and wore a large fake phallus strapped around his waist. Smoking continually from a traditional tobacco pipe, he wheezed and coughed in exaggerated fashion until, in a spasm of sickness, he toppled over with a loud thud. This attracted the attention of a spirit medium, played by Damya, the son of Nolop. Damya's costume was absurdly traditional, including an upside-down cassowary headdress and a bark belt that was so oversized that it slid down whenever he got up. Mora proceeded to cry that he was going to die. This prompted Damya to lean over him and screech directly into his ear. This parodied the traditional Gebusi custom of yelling to keep a person's spirit from leaving his body when he or she was near death. Damya's efforts were ineffectual, and Mora rapidly "died." After energetic but farcical wailing, a sorcery suspect was paraded up to Mora's corpse. The suspect was Kawuk, a senior man of Gasumi Corners and staunch supporter of the Catholic Church. (During the early years of colonial influence, Kawuk had, in fact, killed a family of three—a husband and wife accused of sorcery plus their son.) In the skit, Kawuk was brilliantly made up with black paint, white body markings, leaf strips, and feathers. Now it was his turn to be the "victim." He was forced to wail over Mora's corpse in an attempt to prove his innocence. As he did so, the corpse gave a dramatic "sign." A fishing line that had been tied to the tip of Mata's fake phallus was surreptitiously pulled. As the corpse dramatically arched its back and moaned, this large organ raised up suddenly as a monumental erection. Audience members could scarcely contain themselves in laughter. Needless to say, the corpse had indicated that Kawuk was "guilty"—the sorcerer responsible.

Now judged to be guilty, Kawuk was taken by Damya and farcically interrogated by him and by the kin of the dead man. Kawuk cried like a baby as they hit him. He initially denied but finally admitted that he had killed Mora with sorcery. His captors then untied him and beat him until he fell down. Then Bulobey—who is Mora's real-life cousin and a former spirit medium who was himself implicated in sorcery killings—took up a large piece of wood. Winding up with histrionic ferocity, he finished Kawuk off with a great wallop (striking the ground right next to where he lay). With Kawuk now "dead," his kin in the skit became incensed and took up their bows and arrows. With great buffoonery, the two sides squared off for a mock bow-and-arrow fight—until they all ran off. That was the end of the skit. To conclude the act, however, the performers now distanced themselves even more clearly from the roles they had been playing. They marched solemnly back into the performance area, lined up in a neat row, and stood at attention in front of the judges. Formally and soberly, they bowed in unison to each side of the audience that encircled them—to the left, to the right, to the rear, and to the front. Finally, with military precision, they marched out, to the cheers of the crowd.

What was I to think? On the one hand, the richness of Gebusi spirit beliefs, the poetry and aesthetics of their spirit mediumship, their cosmology, and even their concern for the sick and dying had been turned, as it were, into mincemeat. On the other hand, the skit represented a stinging critique of the sorcery beliefs, inquests, and fights that had killed many Gebusi in the past. That persons such as Kawuk and Bulobey could play lead characters in this mocking retort—having themselves participated in sorcery violence in years gone by—underscored this rejection. The skit was funny, smart, and very well performed. It left me with much to ponder.

In all, over two nights, a total of forty-two dramas were performed. The majority, like the one just described, were spoofs of tradition. But these were thrown into relief by the remaining acts. Some of these were Christian morality plays, with large posters upon which verses from the Bible were written. Others were skits of first contact. In these, local villagers were portrayed as stupid, violent, and clumsy until they were shown the fruits of modern civilization—peace, trade goods, and store-bought food—by benevolent Australian patrol officers (played by villagers). It was hard to watch these acts without thinking that a core insight of anthropology—that indigenous ways of life should be respected—was here being turned upside down by local people themselves. Certainly, there were features of Gebusi tradition that I was glad to see disappear. But much of beauty had been lost in the bargain. And the new inequalities that Gebusi were now experiencing—in church, in school, and at the market—were not always preferable to the social relations they replaced.

The final skits, though few in number, suggested a more sensitive view across these extremes. These enacted some of the traumas and foibles of trying to live a modern life. The skits portrayed the problems of trying to earn a living in Kiunga, of scrounging medicine for a sick child from a pompous official, and of coping with children who drift into trouble after school. In one poignant little play, an impoverished city youth stole and ran off with a suitcase full of money. When the owner in the skit returned, he pulled out a gun, and shot dead the two security guards he had employed to guard his wealth. Here, the hungry boy had turned into a criminal, but even worse, the powerful boss had become a murderer. Obviously, modern life was not all that it was cracked up to be. Indeed, the skit echoed the life of the provincial premier, who had recently been charged with attempted murder. Despite the seriousness of such themes, the skits maintained a humorous tone. In this way, they promoted a sense of alternative outcomes and different scenarios rather than foregone conclusions.

Taken together, the dramas were so rich and varied that I could probably write a whole book about them. But even so, they represented only one slice of the larger festivities surrounding Independence Day—and these continued day and night for several more days! The remaining events supplied yet more missing pieces to the puzzle of contemporary culture in and around Nomad. It was all coming together in my awareness, but only gradually.

Although local traditions had been lampooned at night, they were honored the following day. Troops of performers in gorgeous, meticulously arrayed costumes danced in full customary fashion. The throngs of people who watched the performances were even larger than they had been at the evening "dramas"—more than a thousand strong. A wide range of ethnic groups displayed their dance and initiation rites: Bedamini, Kubor, Samo, and even the Pa from across the Strickland River. Their costumes were spectacular, a photographer's dream. Gasumi Corners was represented by Halowa, Yuway's brother and an Evangelical Christian, who drum-danced in stately costume accompanied by a traditionally dressed Gebusi woman from another settlement. But the performance that stole the heart of the audience—and of the judges—was by a group of dancers from the distant Kabasi peoples, who lived three days' hard walk southeast of Nomad. Dancing in a slow and dignified manner while singing haunting songs, they performed both sitting and standing for over half an hour. Many in the audience were visibly enthralled and appeared to never have seen their style of performance.

I couldn't help but think that Independence Day was expanding on traditional practices at the same time that it transformed them. Rather than being performed at night in the darkened longhouse for kin and friends, rituals were now re-enacted on the official grounds of the Nomad Station for a thousand strangers in the harsh light of day. Even a member of the national parliament was present. The instrumental purpose of the performances was not to initiate a young man, cure a sick person, celebrate a local accomplishment, or reenact the spirits. Rather, it was to celebrate the nation of Papua New Guinea and to provide a secular display of body art and dancing. This was underscored by the rating and judging of the performances by officials, who both enjoyed the proceedings and grumbled about the extra hours of work that it took to organize and orchestrate them. As the men of Gasumi Corners had emphasized, the small amount of prize money given to winning performers was a major motivation for many participants. Some villages dressed up practically anyone they could, including young boys, regardless of whether the person was qualified to wear the costume. For many and perhaps most of the performers, the displays did not reflect current practices, beliefs, or rituals in their own villages. Indigenous culture was increasingly re-enacted as historical folklore for regional and even national consumption.

If the Independence Day festivities alternately spoofed and then celebrated traditional dances as a kind of secular folklore, they also played with features of contemporary life. Toward the end of the week, a range of additional contests was held. These included such playful competitions as drinking quantities of hot tea, pillow fighting while sitting on a beam, having blindfolded women try to split papayas with bush knives, and climbing a greased pole. The atmosphere was similar to that of a country fair. Hundreds of people milled about. Scattered along the walkways were stalls of blaring boom boxes where villagers sold cooked food. Tables of ring toss and even rudimentary gambling were set up for those willing to risk 5 or 10 cents in a game of skill or chance. In the afternoon, an avidly attended "disco contest" was held. The dance ground was thronged with bodies gyrating to the throb of Papua New Guinea rock music broadcast over speakers. Although a few brave women were there, including mothers dancing with their daughters, the dance ground was dominated by the older boys. The dancing appeared to be entirely same-sex: guys with guys, and girls with girls. The dancers' outfits presented a mélange of styles ranging from spiffy modern shirts and jeans to hip-hop clothes or traditional costumes. Some young men dressed up and danced buffoonishly as women.

What sense could be made of this hodgepodge? If local traditions were parodied, the same was also true, at least somewhat, of modern customs. Ultimately, the festivities were a smorgasbord in which diverse cultural practices—traditional and modern, nearby and distant—were put on display for performance, reflection, and playful combination. The audience of these displays was at one level the few government officers, who seemed to enjoy them thoroughly. But more prominently and powerfully, they were performed for the large crowds of local people themselves.

Within this potpourri, traditional customs were being strongly if not radically transformed. Although local traditions were the centerpiece for much of the action, their display was either divorced from traditional meanings or explicitly debunked. At the same time, what we might call rites and rituals of being modern were also portrayed in fragmented, satiric, and playful ways. If rituals reflect and symbolize the structure of people's social life, as Émile Durkheim long ago suggested, then the Independence Day celebrations reflected the fact that life in and around the Nomad Station had become diverse, multifaceted, and fractured across lines of tradition and modernity and between local affiliations and regional or national identities. For the people of Gasumi Corners, the festivities of Independence Day symbolized the challenge of new alternatives in their locally modern lifestyle. Gebusi themselves have willingly engaged this new lifestyle when they moved from the deep rainforest to the edge of the Nomad Station. In reciprocal fashion, the multifaceted culture that was expressed in the Independence Day festivities had become a principal part of their own lives as well.

In the aftermath of Independence Day, the Nomad area seemed to relax. Having worked and played so hard, people unwound in a kind of collective morning after. A few settlements held subsidiary feasts and celebrations, like a series of happy aftershocks following a marvelous large quake. In Gasumi Corners, the period of respite lasted several weeks before gradually giving way to planning for another festivity. This next occasion would be especially poignant for me—the feast to commemorate my own departure. As my time to leave inched gradually closer, my days became increasingly bittersweet. My friendships had been so deeply rekindled, and new ones had taken root. How could I go?

It ended up being an incredible finale, and I can't claim to be the only reason for its success. Village celebrations have always served multiple purposes. And the Gebusi are the first to keep anyone from getting a big head. But it was hard not to cry when I first heard the song that the Gasumi string band composed to thank me for having come back to them.

With their typical casual gusto, the village started to buzz with preparations. Firewood and cooking leaves were stockpiled, sago was processed, and game was hunted deep in the forest. As a contemporary twist, profits were pooled from our local store to buy a large stock of tinned fish and rice. Added to these were my own gifts to the community, both to individuals and for our collective feast. The latter included additional cartons of store-bought food and a score of coveted shotgun cartridges, which Wayabay and the other young men used to hunt a stunning array of wild pigs and cassowaries.

During the numerous weeks of preparation, everyone was so busy gathering food and materials in the forest that I started to feel lonely in the village. I longed to be with them in their timbered hideaways, and I was nostalgic for the rainforest. So Sayu, Didiga, and I set off to visit those from my immediate hamlet in their makeshift forest camp at Harfolobi. On the way, we traveled the Kum River, under the stately canopy of the towering trees that lined the banks. We climbed up the bluff at Yibihilu. My lip quivered to see our former village and even the site of my first house with Eileen. It was all overgrown, not just with weeds but with good-sized trees turning into forest. Gone as well were so many of my friends from the early 1980s, reclaimed by nature in graves that dotted the former settlement. Up at Harfolobi, I visited the grave of Sayu's wondrous mother, Boyl, and it was hard not to weep. I sat in the crystal waters of the little waterfall where I had bathed. And I enjoyed for the last time the easy rhythm of rainforest living—husbands, wives, and children relaxed and peaceful, and I at home among them.

After several days, obligations drew us reluctantly back to Gasumi Corners, where the buildup for the celebration continued. Although I knew the general contours of the event to come, both from planning and from precedent, what my friends were devising by way of entertainment remained a mystery. I sensed that it would be a vintage Gebusi mix of joy, sadness, and bittersweet remembrance of the past.

On the day of reckoning, visitors came from near and far—all of those still living whom I had known so well, many others whom I had seen occasionally, and a few who knew of me only by reputation. For several days ahead of time, the piles of coconuts, a ton or more of sago starch, mounds of dried game, and stashes of rice and fish spawned a veritable village industry of cutting, cleaning, wrapping, and cooking. Now it was time to pull it all from the cooking fires, divide it up, and give it away. Hundreds of visitors had come. Amid our shouts of laughter and whoops of celebration, the gift giving continued long after dusk turned into night. I was no longer a bystander but a primary host, and I tried to make sure that my friends and acquaintances, the government officials, and even the hangers-on each got an appropriate share.

Then came the entertainment. Would this be a traditional dance, linked to my widely known appreciation of historical customs? Or would it be modern? Instead of choosing a single course of action, my friends had opted, as it were, to let all the flowers bloom. On one side of my hamlet, in the dim light of a darkened house, a visiting performer danced in the full dignity of traditional costuming. Older men and women were especially drawn to this proud display of days gone by. Mothers held their smallest children, some of whom were possibly seeing a fully traditional Gebusi dance for the first time. From the other side of the village came the strains of a visiting string band, replete with guitar and ukulele, playing wonderful songs that I had never heard. I flocked with others to bask in the rhythms and harmonies of their music. In the middle of the hamlet, in the central clearing, was the festive pièce de résistance: a modern disco. My friends had finagled one of the really nice boom boxes and a set of speakers from workers at the Nomad station and had lugged them all the way to Gasumi Corners. A bright lantern illuminated the area, and the music poured forth. As older folks looked on, youngsters picked up the beat. Within minutes, they were moving and grooving in ways that would have passed quite tolerably in most dance clubs in the United States.

In the moonlight and gentle breeze, the joy and sadness of nostalgia blurred together. For me, it was the modern Gebusi equivalent of old *fafadagim-da*—the wistful enjoyment of intense and indescribable longing, of being together while thinking of loneliness and loss. Swaying to different beats from one end to the other, the village became a three-ring circus of bittersweet pleasure. I shuttled back and forth between the traditional dance, the string band, and the disco in the middle, delighting in each for their part. Together, they formed a fugue of contemporary cadences that were at once discordant and yet strangely harmonious. No one seemed to mind this jumble of aesthetics and experiences, and neither did I.

Perhaps I had learned something new after all—not just to accept the fragmentary nature of Gebusi culture as it currently expressed itself, but to enjoy and be part of it.

I thought back to Sayu's dance and all the years of ritual splendor that had preceded it. Was Gebusi ritual life now a past tradition, or was it a spirit of new things to come? I finally realized that the answer could not be one or the other; it was both at the same time. I had long been partial to many of the indigenous Gebusi customs that I had observed sixteen years earlier. But now I genuinely appreciated the Gebusi's relaxed ability to mix old and new, to not fear the future while also not fearing departures from the past. Outpacing my understanding, the people of Gasumi Corners had become modern in their own unique way. On the eve of my departure, I contemplated again what had they given me. Their truest gift had gone beyond the present or the past of their culture. It was something more. They had shown me the surprise of discovery in the path of cultural unfolding and of human connection.

PART THREE
2008

CHAPTER 12

Villagers on the Gasumi Corners path, 2008. (PHOTO: Bruce Knauft)

Gebusi 2008

I HAD TRIED TO send word to my Gebusi friends ahead of time that I was coming back. This would be a briefer visit, to be sure, but no less important for that. Ten years later, what had changed? Would my Gebusi friends be yet more engaged in an outside world, the old customs further gone, the Gebusi's rush to be modern, albeit in their own way, yet more intense than before?

My first inkling was the challenge of getting there. Flights were no longer going to Nomad Station at all. I looked in amazement at my computer screen to see the e-mail from the Mission Aviation Fellowship (MAF); it said that the Nomad airstrip was closed. How could this be? For forty-four years that airstrip has been the lifeline to the outside world for Gebusi and their neighbors. Since Nomad still has no roads to anywhere, what did this new isolation mean? Had it made Gebusi yet more remote than they had been in 1998? How had they responded, given all their new aspirations and the changes they had experienced?

These questions filled my mind as I made plans. My sinking fear was that I would not see my Gebusi friends at all. With no air transport, what would I do? The overland trip to Nomad from Kiunga still takes up to a week to complete on foot, including across swamps and the dangerous Strickland River. I was almost tempted to try this route, but the extended time of walking there and back again would have greatly limited my visit with Gebusi themselves. Fortunately, the MAF agent had another idea. He suggested that I fly north of Nomad and land at a tiny mission airstrip that was still open—and then hike with my gear from there to Nomad and on to Gasumi Corners. If I was lucky, the Nomad strip might be fixed and reopened by the time I arrived in Kiunga. If all else failed, I would simply remain in Kiunga and make contact with whichever Gebusi happened to be residing in the corners of the town.

When I left Atlanta, I didn't know which of these options would come to pass. My best guess was that I would land north of Nomad and trek south to the Gebusi. But twenty-eight years after my first trip, I was to be surprised yet again—and I was not disappointed.

After the grueling trip from Atlanta to Los Angeles to Australia to Papua New Guinea's capital of Port Moresby, and then to Kiunga, I finally got some word about Gebusi. Though none of my advance communications had gotten through, Father Eddy at the Kiunga Catholic mission recognized my photo of Sayu. He said that Sayu was now married, that he had several children, and that he previously had been working with Father Aloi at the Catholic Church at Nomad. My appetite whetted, I was all the more eager to see my Gebusi friends. But first I had to get there.

※　　　※　　　※

The logistics that surround key features of infrastructure such as airstrips are practically and even culturally important in developing countries such as Papua New Guinea. On arriving in the country's Western Province, my desire to return to the Gebusi directly engaged these dynamics. In the case of Nomad, the local government had run out of funds to pay Gebusi and other workers for cutting and clearing grass on the airstrip. Laborers had continued for several months but eventually gave up and stopped working without wages.

As the grass shot up and the airstrip deteriorated, incoming planes could barely land. Nomad's government officials, most of whom hailed from other towns and cities in Papua New Guinea, responded by leaving altogether and flying out on the last planes. Amazing as it may seem, politics and networks allowed them to reside in Kiunga or elsewhere and continue collecting their government salaries while not living or working at Nomad at all. Officials themselves viewed this arrangement as a kind of extended or semi-permanent business trip, paid at government expense, because they did not consider their job postings at Nomad to be viable. Government presence at Nomad hence declined to almost nothing. The grass on the strip continued to grow and the airfield was eventually closed.

In Papua New Guinea and many other developing countries, decline or closure of rural infrastructure is a great problem. Even for Papua New Guinea's extensive Western Province, however, the closure of the large Nomad airstrip was a worst-case scenario, and one which had great impact on the various ethnic groups and thousands of people who live in the Nomad Sub-District.

Back at the Nomad Station, one lower-level government worker from the area and another who had married a local woman continued to stay on. After months of persuasion, cajoling, and diligence, they managed to get some money and pay part of what was owed to local airfield laborers, who then started to re-clear the airstrip. Even when their work was finished, however, the landing area was soft and easily saturated by rain. By the time I had hoped to arrive, the airstrip had been closed for nine months.

In Papua New Guinea's Western Province, the only regular flight service to outstations is provided by MAF. By early 2008, officials there wanted to know if and how the Nomad airstrip could be reopened. Their test case turned out to be me. When I finally arrived in Kiunga, Nick Swaim, an accomplished young MAF bush pilot, said that he would try to fly me to Nomad if I would pay full charter fare—almost 3,000 kina—for a flight of less than ninety minutes. I could take only a few supplies, so the plane would not land too heavily on the soft airstrip. Before touching down, Nick would fly over the Nomad strip and inspect it. If it looked okay, we would land; otherwise, we would fly north to Honinabi and I would walk south to Nomad and Gasumi Corners. If it was raining or had rained the day before, the strip would be wet and we wouldn't go.

Luckily, the weather cleared. I loaded my few things and was finally bound for Nomad. As we took off and ascended, I marveled as if for the first time again at the full magnificence of the rainforest, from horizon to horizon. A rush of awe and also sorrow swept over me as I realized how rare such unbroken vistas of rainforest have become—one of the most endangered sights across our shrinking planet.

Almost before I was ready, the Strickland River passed beneath us and we approached Nomad Station. Nick circled and we careened down to just six or eight feet above the airstrip so he could inspect it carefully. As I looked across anxiously, he pulled up suddenly to get us back over the treetops. Then he gave me the thumbs up; we were going to land. My pulse continued to race as we circled again. On finally touching down, we caught a rut and the plane skidded to the right and then to the left. But Nick calmly got us straightened out and brought the plane to a gentle stop. It was only later that he told me the greater risk—that if the plane had hit a deeper rut, it could have been catapulted sideways or forward. If the lone propeller hits the ground, it typically flips the fuselage to disaster.

But, oh, to be safely back! I gazed out eagerly as we taxied, remembering how I had done the same thing in 1980 and again in 1998. Who would be there? What would I find? Each time was a new beginning.

As I later found out, word of my arrival had gotten to Nomad only that same morning. Many of my friends had been out in their gardens, but Sayu and Didiga had heard the news and rushed to the airstrip; there they were to greet me! I could hardly believe it. We hugged and hugged and snapped fingers. At first we could barely say anything, overcome by the joy and speechless grins of simply being together once again. Their faces were now middle aged, but their smiles were bright and deep as ever.

As I caught my bearings, I realized that most of the clothes on those gathered around me were plainly ragged. This caught me off guard, as the Nomad airstrip is quite a public place. I then looked up and across to the Nomad Station. It, too, was ragged. Most houses were deteriorated and boarded up. The Nomad school-yard, which had been full of pupils running to meet the plane ten years ago, was devoid of life; even the grass was burned away and charred black. Turning to the right, I saw the remains of the Nomad ball field that had seen so many challenges and triumphs played out—now grown over with two feet of grass. Gebusi them-selves were smiles all over. But what had circumstances done to them?

Not wanting to linger at Nomad, we gathered my few supplies and prepared to go. I shook hands and exchanged warm greetings with Father Aloi, the Gebusi's Catholic priest. News of him had been encouraging when I had passed through Kiunga—that he loved the Gebusi, was actively learning their language, supported their customs, and was molding the church to local needs. I was sorry to see him go so quickly. But after waiting months to leave Nomad for a much-needed break, he was eager to board the plane that had brought me. Departing the airstrip, we trotted off in high gear to Gasumi Corners.

Along the way, I explained to everyone with apologies that I had not been able to bring as many supplies and gifts as I would have liked; the weight limit on the plane was the price of my being able to arrive at all. To my surprise, my friends not only understood but hardly seemed to care. My wonder and curiosity grew at how Gebusi had been dealing with the fact that their material circumstances had so obviously declined. My questions deepened when I got to the village and saw that my friends' possessions were indeed fewer, their clothes more torn, their pots more battered, and their knives and axes more worn than they had been before.

My first priority, though, was simply to find out who was still alive. To my huge relief, most of my closest friends had survived. A surge of welcomes came from Kilasui, Mosomiay, Hogaya, Wobebiay, Agiwa, Yokwa, and my great old friends Yuway, Keda, Uwok, and Hawi. Among the women, Mus, Dohayn, Dasom, Tabway, Kuni, To'ofun, Towe, Hahap, Oip, and many others were still living. Along with the adults was a bounding gaggle of new children who had been born since my last visit. I struggled to record and remember their many names. As my tabulation finally showed, the work of time has been kind to the population of Gasumi Corners, which grew 38 percent in the ten years between 1998 and 2008, from 122 to 168. Among the additions is one new "Knauft" in the world: Didiga's first son, to whom he gave my last name. I was deeply touched.

Among many peoples across the developing world, growing numbers of children pose a major challenge. High rates of fertility mean more mouths to feed— and can easily increase and intensify poverty. But Gebusi have extensive tracts of land. Given their history of being preyed upon and depopulated by Bedamini raiders, the Gebusi's current surge in numbers is more a healthy replenishment than a crisis condition. The total number of Gebusi is still under 1,000. The main stress caused by their population growth is competition for land in and around settlements such as Gasumi Corners itself. But as developments at Nomad Station have become moribund or been scaled back, the people of Gasumi Corners have oriented increasingly to their forest gardens, to foraging, and to other activities in the rainforest, where land remains plentiful.

This trend has impacted basic patterns of subsistence. In 2008, those in Gasumi Corners were not raising anywhere near as many sweet potatoes or other root crops as they had ten years earlier. This was not surprising since the local market for these foods had been driven by purchases made by now-absent government workers and their families. Gebusi now rely more firmly on their traditional starch staples, especially bananas and sago, and they no longer work to keep pigs away from their erstwhile root crop gardens.

❧   ❧   ❧

How else had the community changed? As I strolled along with a throng of friends on that first day, the biggest change was also the most obvious—a great

Children in Gasumi Corners, 2008. (PHOTO: Bruce Knauft)

Gebusi in traditional costuming for a Catholic welcoming ceremony, 2008; Sayu is on the far right. (PHOTO: Father Aloi, SMM)

new longhouse in the middle of Gasumi Corners. I knew right away what this meant: a whole new generation of Gebusi had been initiated since the last time I had been there. Their transmission of core cultural features across generations has been resuscitated and maintained. What a joy! Given this, I strongly suspected I might soon learn of other traditions that were also being reasserted.

As I entered the house, as if there were any doubt, I was besieged by a full flurry of traditional welcoming. My fingers were snapped again and again, my gift exchange names called out, and the floor swept clean. After being begged to sit down, I was offered water, bananas, and, most importantly, round upon round of strong sweet tobacco from traditional bamboo pipes. In short order, the festivities were punctuated by waves of good-natured sexual joking, just like I had remembered from 1980. In marked contrast to 1998, the men were delighted almost to tears that I was able to joke back with them in their own traditional terms.

As the conversations started in earnest, I found that my own interest in long-standing customs of Gebusi culture was no longer as marginal to my friends in Gasumi Corners as it had been a decade before. Alongside a resurgence of older traditions was a surprising new curiosity about details from the past, including the historical records and old genealogies that I had photocopied and brought with me. In 1998, this information elicited scant attention from Gebusi. Now, however, men in the community took interest and pleasure in my tabulations and charts of kinship connections, residence histories, and genealogies, including who had been married to whom, the names of their children, and where they had lived in days gone by. Enough time had passed that much of what I had recorded from those early days was unknown to a number of the men gathered around. They seemed to marvel at my ability to resurrect facts and to punctuate them with accounts of my personal experience from almost three decades before. They heartily supported the idea that I give a complete copy of my Gebusi clan genealogies to my friend Didiga Imba, who could read and recite the information as a kind of community history. That night, I stumbled to bed amazed: the Gebusi were reclaiming their past.

When I got up the next morning, I found my friend Keda, now dominantly called Joseph, reading one of my books about the Gebusi that I had brought with me. I had given copies of these especially to Sayu and Didiga, and they had already started circulating in the community. My first surprise was that Keda could read. I had known that he could speak and understand the national pidgin-English language, *tok pisin*. But I hadn't known that he could read English. In fact, he had just finished reading my story of Doliay—how as a young man he had beheaded Basowey as a sorcerer and how he later became a staunch Christian. Unfortunately, Doliay had died since my last visit. He had been one of those whom we had helped initiate in 1981. Now only two of those six young men were still alive.

Putting down the book, Keda told me how interested he was in the story and how glad he was that I had written it down. But it was especially Didiga who liked to read my writings on the Gebusi. (The cover photo of this second edition of *The Gebusi* shows Didiga in Gasumi Corners in 2008 reading the first edition of the book.) If Gebusi are recreating their traditions, they are certainly doing so with all the tools they have at their disposal, including modern literacy as well as traditional memory and experience.

I am at pains to convey how meaningful and satisfying the Gebusi's cultural renaissance is to me personally. In 1998 I had tried hard to respect and document their desires for change and the forces that were so strongly affecting my friends and their local world at that time. I wondered then how, or if, they would be able to benefit from greater interaction with the outside world without losing what was distinctly theirs. What I observed this time was a greater sense of self-determination by Gebusi, who now seemed to be seeking a balance between their desire to be modern and an appreciation of their cultural past.

To my surprise and delight, this balance now includes the performance of traditional dances. Within three days of my arrival, a dance in full regalia was held in a large house just a ten-minute walk from the center of Gasumi Corners. In good classic style, the dancer was from a distant village; he came to help cure a man who had been stricken with illness. In style, form, and costume, the dance was just what I had witnessed so many times twenty-eight years earlier. In fact, the custom of men drinking kava, the local root intoxicant, was even more prevalent than it had been during that earlier period. The young men were the most active drinkers.

∗∗∗   ∗∗∗   ∗∗∗

Thankfully, some traditional beliefs that had become moribund by 1998 remained in abeyance. Sorcery inquests, for instance, were still no longer practiced. When I asked why, my Gebusi friends noted the continuing absence of spirit mediums; the last ones had died or given up the practice, and no new ones had been indoctrinated. As in 1998, they said: "If we could talk with the spirits through our traditional spirit mediums, we could find out who sent the sorcery and perhaps take action. But without our spiritual go-betweens, we just cannot know. So we leave it up to God, if he wants to take action."

Instead of spirit séances, the lovely string-band singing that had come to the fore during the 1990s has persisted and expanded. Rather than singing to traditional spirits via a spirit medium, Gebusi continue to enjoy non-spiritual plaintive songs of longing, sexual attraction, and allure accompanied by guitar and ukulele—and now accompanied as well by bouts of intense sexual humor and joking.

Figures bear out the link between Gebusi's changed forms of music, spiritual belief, and violence. Of the various deaths that occurred in Gasumi Corners since 1998, not one was a homicide. For instance, there have been no killings of those who might have been suspected as sorcerers. The community homicide rate has hence been zero from 1989 to 2008—for almost two decades. Given that previously almost one of every three adult Gebusi had been violently killed, this is a major, and, to my mind, wonderfully positive change. Among other things, it testifies to and underscores the human ability for aggression and violence to be effectively managed and reduced through social and cultural change.

∗∗∗   ∗∗∗   ∗∗∗

Influencing if not underlying the reduction of violence in Gasumi Corners is the St. Paul Catholic Church. As I quickly found, the Nomad Catholic Church is one non-traditional institution that has grown and intensified rather than diminished for the people of Gasumi Corners. Its influence has persisted despite decline of government services, wages, and the small cash economy—and despite the relative decline of many other Christian churches in the Nomad area, including Evangelical and Seventh Day Adventist congregations. In 1998, these churches as well as the Gebusi's Catholic Church were quite strong. But all of these were also commandeered by pastors and catechists from outside the Nomad area. My own impression had been that Gebusi seemed to be passive if not submissive "sheep" under the direction of spiritual leaders from elsewhere.

Now, however, the relationship between the people of Gasumi Corners and the Catholic Church had grown. These changes have been encouraged by the smart and compassionate young priest of Gasumi Corners, Father Aloi—a native of Indonesia. As later explained to me in Kiunga by Bishop Gilles Coté, a dearth of new priests from the United States, Canada, and Europe forced the Catholic Church in Papua New Guinea to look farther afield to find young priests, in particular, to South and Southeast Asia. According to Bishop Coté, the experiment was a great success. As he said with a laugh, he wished he had thought of it years earlier. In the case of Father Aloi, who I later came to know well, I agreed heartily. An engaging and energetic polyglot, Father Aloi spoke a half-dozen or more languages, including Indonesian, English, *tok pisin*, a vernacular from interior Borneo, and a strong complement of Gebusi and other tongues from the Nomad area.

More importantly, he understood and respected the intricacies of Gebusi's spirit beliefs, marital dynamics, social disputes, and general ethos—more than I would have thought possible for a young Catholic priest. Perhaps this was due to his own background and rigorous service in Indonesia, including in a Jakarta slum and with a Borneo hill tribe. Whatever the reason, he cared about Gebusi on their own terms—and had gained their affection as well as their respect.

From his main residence on the fringe of Gasumi Corners, Father Aloi has kept his mission materially supplied from Kiunga, which was no mean feat in an environment of declining or defunct government services. He had further taken responsibility to spread church outreach by visiting a very wide range of settlements, including in the deep bush. These long excursions to distant areas had little real precedent in the Nomad area since the patrols of the intrepid Australian colonial officers and a few white missionaries some thirty-five years before. Often gone for weeks at a time, Father Aloi traveled on foot and canoe or motor boat, accepting local food and trying to appreciate local customs wherever he went. He recounted with a laugh having unwittingly smoked a large amount of marijuana that was "innocently" put in a traditional tobacco pipe by a mischievous welcoming villager in a distant Bedamini settlement. As it turned out, the raising and selling of marijuana has become a major problem in the general Nomad area, especially to the east of Gebusi. This problem has intensified as the local cash economy based on garden produce and other forest products has almost collapsed.

Amid his travels and activism, Father Aloi has both entrusted and encouraged those from Gasumi Corners to take charge of the Catholic mission church in his absence, including the running of the Sunday service. This was the case during my own time at Gasumi Corners. On one occasion, for instance, Yamdaw (now "Luke") led the service while Anagi (now "John") read the scripture and Keda (now "Joseph") gave the sermon—while Sayu and others played guitar and ukulele to lead the singing.

Amid the strength and compassion of Catholic leadership, many Gebusi in Gasumi Corners have taken new responsibility and expanded their role in their church. In the process, they have also mixed and combined ritual practices of Christianity with those of traditional custom. Father Aloi has been in favor of these developments, just as he supported the building of a new longhouse and the holding of Gebusi initiations. Now, the people of Gasumi Corners actively cooperate in creating indigenous-style costumes and performances that help celebrate Christian events, activities, and special occasions. As a result, the separation and the inequity between Catholic leadership and Gebusi culture seem less in 2008 than they did in 1998.

This state of affairs illustrates how Gebusi, like other peoples, do not simply reproduce their past even as they draw upon it as an inexhaustible resource—the resource of culture. In the process, they extend and develop their culture as they confront new realities, explore new ways to express themselves, and find new means of creating meaning and finding value in their lives and livelihood.

Amid their other changes, what has happened to the external factors and forces that loomed so large in Gasumi Corners during the 1990s? At that time, of course, the Nomad school, police, government officials, development projects, health clinic, sports league, and twice-weekly market were all not just strong but powerful magnets of interest and activity. Now all of these institutions and activities are dormant or defunct. The elementary school is closed, the health clinic is all but shut, the police are gone, the central government station has no officers or radio, the Nomad market is desultory, and the sports leagues are no more. Maybe they will come back again some day, but for now, they are gone.

Gebusi themselves say simply, "The government has died" (*gamani golom-da*). But to my surprise, they say this with a glint in their eye, almost with a sense of "good riddance" rather than pining for lost advancement or opportunities. True, their material standing is less than it used to be when judged on the basis of income, manufactured goods, or employment. And yet, though they certainly earn less than one U.S. dollar per day—the international standard of extreme poverty—Gebusi reliance on their traditional economy and customs is stronger and prouder in 2008 than it was a decade before.

Gebusi do lament and criticize the inefficiency and waste of the Papua New Guinea government, including the continued payment of salary to Nomad's civil servants while they live outside the area. But those from Gasumi Corners do not sit on their hands or degrade their own culture as a result. They do not agree with the opinion of government officials that the people of the Nomad area are undeserving of government presence, programs, and support. Instead, they have taken it upon themselves to develop and reassert their own customs and beliefs and their integrity as an indigenous people. In the process, they have taken responsibility and initiative, drawn on their cultural and environmental resources, and influenced their own destiny.

In terms of the Gebusi's physical environment, this last point bears emphasis. Unlike many remote and marginalized peoples, Gebusi have not had their lands taken away, exploited, or cut up or pockmarked by loggers or miners. Their paltry cash economy, especially in terms of daily subsistence, is counterbalanced by their ability to reassert themselves by utilizing and fully controlling their natural environment. Many other marginalized peoples in the world are not so lucky.

What Gebusi do illustrate more generally is the ability of peoples across the world to create dignity and shared meaning in their individual and communal lives. In Western perception and scholarship, it is commonly thought that social and economic developments are converging globally and becoming more homogeneous. In complementary fashion, it is often asserted that those left behind in the process of global development are becoming more disempowered and dehumanized. Both of these assumptions are effectively pushed aside by people like the Gebusi. The resurgence of local cultures such as theirs cannot be discounted in our twenty-first century.

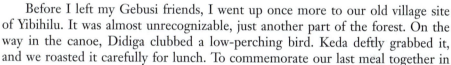

Before I left my Gebusi friends, I went up once more to our old village site of Yibihilu. It was almost unrecognizable, just another part of the forest. On the way in the canoe, Didiga clubbed a low-perching bird. Keda deftly grabbed it, and we roasted it carefully for lunch. To commemorate our last meal together in the forest, we stuck the bird's feathers in the rafters of the tiny lean-to that is now the only structure in the general vicinity of Yibihilu. We talked and laughed and sighed about days and people gone by, about the passage of time. On our way back to the village, we brought food to a party of men from Gasumi Corners who were carving a canoe from a big tree along the river. We stopped and joked, smoked tobacco, cursed the mosquitoes, and danced around in horseplay. The canoe being built was for Father Aloi, and the workers would be paid in cash. But the power of traditional practices, and especially of good company, was as strong as ever.

Regardless of how many times I return to the Gebusi, their story will never be predictable. Time and again my own expectations of what Gebusi were, or could be, have been wonderfully shattered. In the process, not just my understanding but my life has become richer through the power of human connection. My friendships with Gebusi continue to grow, and when I go back yet again, I feel sure that this will again be the case.

What my most recent visit to the Gebusi has taught me is that our understanding of other peoples and cultures—across the world or around the corner—is never finished. Today's new finding could be either reinforced or overturned tomorrow. This does not mean that our efforts as cultural anthropologists are either random or doomed to obsolescence, on the other. It means simply that our work, like our lives, thrives on new cycles of experience that freshly engage both our hearts and our minds.

So, too, my Gebusi friends, their families, and their future will always be meaningfully growing and changing. As long as I live, I hope to keep contact with Sayu, Didiga, and my other Gebusi friends. Since 1980, their culture has been transformed for me from an alien world to one of powerful value and then to one of friendship and deep human connection.

Across the miles and the years, what more can one ask?

Conclusion
Twenty-Eight Years amid Worlds of Change

AROUND THE WORLD, TRADITIONS fade. But important parts of them are rediscovered, reinvented, and expressed in new ways. The paths of the past continue to fertilize those of the present, even if the latter are large and increasingly well trodden. People like the Gebusi experiment continually with this mix. Although the two sides of this coin are often written about separately, the traditional and the modern, I think not only that they are connected but also that they mutually determine each other. As an ethnographer and as a person, engaging this process has been an important intellectual challenge and also an emotional one. Personally, I think that confronting the dynamics of culture change in lived experience requires a reciprocating balance and a healthy tension between the reflections of our minds and the feelings of our hearts. Where would we be without both of these in our lives and in our works?

Over the years, as I have thought about and felt changes in Gebusi culture, I have moved increasingly beyond a view of Gebusi as either fundamentally traditional or as orphaned from their rich past. I view them rather as simply vibrant in their present. I have realized that Gebusi themselves negotiate these tensions better than I have been able to do in my reflections and analyses. I think they have been able to do this in part because of their abiding sense of playfulness and flexibility. My friends might embrace new events and activities as if they were separate from their past, or they may rediscover older customs in a new light. But in either case, they convey strong awareness—through humor and irony, play and performance—that these developments are neither as fixed nor as serious as they might appear to an outsider. Even as some of their beliefs or practices may be left aside or in some cases actively abandoned, strands of their deeper influence may be revived, retooled, and made newly imaginative at a later time.

In 1980–82, I was able to appreciate the richness of Gebusi indigenous customs—their subsistence, kinship, sorcery, sexuality, spiritual life, ritual performances, and the rest. I became increasingly mindful of how remarkable and fortunate Gebusi had been to develop and expand their customs, to a significant extent, with only a modicum of outside pressure. Since then, of course, the people of Gebusi Corners have increasingly combined older traditions with newer influences coming from outside the area, and they have done so in their own unique way. During the late 1980s and 1990s, their changes during a few scant years were remarkable. In addition to most members of the community going to church, children attended the Nomad school, men played soccer and rugby in the Nomad sports leagues, and women became food-sellers at the Nomad market. Gebusi gave up spirit mediumship and active sorcery investigations and were increasingly cut off from their rich indigenous cosmos. In the mix, their high rate of violence and killing plummeted, and their lives became much more peaceful than before. Oriented increasingly around tape cassette players and boom boxes, their music and dance pulsed to the beat of string bands and disco.

In more recent years, as government presence has withered, the Gebusi's connection to and interest in activities and lifestyles associated with the Nomad Station have declined significantly. By 2008, the Gebusi of Gasumi Corners had rediscovered or reasserted a range of their older customs, including social life centered around a communal longhouse, traditional dancing and joking, and increasing commitment to life in the rainforest. Their patterns of kinship and residence had also endured. But some practices that Gebusi had previously given up remained defunct or moribund, including, thankfully, the sorcery inquests and divinations that had led to such a high rate of Gebusi violence and killing. In complementary fashion, Gebusi affiliation with some newer institutional forms and activities had intensified and expanded rather than been reduced. Prominent here has been the growing commitment of those in Gasumi Corners to the local Catholic Church. The community's increasing involvement with and leadership in the church has increased not only their shared sense of Christian commitment but also their motivation and ability to employ traditional performances and aesthetic expressions in Catholic activities and celebrations.

Gebusi still desire money, modern goods, and more contemporary styles of life. But they are no longer as subordinate to outside authority figures—pastors, teachers, referees, buyers at market, and government officials—as they had been during the 1990s. Their lives then embraced a larger and more complicated social universe at the Nomad Station. At the time, Gebusi engaged diverse modern institutions in and around Nomad—the market for economic transactions, the police station for social control, the aid post for health, government offices for politics, the churches for religion, the interethnic league for sports, and Independence Day for national-cum-local celebration. But since the 1990s, the people of Gasumi Corners have reasserted their own social world and have emphasized greater social integrity in their own community, including in relation to the rainforest.

Gebusi cultural and symbolic developments illustrate these changes. In 1980–82, Gebusi performance and aesthetic expression emphasized reciprocity and exchange with their natural and spirit world, both in spirit mediumship and in the beautiful spirit forms embodied by the sublime Gebusi male dancer. By 1998, Gebusi cultural identifications had expanded to include a much wider web of meanings. These included broader ethnic, interethnic, regional, and national affiliations as well as identification with Christian denominations. Gebusi's avid participation in the 1998 Nomad Independence Day ceremonies exemplified the complex and varied nature of these diverse and sometimes fragmented cultural and symbolic ties. These identifications have not been entirely given up since that time but are now tempered and complemented by greater core reliance on customs and rituals associated with the Gebusi's own past. These customs are not reasserted or rediscovered just as they had been historically but are rejuvenated in new ways that reflect the selected value of past orientations in present circumstances.

Like other peoples in the contemporary world, Gebusi are becoming both more modern and more traditional at the same time—and in their own distinct way. Gebusi still value quiet moments in the rainforest, the bonds between kin and friends, and the aesthetic splendor of their traditional costuming and performance. They also engage and aspire to features of so-called modern life, including reliance on steel tools and manufactured implements, clothes, a desire for money, strong involvement with their local church, and interest in new cultural forms of aesthetics and music. The resulting combinations are distinctive to Gebusi and not the same as they may be in other countries or even in other parts of Papua New Guinea. Like the mixed vocabularies that pervade their string band songs, contemporary life for Gebusi cannot be framed solely in terms of either outside influences or traditional dispositions.

The Gebusi are fortunate to have the continuing bounty of their land. They own not only their own settlement sites but also the gardens and pristine forests that provide them with their food, and a surplus to boot. Many peoples who experience so-called modernization are not so lucky. The inhabitants of Gasumi Corners are additionally fortunate that part of their land is within a few minutes walk of the largest outpost for many miles in any direction—the Nomad Station. This provides them the flexibility, depending on conditions and their disposition, to orient to a greater or a lesser extent to the events and activities of the Nomad Station, on the one hand, or the deeper rainforest, on the other.

I have been fortunate as well. I have had the rare opportunity to know the Gebusi, to be part of their lives, and to share in their customs across a rich spectrum of traditional, modern, and combined practices and orientations. That these have spanned such broad cultural distance during less than three decades makes my fortune all the greater. The Gebusi in 1980 were neither pristine nor fully "traditional," but their particular history gave them a special opportunity to develop their culture, in significant part, on their own terms. By 1998, the Gebusi's path of cultural change had not just taken off but had run circles around its previous scope and scale, including alterations in subsistence, economy, religion, marriage, politics, aesthetic life, and even their sense of time. Due to these changes, Gebusi will never be as independent or remote from outside influence as they once were. But by 2008, a new of turn of the wheel had informed Gebusi culture. Now their deeper traditions are more fully reasserted and more fully combined with selected recent developments. Gebusi traditions are resurgent, not as an exact replica of the past, but in ways that draw upon longstanding customs as deep and powerful resources.

A special good fortune is that the people of Yibihilu and now Gasumi Corners have to a large extent engaged the outside world through their own choices. They have not been subject to the worst excesses of colonialism or modern development. They have not had to endure slavery, violent subjugation, land alienation, heavy taxation, exploitative wage labor, depletion of natural resources, or degradation of their natural environment. In all these respects, they have been very lucky, indeed, notwithstanding their own sense of lagging behind on a modern path of progress.

The final fortune is my own. As part of their openness, the Gebusi warmly welcomed me from the start, and they continue to do so time and again. They have given me the greatest gift that people can give and one that we can all appreciate: to share life across differences of culture.

Farewell

ON THE DAY OF departure, I had no shame. The morning started rainy, and I hoped it would continue so the plane wouldn't come. I didn't care that my few boxes were already sealed up and that everything else had been given away. Eventually, though, the rain lessened, and I trudged in sorrow with everyone else to the airstrip.

I started choking up well before the plane emerged on the horizon. I knew it would happen, just as it had for the past few days as I gave things away to so many good people. I fought back the tears, but they kept coming. I had known the people of Yibihilu and of Gasumi Corners so well before and now again through many years—first when they were children or young adults and now with their own children in their place. It always remains a question whether I can return to the Gebusi yet again. Nomad is so remote, and the logistics of getting to my Gebusi friends are difficult. The tropics grind hard on my middle-aged body, and my obligations back home remain packed in a whole other life. My Gebusi friends know this. Those who are older know that I may never see them again; they may be dead by the time I can return. Despite other changes, their lives remain short.

Instead of using my camera that last day, I took mental pictures that were more indelible. As I moved down the sorrowful line of those gathered to say their good-byes, I forced myself to peer in the face and gaze into the eyes of each man and woman, each boy and girl from Gasumi Corners. Snapping their fingers in my best and most forthright manner, I burned into my mind the living image of each of these unique persons so as never to forget their exquisite humanity. Their tear-streaked faces mirrored my own as they fought the impulse to turn away. I sobbed along with them, oblivious to onlookers—a six-foot, short-haired white guy crying with a crowd of villagers.

I lost it when I came to Sayu and Didiga. I have become so close to them over the years, since they were very small. They have shared much about their lives with me, and I with them. It is hard to think that I don't know when again I will see them, and that in the interim I will have but fleeting contact with their lives.

Then there was Yuway, who is older, a truly senior man. He is now the father of five children, most of them grown or nearly so. Yuway helped lead us on our very first patrol in 1980. He was my most sensitive and caring helper when I was first learning the Gebusi language. He was my best friend during my initial field-work and remains one of the nicest and most decent people I have ever met. I looked into his eyes and suddenly blurted out, "Friend, oh friend, when will I ever see you again?!" His wisdom was greater than mine. With a weepy and yet dignified smile, he told me, "I'll see you later, in heaven."

I don't remember much after that. The plane taxied and took me away in the dampness. My last sight at the end of the airstrip was Yuway. He had walked all the way down the path, waiting to wave one final time to me. Then I sailed up toward the heavens of Kiunga, while Yuway awaited his own.

Who can deny the world of change in cultures? Or that richness of humanity that persists despite all that would repress it?

List of Persons

Bosap: 1998 — older woman, never married, mother of Kuma, regular market seller; **2008** — deceased

Boyl: 1982 — mother of Sayu, wife of Silap; friend of Eileen; **1998** — deceased

Bulobey: 1982 — active spirit medium, newly married; **1998** — Evangelical Church member, married with five children; **2008** — deceased

Damya: 1982 — young boy, son of Nolop and Wosip; **1998** — married with children, lead Gasumi string band singer, devoted member of the Catholic Church; **2008** — Catholic prayer and service leader, father of three children

Didiga: 1982 — young boy, son of Imba; **1998** — grade six graduate, good friend and helper of Bruce; **2008** — son had been named "Knauft"

Doliay: 1982 — initiate, friend of Hawi, transient tryst partner of Nolop; **1989** — widower of Boyl, killer of Sabowey, begins prison term in Port Moresby; **1998** — married with three children, devoted member of the Catholic Church; **2008** — deceased

Dugawe: 1980 — husband of Sialim, committed suicide by drinking fish poison, died childless

Gami: 1982 — born in Yibihilu very shortly after Bruce and Eileen's departure; **1998** — temporary wife of Guyul; **2001** — wife of Wayabay; **2008** — mother of three children with Wayabay

Gono: 1980 — carrier for Bruce and Eileen on first expedition, forewent initiation to marry early; **1998** — husband of Nolop, father of teenage girl; **2008** — deceased

Guyul: 1982 — young boy; **1998** — temporary husband of Gami

Gwabi: 1982 — young boy; **1998** — builder and owner of Bruce's house, married with one son

Halowa: 1982 — young boy, younger brother of Yuway; **1998** — member of Evangelical Church, married with four children; **2008** — father of six children

Hawi: 1980–82 — carrier for Bruce and Eileen on first expedition, initiate, friend of Doliay; **1998** — married with four children, lived at Nomad Station, devoted member of the Evangelical Church, helped keep track of aircraft cargo; **2008** — still alive

Haymp: 1982 — initiate, incipient father of Kubwam; **1998** — deceased

Hiali: 1981 — younger brother of Silap, died of sickness eleven days after being initiated

Howe: 1982 — young boy, son of Kawuk; **1998** — young man; member of Catholic Church, singer in the Gasumi Corners string band

Huwa: 1998 — orphaned teenage younger brother of Sayu, Gasumi string band singer

Imba: 1982 — senior man of Yibihilu, father of Didiga; **1998** — deceased

Kawuk: 1982 — co-founder of Yibihilu longhouse, married man with two small children; **1998** — senior man of Gasumi Corners, devoted member of the Catholic Church, married with five children; **2008** — security guard for the Catholic Church, five children and six grandchildren

Keda: 1982 — teenage younger brother of Yuway; **1998** — married with children, active Catholic Church member; **2008** — Catholic church lay leader; father of three children

Kubwam: 1982 — born in Yibihilu shortly after Bruce and Eileen's departure; **1998** — temporary wife of Mako; **2008** — divorced Gebusi husband, married Bedamini man, moved to Bedamini territory

Kuma: 1982 — young boy, son of Bosap; **1998** — marriageable bachelor

Kwelam: 1998 — teenage daughter of Nolop

Mai: 1982 — young daughter of Tewo; **1998** — adult woman, living with Tewo outside of Kiunga

Mako: 1982 — young boy; **1998** — young man, temporary husband of Kubwam

Marbwi: 1998 — young girl, adopted daughter of Gwabi; **2008** — outmarried to a Sirigubi settlement

Mokoyl: 1979 — mother of Sialim, killed by Swamin for the sickness death of his wife

Momiay: 1982 — initiate; **1998** — deceased

Mora: 1982 — teenage boy, solicitor of Bruce; **1998** — married with three children; **2008** — deceased

Nolop: 1982 — mother of Damya and Korlis, incipient mother of Kwelam, wife of Wosip, transient tryst partner of Doliay; **1998** — older woman, market seller, wife of Gono

Sabowey: 1989 — adult man, killed by Doliay for the sickness death of Boyl

Sialim: 1982 — widow of Dugawe, mother of one daughter, wife of Swamin; **1998** — deceased

Silap: 1982 — cofounder of Yibihilu longhouse, husband of Boyl, father of Sayu; **1998** — deceased

Sagawa: 1982 — forewent initiation to establish a temporary relationship with Sialim; **1998** — deceased from a death adder bite

Sayu: 1982 — young boy, son of Boyl and Silap, friend of Bruce and Eileen; **c. 1994** — lived in Kiunga; **1998** — bachelor, friend, helper, and confidant of Bruce; **2008** — father of four children by two wives in sequence

Swamin: 1980–82 — carrier for Bruce and Eileen on first expedition, main spirit medium of Yibihilu community, widower, father of Wayabay, married Sialim; **1998** — deceased

Tewo: 1982 — incipient mother of Gami; **1998** — living with husband and family outside Kiunga

Uwano: 1982 — Young adult man, "breadfruit" exchange partner of Bruce; **1998** — deceased October 9, 1998

Warbwi: 1982 — new wife of Yuway; **1998** — wife of Yuway and mother of five children; **2008** — still alive

Wayabay: 1982 — young boy, son of Swamin; **1998** — bachelor, hunter, and house builder; **2001** — husband of Gami; **2008** — father of three children

Willy: 1998 — boy, son of Doliay

Wosip: 1982 — husband of Nolop, father of Damya and Korlis; **1998** — deceased

Yaba: 1982 — widower, jokester in Yibihilu; **1998** — deceased

Yuway: 1980–82 — initiate, carrier for Bruce and Eileen on first expedition, language helper and friend of Bruce; **1998** — husband of Warbwi, father of four children, member of the Seventh Day Adventist Church; **2008** — member of the Catholic Church, father of five children

Study Questions
for *The Gebusi, Second Edition*

Introduction: In Search of Surprise

A. In what ways is being surprised a good or a necessary feature of being a social and cultural anthropologist?

B. During what three time periods did the author study with the Gebusi? What general patterns of social change are described across these times?

C. What does the author say about the appreciation of cultural diversity and the critical exposure of human inequality and domination? What does he assert about the relationship between these aspects of culture in anthropology? In thinking about your own culture, do you agree or disagree with his point of view, and why?

Chapter 1: Friends in the Forest

A. How did the author come in contact with the Gebusi? How were he and his wife treated at the beginning? In what ways was it challenging for them to learn the Gebusi language?

B. How were the lives of Gebusi shaped by the neighboring Bedamini people, on the one hand, and intervention by Australian colonial officers, on the other?

C. What is *kogwayay?* What does this term reflect about Gebusi culture, and why is this significant?

D. What important aspects of Gebusi culture and of Gebusi gender relations were downplayed or covered up by emphasis on *kogwayay?* What do these patterns reveal about the use of culture in general?

Chapter 2: Rhythms of Survival

A. Describe the connection between sharing and the making of social relationships in Gebusi society. Give specific examples of Gebusi gift giving. In what ways were the resulting relationships similar to or different from those in your own society?

B. What do Gebusi eat? How do they make their houses? Across the spectrum of human subsistence patterns, what type of subsistence and of residential organization do Gebusi exhibit most strongly?

C. How would you describe the physical environment and health situation of the Gebusi? In what ways were conditions of environment and health experienced similarly or differently by Gebusi, on the one hand, and the author, on the other?

D. In what way are Gebusi "in-betweeners," and what does this reveal about the use of concepts in social and cultural anthropology?

Chapter 3: Lives of Death

A. Describe key features of Dugawe's death, his funeral, and the investigation that resulted. Reflect on how you would have or might have reacted to these events.

B. Summarize key features of Gebusi sorcery beliefs and practices. Describe how beliefs and practices concerning sorcery affect Gebusi responses to death.

C. In what ways did events concerning the death of Dugawe and the fate of Sialim reflect general features of Gebusi culture? In what ways were these events distinctive or even unique?

D. What does the author say about the experience of fieldwork in relation to establishing ethnographic facts and making generalizations?

Chapter 4: Getting Along with Kin and Killers

A. Describe Gebusi kin groups, the role of clans and lineages, and the composition of Gebusi settlements.

B. What types of marriage are characteristic of Gebusi, and how do they relate to Gebusi patterns of kinship, exchange, and reciprocity? What structural tensions or fault lines result from marriages that are "romantic" in nature and not reciprocated? What connections are there between Gebusi sorcery accusations and their patterns of marriage and social organization?

C. Describe the pattern and degree of violence and homicide among Gebusi as described in this chapter. How did the Gebusi rate of killing compare with that in other societies and cultures? Does an understanding of Gebusi violence suggest anything about the causes and conditions of violence elsewhere?

D. For Gebusi and more generally, what is the value of social organization and kinship for understanding problems and tensions that societies face? How does the study of social organization help uncover the variable relationship between what people say or believe and what they actually do?

E. According to the author, what place is there in anthropology for structural or statistical depictions of social behavior? What is the proper relationship between these depictions and the more nuanced and humanized description of specific events and people?

Chapter 5: Spirits, Sex, and Celebration

A. According to the author, what are some of the important reasons why sexual culture is a valid and significant topic of study for anthropologists? What does the author's experience reveal about the potential benefits—and risks—of investigating sexual beliefs and practices in another culture?

B. Describe the shifting sexual practices of Gebusi males from early adolescence to middle age as described for 1980–82. What role do spiritual beliefs play in influencing their sexual orientations and practices?

C. Do you think Gebusi men are in fact more strongly attracted sexually to other men, or to women? What evidence could you use to support your claim either way?

D. Describe the attitude and orientation of Gebusi women concerning: (a) their own heterosexual relations with men, (b) men's sexual relations with each other, (c) men's ritual representation of female sexuality and of spirit women, and (d) the potential for sexual relations between Gebusi women themselves.

E. In what ways are Gebusi sexually tolerant? In what ways are they restrictive or conservative? Do women enjoy the same degree of sexual toleration or restriction as men? Why or why not, and under what circumstances?

F. What do the Gebusi illustrate about the nature of human gender and sexuality generally?

Chapter 6: Ultimate Splendor

A. Summarize the basic sequence of Gebusi initiation activities—what comes first and what comes next. Describe the ways that Gebusi from different settlements are thereby brought together.

B. The author states that Gebusi initiations combine (a) spirituality, (b) sexuality, (c) material gifts and exchanges, (d) kinship, (e) friendship, and (f) gender. Identify a key example of each of these features in the Gebusi initiation, and describe its connection to the other features.

C. What do you think the experience would be like to be initiated as a young Gebusi man? What parts of this process do you think would be most enjoyable and which most difficult?

D. What prevented the climactic celebrations of the Gebusi initiation as described from going forward smoothly? How did Gebusi react to this problem—and what did their reaction reveal about Gebusi culture?

E. What special role did women play at the final conclusion of the initiation festivities—and what was significant about their concluding roles? In what way did this "final act" of the initiation change your view of the entire event—or not?

Chapter 7: Reentry

A. Describe how changes in anthropology—and changes in the author's own circumstances and disposition—affected his expectations and initial experiences among the Gebusi in 1998.

B. What general features, according to the author, are associated with being or becoming "modern"? Which specific new activities and institutions were associated with becoming modern for the people of Gasumi Corners in 1998?

C. How did Gebusi notions and experiences of time change between 1980 and 1998? What examples does the author provide to illustrate these changes? Why are changes in Gebusi notions of time significant?

D. What factors help account for the fact that Gebusi so willingly accepted modernizing influences between 1982 and 1998? How much of this acceptance was based in factors of culture or belief rather than actual economic improvement?

Chapter 8: Yuway's Sacred Decision

A. By what means had Gebusi become Christian by 1998? What was the respective role of (a) white missionaries, (b) Papua New Guineans from other parts of the country, (c) cultural beliefs and orientations to modernity, (d) the prospect or lure of material rewards, and (e) the decisions and actions of Gebusi themselves?

B. Why did Yuway choose to become a member of the Seventh Day Adventist Church (SDA)? What does his choice reveal about local perceptions of different Christian churches, and about the extent of Gebusi religious freedom?

C. What has been the relationship between Christianity and sorcery violence among Gebusi over time? In what ways is the impact of Christanity upon Gebusi sorcery evident in (a) the life story of Doliay—the man who beheaded a Gebusi as a sorcerer in 1988, and (b) the death and funeral of Uwano in 1998?

D. The author suggests that Christianity among Gebusi in 1998 was linked with politics, government, and desires to be or become modern. What evidence is used to support this claim?

E. What does the author assess as the cost and the benefit of Christianity among Gebusi relative to their traditional spiritual beliefs and practices? What is your own opinion, and why?

Chapter 9: Pennies and Peanuts, Rugby and Radios

A. How successful were Gebusi women in selling goods at the Nomad Market in 1998? Describe the cultural as well as the economic features of the Nomad market—and how these help explain the continuing participation of women.

B. Describe Nolop's achievements and challenges in life, and reflect on her status in Gebusi society.

C. How was the author able, as a man, to obtain information in direct conversation with Gebusi women? Describe the opportunities or constraints that you think you yourself would face, given your gender and disposition, in engaging the lives of Gebusi men and women.

D. How did Nomad school children envisage their future lives in 1998, and what were the differences between boys and girls in this regard? Why is this significant?

E. What difficulties had arisen at the Nomad Station by 1998 due to increasing or inflated expectations of future success? What differences are there between young men and women in this regard, and how do these differences appear to affect gender relations?

Chapter 10: Mysterious Romance, Marital Choice

A. What does the story of Wayabay reveal about (a) new ways of finding a bride in Gasumi Corners, (b) changes in Gebusi sexual orientations and practices, and (c) the challenges of communication across cultures?

B. What does the story of Gami illustrate about (a) changing patterns of Gebusi sister-exchange, (b) the ability of Gebusi women to make their own marital choices, and (c) the dilemma faced by outsiders such as anthropologists when they try to help local people?

C. Based on the stories of Wayabay and Gami, what guidelines do you think would reduce the chances that well-intentioned attempts by outsiders to help local people will fail or be counter-productive?

D. Describe changes in marital choices and in marital risks as experienced by young people in Gasumi Corners. In your own opinion, among Gebusi and in your own culture, is there any potential benefit to trying to reduce rather than maximize the number of people from whom one might choose a partner?

Chapter 11: Sayu's Dance and After

A. What were the major stages and transitions in Sayu's life as recounted by the author? How would you characterize the changes and challenges of Sayu's life up to 1998? What was the author's history with Sayu—and his relationship with him in 1998?

B. In what ways did ritual life as performed in Gebusi villages change between 1982 and 1998? Use Sayu's dance and the author's departure feast as examples.

C. Summarize the basic events and activities of the Nomad Independence Day celebrations of 1998. Describe how traditions and traditional dancing were presented—and their relationship to contemporary or modern forms of entertainment or display at Nomad.

D. What did the Nomad Independence Day celebrations reveal and reflect about (a) changes in Gebusi culture, (b) Gebusi's relation with their ethnic neighbors, (c) Gebusi in relation to their government and the Papua New Guinea State, and (d) the general relationship between culture, ritual, and social change?

Chapter 12: Gebusi 2008

A. How difficult was it for the author to return to the Gebusi in 2008, and why? What was the larger significance of this difficulty for the Nomad area and for the Gebusi?

B. What were the author's first reactions and impressions upon returning to the Gebusi in 2008, and what did these reveal?

C. List and give examples of the major features of change that the author describes for the Gebusi in 2008, including (a) engagement with their physical environment, (b) population, (c) economic status, (d) government, (e) institutional religion, (f) dance and performance, (g) social etiquette, and (h) residence, community relations, and social integrity.

D. Describe and draw implications from developments of the Gebusi's local Catholic Church as portrayed for 2008.

E. What is the author's final conclusion in 2008 concerning the end point of culture change among Gebusi? What does he assert as the meaning of his own continuing fieldwork among Gebusi?

Conclusions: Twenty-Eight Years amid Worlds of Change, and "Farewell"

A. Summarize the key patterns and differences across time of Gebusi as described by the author for (a) 1980–82, (b) 1998, (c) 2008. Given this sequence of changes, what future does the author predict, or not predict, for Gebusi in the future?

B. What does the author say about the reassertion or rejuvenation of customary practices? Can these ever be re-enacted just as they were before? Conversely, can customs or practices be abandoned and left behind with no impact at all on the present or the future?

C. What key features of environmental change, and of colonialism and modernity more generally, have the Gebusi been fortunate to have avoided? How does their fortune in this respect impact the Gebusi's ability to develop their own livelihood and culture?

D. What is the ultimate gift that the author finds the Gebusi have given him?

E. Farewell: How does the author feel when he finally leaves the Gebusi, and why? If it were you, how would you feel, and why?

Index